Ryan marsen

William Shakespeare

Romeo and Juliet

for Junior Cycle

with annotations, analysis and commentary by

Patrick Murray

Edco

The Educational Company of Ireland

First published 2014

The Educational Company of Ireland
Ballymount Road
Walkinstown
Dublin 12

www.edco.ie

A member of the Smurfit Kappa Group plc

ISBN: 978–1–84536–596–7

The paper used in this book comes from Managed Forests in Northern Europe For every tree felled, at least one new tree is planted

Editor: Jennifer Armstrong

Design, layout and cover: Liz White Designs

Front cover photograph: TopFoto

Back cover photograph: Karl Hugh, courtesy of the Utah Shakespeare Festival, 2011

Photograph acknowledgements:

Pages iv, 7, 10, 42, 54, 92, 107, 129, 154, 204, 207, 210, 213, 217, 220, 223, 227, 228, 229, 231, 232, 233, 235: TopFoto.

Pages 1, 2, 8, 9, 21, 51, 53, 74, 90, 96, 123, 142, 173, 175, 200, 242: Shutterstock.

Pages 4, 5, 35, 55, 57, 67, 95, 125, 151, 161, 180, 181, 183, 203, 214, 221, 222, 224, 240, 241, 248, 251, 252: Alamy.

Pages 15, 23, 29, 36, 59, 75, 86, 136, 155, 156, 165, 195, 202, 219, 237: photos by Karl Hugh, courtesy of the Utah Shakespeare Festival, 2011.

Pages 69, 84, 98, 108, 140, 144, 185, 212, 216, 218, 245: photos by Karl Hugh, courtesy of the Utah Shakespeare Festival, 2005.

Pages 109, 160: photos by Karl Hugh, courtesy of the Utah Shakespeare Festival, 2013.

Page 116: Rex Features.

05M22

Preface

THIS NEW EDITION OF *Romeo and Juliet* provides for young students an attractive introduction to the world of Shakespeare, a world that they may be encountering for the first time. All aspects of the play are dealt with in a manner that will help them to enjoy this much-loved play and work through the difficulties associated with reading material that was written more than four hundred years ago.

One of the problems facing modern students of Shakespeare's plays is that there is a significant difference between the language of Shakespeare and present-day English. Some of the words in *Romeo and Juliet* are no longer in common use, and some have different meanings from those they had when the play was written. As well as that, the syntax, or ordering of words, can be complex, even puzzling. In response, this edition of the play provides detailed notes in the margins of the text, explaining the meanings of unfamiliar words. Additionally, there are summaries for each scene and detailed commentary on the play as a whole. These features will ensure that students fully understand the text.

To appreciate *Romeo and Juliet*, we must think about what is happening to and within the characters, as revealed by their actions, their speeches, their soliloquies and asides. There are questions at the end of each scene and activities at the end of each Act to stimulate such thinking. These questions and exercises are designed to suit both Ordinary and Higher Level students. Detailed accounts of the characters are provided at the back of the book.

It is also important to be aware of the kind of world in which the play was written, and the kind of world in which the play is set. This edition gives information on the historical background to the action and on the type of theatre and audience for which Shakespeare wrote.

Topics discussed include the kind of play *Romeo and Juliet* is (a tragedy), the main themes of the play, character change and development, and the relationships between characters. Colour photographs from various theatre and film productions of *Romeo and Juliet* are displayed throughout the book. These images remind students that they are reading a play and provide an opportunity for students to consider different casting and staging decisions.

To assist with revision and exam preparation, the edition identifies the key moments in the play and highlights useful quotations. A helpful diagram makes clear the family relationships between the characters, as well as the impact of characters on each other. A timeline is included to illustrate the progress of the action. A final section is devoted to typical exam questions and contains tips and sample answers.

The approach taken to *Romeo and Juliet* in this edition will help students to:

- develop an appreciation of Shakespeare's use of language
- acquire a sound knowledge of the text
- understand the workings of the plot
- study the characters, their motives and how they interact with each other
- learn about the social and cultural background to the play
- identify themes and issues in the play and discuss their relevance today
- remember that *Romeo and Juliet* was written for performance
- learn about the early seventeenth-century stage and Shakespeare's audience
- consider how the play might be performed and produced today.

Teachers can access the *Romeo and Juliet* e-book at **www.edcodigital.ie**.

Contents

Introduction

About William Shakespeare

THE MOST REMARKABLE THING about Shakespeare is how little we know of him. We know that he was the son of John Shakespeare, who made gloves and traded in wool in Stratford-upon-Avon, England, and that he was baptised there on 26 April 1564.

The Royal Shakespeare Theatre in Stratford-upon-Avon

We also know that in 1592, he was working in London as an actor and a playwright. Between these two dates, the Stratford records show that he was married in 1582, his first child was baptised in 1583, and his twin children in 1585. Apart from these few facts, we have no certain knowledge of where Shakespeare was, or what he was doing, during the first twenty-eight years of his life.

It is very likely, though not certain, that Shakespeare was educated at the free grammar school in his home town. The standard of education at this kind of school was very high. Education was entirely in Latin, and students were not allowed to speak English. If Shakespeare attended this school, he would have learned the rules of Latin grammar, and been taught to read the works of famous Roman authors. He would also have studied Roman history and mythology, as well as rhetoric, which is the art of public speaking.

Why or how Shakespeare became a playwright is a mystery. If he chose this career with the aim of making his fortune, he was taking a gamble that paid off. Many of his fellow playwrights died in poverty and none was prosperous. Shakespeare was the exception: he wrote extremely popular plays over a twenty-year period, one of the most popular being *Romeo and Juliet*.

Shakespeare was also an actor and a poet and he earned a share of the profits of one London theatre. All of these activities made him an extremely wealthy man. He acquired valuable properties in London and Stratford. He was a shrewd businessman who avoided taxes and sued debtors, even those who owed him very small sums.

He retired to Stratford in 1611, and died there in 1616, aged fifty-two.

Shakespeare's collected plays were first published seven years later, in 1623, in an edition known as the First Folio. This book was prepared for publication by two of his fellow actors. We may not know much about Shakespeare but we can be certain that he did not expect his plays to be studied in classrooms more than four hundred years after his death. When reading Shakespeare's plays, always remember that his works were written for performance on stage rather than to be read. He wrote plays to entertain his audience.

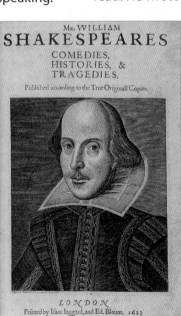

Title-page of the First Folio (1623)

Shakespeare's reputation as the world's greatest playwright is secure. His plays are constantly performed throughout the world. Countless books have been written about him and his works, and despite the shortage of established facts, new biographies are still appearing.

About Shakespeare's theatre

THE THEATRES FOR WHICH Shakespeare wrote his plays were public, open-air ones. Shakespeare owned a share in one of these theatres, the Globe, which opened in 1599 and was situated close to the River Thames in south London.

Modern-day Globe theatre, London

Another famous London theatre at that time was the Swan. A Dutch visitor to London, Johannes de Witt, made a drawing of the Swan theatre around 1596. A copy of this drawing is shown opposite. It is the only surviving sketch of the kind of theatre in which Shakespeare's plays were first performed.

De Witt estimated that the Swan could hold 3,000 spectators – many more than Ireland's largest modern (seated) theatres such as the Belfast Waterfront (2,200), Bord Gáis Energy Theatre, Dublin (2,100) or Royal Theatre, Castlebar (2,000). The modern-day Globe in London has a capacity of almost 1,600 (including 700 standing), and Cork's Everyman seats 650.

The drawing, which De Witt labelled in Latin, shows a round, open-air playhouse. The main feature is the large stage (*proscaenium*), with its overhead canopy known as 'the heavens'. The stage extends into an open yard, described as level ground without sand (*planities sine arena*).

For the price of a penny, spectators called 'groundlings' stood in the yard looking up at the actors. There were also three tiers of galleries where, for an extra penny or two, people could sit and enjoy some shelter under the projecting piece of roofing (*tectum*).

The wealthiest members of the audience wanted to have a clear view of the stage, and also to be seen by the rest of the audience. They would sit in a private gallery above the stage. The gallery was part of the tiring-house

(*mimorum ades*) at the back of the stage. This housed a dressing area where actors changed their costumes or attire, hence the term tiring-house. They also stored props there.

The tiring-house was topped by a storage loft and a flagpole. A flag with the symbol of the theatre (e.g. a globe or a swan) was hoisted to indicate that a play was about to be staged that afternoon. When members of the audience entered the theatre, they would be able to tell what kind of play to expect. For example, if *Romeo and Juliet* was to be performed, the tiring-house would be covered with black cloth to indicate a tragedy (a lighter colour was used for a comedy).

The man shown outside the loft in the drawing is sounding a trumpet. The trumpet would be played more and more loudly as the time for the performance drew near. Plays began at two o'clock in winter and somewhat later when the days grew longer.

Actors entered and exited the stage through two sets of large doors in the front of the tiring-house. All actors were male, with most female parts being played by boys. These boy actors were chosen for their public-speaking skills and then trained by the adult actors to play female roles convincingly.

The audience could be very noisy. People would move around, talk, munch apples and crack nuts. If an actor was not doing a good job, the audience would be sure to let him

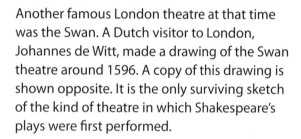

Sketch of the interior of the Swan Theatre, by Johannes de Witt, as copied by Aernout van Buchel, c. 1596

KEY

1. Playhouse flag
2. Storage loft
3. The heavens
4. Gallery over stage
5. Tiring-house
6. Stage doors
7. Upper gallery
8. Middle gallery
9. Entrance to lower gallery
10. Stage
11. Hell (under stage)
12. Yard

know about it. If a play was boring, spectators would find other ways to amuse themselves, such as playing cards or dice games. Even when the play caught their interest, they would be more likely to make loud comments about it than to enjoy the action in silence.

There was no painted scenery to indicate where the action was taking place. Playwrights like Shakespeare were experts in using words to set the scene, and the audience accepted that the stage could be any place that the action required, from a palace to a graveyard, or a public street to a private bedroom.

One problem Shakespeare had to solve for *Romeo and Juliet* was how to present night

scenes when performances took place in daylight. To overcome this problem, Shakespeare makes the actors suggest darkness through the words they speak. For example, the scene in which Romeo and Juliet express their love for each other takes place late at night, and this is emphasised in the speeches of both characters. Romeo refers to 'the envious moon', 'the fairest stars', 'this night'. He tells Juliet that he has 'night's cloak' to hide himself from being seen by her family. Juliet says Romeo is hidden or 'bescreened in night', notes that 'the mask of night' is on her face, and refers to 'the dark night'.

About *Romeo and Juliet*

THE STORY OF THE young lovers Romeo and Juliet had already appeared in many versions (in Italian, French and English) before it reached Shakespeare. As far as Shakespeare was concerned, the most important of these was a long poem (3,020 lines) with the title *The Tragical History of Romeus and Juliet* by the English poet Arthur Brooke. This poem was published in 1562, two years before Shakespeare was born.

Shakespeare found all the details he needed for *Romeo and Juliet* in Brooke's poem, and presumably had this poem beside him as he wrote his play. Shakespeare did not invent his plots. He borrowed these from works by other writers, English as well as European. At the time it was not considered necessary to invent new stories. It was about being creative with well-known stories and making them your own.

Romeo and Juliet is believed to have been written between 1594 and 1595. It is set in the cities of Verona and Mantua in northern Italy in the fourteenth century.

The play's fame prompts thousands of tourists to visit Verona each year. Of particular interest is Juliet's balcony, where some people stick messages and letters to Juliet on the walls. However, there is no evidence that Romeo and Juliet ever existed. And while there are records of the Capulets and Montagues, it seems the families were not involved in a feud.

Romeo and Juliet is still popular in theatres throughout the world, not only as a stage play, but also in musical, opera, ballet and film forms. In 2013, for example, a new *Romeo and Juliet* film was released starring Douglas Booth and Hailee Steinfeld, while Orlando Bloom starred in a stage production in New York, and a *Romeo and Juliet* ballet ran for two months at the Royal Opera House in London.

The story of *Romeo and Juliet* has inspired many other works. For example, *New Moon* in the *Twilight* series of novels, the animated film *Gnomeo & Juliet*, the film *High School Musical* starring Zac Efron and Vanessa Hudgens, and Taylor Swift's song 'Love Story'.

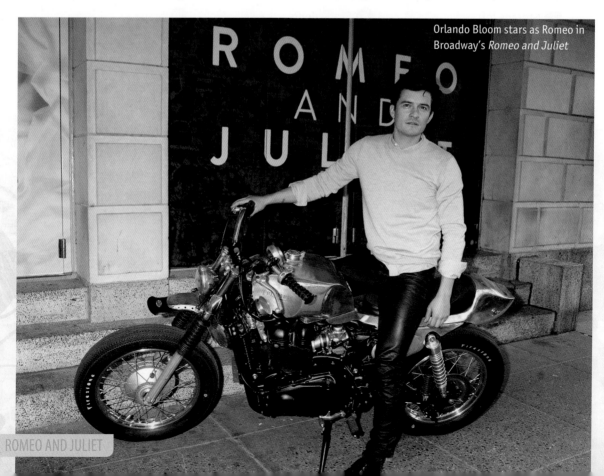

Orlando Bloom stars as Romeo in Broadway's *Romeo and Juliet*

Movie stills from modern adaptations of *Romeo and Juliet* – *Gnomeo & Juliet* and *High School Musical*

ROMEO AND JULIET

Dramatis personae

ESCALUS	Prince of Verona
MERCUTIO	kinsman of the Prince and friend of Romeo
PARIS	a young count, kinsman of the Prince and Mercutio, and suitor of Juliet
PAGE	to Count Paris

THE MONTAGUES

MONTAGUE	head of a Veronese family at feud with the Capulets
LADY MONTAGUE	wife of Montague
ROMEO	son of Montague
BENVOLIO	nephew of Montague and friend of Romeo and Mercutio
ABRAM	servant of Montague
BALTHASAR	servant of Montague attending on Romeo

THE CAPULETS

CAPULET	head of a Veronese family at feud with the Montagues
LADY CAPULET	wife of Capulet
JULIET	daughter of Capulet
TYBALT	nephew of Lady Capulet
AN OLD MAN	of the Capulet family
NURSE	attending Juliet
PETER	servant to Juliet's nurse

SAMPSON, GREGORY, ANTHONY, POTPAN, A CLOWN, SERVINGMAN of the Capulet household

FRIAR LAURENCE	a Franciscan
FRIAR JOHN	a Franciscan
AN APOTHECARY	of Mantua
THREE MUSICIANS	(SIMON CATLING, HUGH REBEK, JAMES SOUNDPOST)

MEMBERS OF THE WATCH, CITIZENS OF VERONA, MASKERS, TORCHBEARERS, PAGES, SERVANTS, CHORUS

Prologue

Plot summary

The Prologue gives the audience a preview of what will happen in the play. It sets the scene: the beautiful city of Verona, where two families are involved in a feud that has been going on for generations. It gives a summary of the plot: a child of each of these feuding families will fall in love with the other and then take his or her own life. This is their fate, their unavoidable destiny written in the stars. Their deaths will bring an end to the feud. Finally, the Prologue asks the audience to listen patiently for the next two hours to get the full story.

Enter: one or more characters arriving on stage

1 *dignity:* rank, importance

2 *lay:* set, locate

3 *ancient grudge:* long-standing feud; the two families have been enemies for a long time
break ... mutiny: are about to quarrel violently again

4 *civil ... unclean:* citizens have the blood of other citizens on their hands

5–6 *From ... life:* the two families are cursed by fate – a child from each family is doomed by the stars to fall in love with the other and to take his or her own life

7–8 *Whose ... strife:* the unfortunate deaths of the lovers bring their parents' feud to an end

9 *passage:* course, history

11 *but ... remove:* only the lovers' deaths could bring to an end

12 *two ... stage:* business of our play, lasting about two hours

13 *attend:* pay attention to

14 *What ... mend:* the actors will try to fill in what is missing in this preview

Exit: the character who has been speaking leaves the stage

Enter CHORUS.

CHORUS

Two households, both alike in dignity

In fair Verona, where we lay our scene,

From ancient grudge break to new mutiny,

Where civil blood makes civil hands unclean.

5 From forth the fatal loins of these two foes

A pair of star-crossed lovers take their life;

Whose misadventured piteous overthrows

Doth with their death bury their parents' strife.

The fearful passage of their death-marked love

10 And the continuance of their parents' rage,

Which, but their children's end, naught could remove,

Is now the two hours' traffic of our stage;

The which if you with patient ears attend,

What here shall miss, our toil shall strive to mend.

Exit

Key points

The Prologue introduces the play and mentions its key elements: 'star-crossed lovers'; 'piteous overthrows'; 'death-marked love'.

- A **prologue** is a short speech to introduce a play or other text. Here it is spoken by the Chorus – this is a single actor (not a group of singers). In the theatre, the Chorus is often the same actor who plays the role of Prince Escalus.

- The first four lines refer to the long-standing feud between two families in the Italian city of Verona. These families (the Montagues and the Capulets) cannot meet without there being a bloody brawl. The feud has been going on for generations and is about to erupt again.

- The next four lines introduce the two lovers (Romeo and Juliet), who are doomed to die as a result of the feud but whose deaths will bring about its end when the two families make peace.

- An important purpose of the Prologue is to suggest that what happens to Romeo and Juliet is inevitable. Romeo and Juliet will die. There is nothing that they can do to avoid this outcome. It is their destiny to meet, fall in love and take their own lives.

- Fate is one of the key themes of the play. Fate is the idea that some unseen power decides what is in store for us as we make our way through life. It was widely believed in Shakespeare's day that the stars governed the lives of human beings. This idea is conveyed in the description of the lovers as 'star-crossed' (line 6) and of their love as 'death-marked' (line 9).

- The final six lines repeat the play's outcome: the deaths of Romeo and Juliet will end the fighting between the families. They also ask the audience to pay attention to the play, which will last for about two hours, so that the actors can reveal the full story.

- When we are told at the start of a play (or a film or a story) how it will end, our attention turns to focus on how that ending will come about. We want to know how Romeo and Juliet will meet, fall in love and die. Also, it is easier to believe in fate when we know what will happen from the start.

- The Prologue indicates what kind of play it is: a **tragedy**. In tragedies, good characters usually make a mistake that eventually leads to their downfall. In this play, Romeo and Juliet will make decisions that in the end lead to their deaths. A tragedy always has an unhappy ending.

- The Prologue focuses on the play's tragic elements: the love of the two main characters is doomed and will lead to their deaths. It does not give a full summary of the plot and does not mention the play's comic aspects.

- The Prologue is in the form of a **sonnet**, which is a fourteen-line poem made up of three quatrains (groups of four lines) and a rhyming couplet (two lines). Shakespearean sonnets have a special rhyming scheme: *abab cdcd efef gg*. Sonnets were very popular in Shakespeare's day and were often about doomed or hopeless love.

ACT 1 † Scene 1

Plot summary

Two servants from the Capulet household, Sampson and Gregory, boast about their part in the feud with the Montagues. When two Montague servants, Abram and Balthasar, approach, the Capulet servants try to start a fight. Benvolio, a Montague, tries to stop the fight; but Tybalt, a Capulet, attacks Benvolio. The fight soon turns into a public brawl, involving the heads of the Montague and Capulet families. Prince Escalus, ruler of the city of Verona, arrives to bring it to an end. He tells everyone to leave on pain of death, which will be the penalty for anyone caught fighting on the streets in future.

With the fighting over, a new theme is introduced: the lovesick Romeo is depressed. Romeo's parents ask Benvolio to find out what is wrong with him. It turns out that Romeo cannot win over the girl he loves. Benvolio believes that the only remedy for Romeo's condition is to wipe out her memory by finding a different girl to love. Romeo does not think that will be possible.

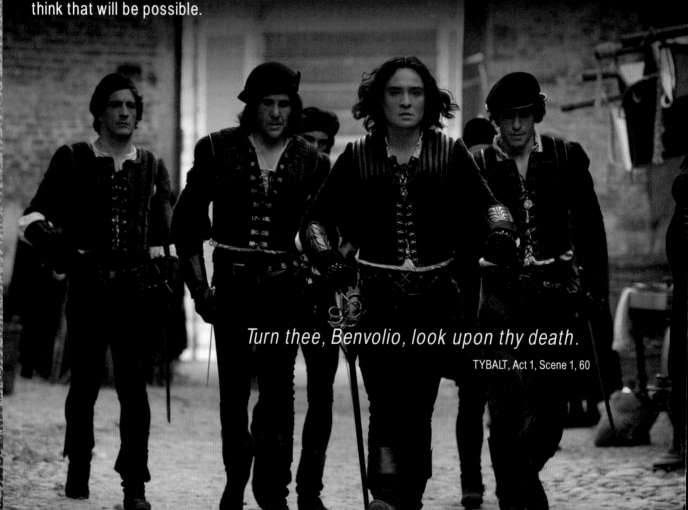

Turn thee, Benvolio, look upon thy death.

TYBALT, Act 1, Scene 1, 60

Verona. A public place.

Enter SAMPSON and GREGORY, with swords and bucklers, of the house of Capulet.

SAMPSON

Gregory, on my word, we'll not carry coals.

GREGORY

No. For then we should be colliers.

SAMPSON

I mean, an we be in choler, we'll draw.

GREGORY

Ay, while you live, draw your neck out of collar.

SAMPSON

I strike quickly, being moved.   5

GREGORY

But thou art not quickly moved to strike.

SAMPSON

A dog of the house of Montague moves me.

GREGORY

To move is to stir, and to be valiant is to stand.

Therefore, if thou art moved, thou runnest away.

SAMPSON

A dog of that house shall move me to stand.   10

I will take the wall of any man or maid of Montague's.

GREGORY

That shows thee a weak slave. For the weakest goes to the wall.

SAMPSON

'Tis true; and therefore women, being the weaker vessels, are ever thrust to the wall. Therefore I will push   15
Montague's men from the wall, and thrust his maids to the wall.

GREGORY

This quarrel is between our masters, and us their men.

SAMPSON

'Tis all one. I will show myself a tyrant. When I have fought with the men, I will be civil with the maids — I will   20
cut off their heads.

---

bucklers: small shields; the two Capulet servants are armed for a fight

1 *we'll … coals:* we won't allow ourselves to be insulted

2 *For … colliers:* if we carried coals we would be coal sellers ('colliers'). This is one of the many puns in the play. The reference to colliers leads to puns on 'choler' (anger) and 'collar' (hangman's noose)
3 *I … draw:* I mean that if we are angry, we'll draw our swords

5 *being moved:* when I am provoked

6 *thou … quickly:* you are not easily

7 *A … me:* I would be ready to strike at any member of the enemy family, the Montagues

8–9 *To move … away:* Gregory pretends to misunderstand Sampson, and to think that 'move' means 'run away'
8 *to be … stand:* to be brave is to make a stand (i.e. not to move or run away)

10 *move … stand:* cause me to stand and fight

11 *I … Montague's:* I will put myself before any man or woman of the Montague family
take the wall: take the cleaner, better side of the footpath
12–13 *For … wall:* because the weakest people are pushed aside, or pushed to the rear

14–17 *women … maids to the wall:* women, who tend to be weaker than men, can be pushed to the wall. Sampson will be able to push Montague's servants away from the wall, and push the Montague women against the wall, to assault or molest them

19 *tyrant:* ruler who uses power in a cruel way

GREGORY

The heads of the maids?

SAMPSON

Ay, the heads of the maids, or their maidenheads. Take it in what sense thou wilt.

GREGORY

25 They must take it in sense that feel it.

SAMPSON

Me they shall feel while I am able to stand; and 'tis known I am a pretty piece of flesh.

GREGORY

'Tis well thou art not fish; if thou hadst, thou hadst been poor-John. Draw thy tool. Here comes of the house of the
30 Montagues.

Enter ABRAM and another SERVINGMAN.

SAMPSON

My naked weapon is out. Quarrel. I will back thee.

GREGORY

How? Turn thy back and run?

SAMPSON

Fear me not.

GREGORY

No, marry. I fear thee!

SAMPSON

35 Let us take the law of our sides. Let them begin.

GREGORY

I will frown as I pass by, and let them take it as they list.

SAMPSON

Nay, as they dare. I will bite my thumb at them; which is disgrace to them if they bear it.

ABRAM

Do you bite your thumb at us, sir?

SAMPSON

40 I do bite my thumb, sir.

ABRAM

Do you bite your thumb at us, sir?

23–4 *Ay . . . wilt:* yes, I will deprive the women of their heads, or of their virginity; you can take whatever meaning you like out of my words

25 *They . . . feel it:* the women who suffer from what you do to them will experience your meaning for themselves

26–7 *Me . . . flesh:* they will feel my attentions as long as I am able to keep them up, and it is well known that I am good at that kind of thing

28–9 *'Tis . . . poor-John:* it is as well you are flesh and not fish; if you were a fish, you'd be like a dried salted hake, fit only for a poor man's dinner

29 *tool:* weapon
of the house: some members of the household

31 *naked weapon:* bare sword

34 *marry:* by the Virgin Mary (a mild oath)

35 *Let . . . sides:* let us have the law on our side

36 *list:* please, like

37 *bite my thumb:* an insulting gesture

38 *bear it:* put up with it

SAMPSON [*aside to GREGORY*]

Is the law of our side if I say 'Ay'?

GREGORY [*aside to SAMPSON*]

No.

SAMPSON

No, sir, I do not bite my thumb at you, sir. But I bite my   45
thumb, sir.

GREGORY

Do you quarrel, sir?

ABRAM

Quarrel, sir? No, sir.

SAMPSON

But if you do, sir, I am for you. I serve as good a man as   48   *for you:* ready to fight you
you.

ABRAM

No better.   50

SAMPSON

Well, sir.

Enter BENVOLIO.

GREGORY [*aside to SAMPSON*]

Say 'better'. Here comes one of my master's kinsmen.   52   *kinsmen:* relatives, members of the Capulet family.
                                                                       Gregory is referring to Tybalt. In fact, it is Benvolio,
                                                                       a Montague, who arrives first

SAMPSON

Yes, better, sir.

ABRAM

You lie.

SAMPSON

Draw, if you be men. Gregory, remember thy washing   55   55–6   *washing blow:* slashing stroke with a sword
blow.

They fight.

BENVOLIO

Part, fools!

Put up your swords. You know not what you do.

Enter TYBALT.

TYBALT

What, art thou drawn among these heartless hinds?   59   *art . . . hinds?* Have you drawn your sword among
Turn thee, Benvolio, look upon thy death.   60   this group of cowardly slaves?
                                                                       60   *Turn . . . death:* turn around and face my sword,
                                                                             which threatens you with death

61–2 *I . . . me:* Benvolio does not want to fight Tybalt. He tells him that he is trying to make peace between the quarrelling servants and asks Tybalt to help him to do this

63–4 *What . . . thee:* Tybalt wants to fight at all costs. He cannot understand how Benvolio, who has his sword drawn, can talk of peace. Tybalt hates peace, all Montagues and Benvolio, as much as he hates hell

65 *Have at thee:* I challenge you

partisans: weapons combining the spear and the battle-axe

66 *bills:* weapons like partisans

gown: dressing gown

69 *A crutch . . . sword?* an old man like you should be calling for a crutch, not a sword. Lady Capulet has a sarcastic tongue

71 *flourishes . . . me:* waves his sword about to defy me

73 *Thou . . . foe:* Lady Montague will not allow her husband to fight
train: followers, entourage

75 *Profaners . . . steel:* you, who misuse your swords by staining them with your neighbours' blood

77–8 *That . . . veins:* you satisfy your rage by causing streams of dark red blood to flow

80 *mistempered:* both badly made, and used in bad temper
81 *movèd:* angry

BENVOLIO

I do but keep the peace. Put up thy sword,

Or manage it to part these men with me.

TYBALT

What, drawn, and talk of peace? I hate the word

As I hate hell, all Montagues, and thee.

65　Have at thee, coward!

They fight.

Enter three or four CITIZENS with clubs or partisans.

CITIZENS

Clubs, bills, and partisans! Strike! Beat them down!

Down with the Capulets! Down with the Montagues!

Enter Old CAPULET in his gown, and LADY CAPULET.

CAPULET

What noise is this? Give me my long sword, ho!

LADY CAPULET

A crutch, a crutch! Why call you for a sword?

Enter Old MONTAGUE and LADY MONTAGUE.

CAPULET

70　My sword, I say! Old Montague is come

And flourishes his blade in spite of me.

MONTAGUE

Thou villain Capulet! — Hold me not. Let me go.

LADY MONTAGUE

Thou shalt not stir one foot to seek a foe.

Enter PRINCE ESCALUS, with his train.

PRINCE

Rebellious subjects, enemies to peace,

75　Profaners of this neighbour-stainèd steel —

Will they not hear? What, ho — you men, you beasts,

That quench the fire of your pernicious rage

With purple fountains issuing from your veins!

On pain of torture, from those bloody hands

80　Throw your mistempered weapons to the ground

And hear the sentence of your movèd Prince.

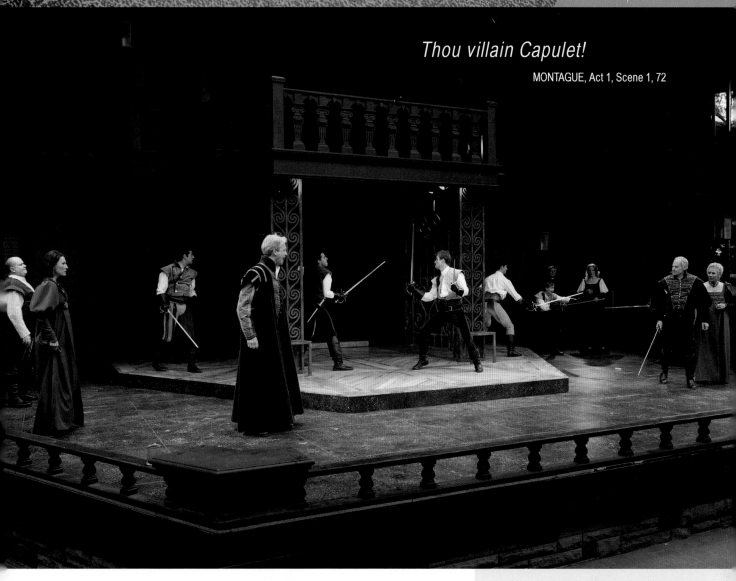

Thou villain Capulet!

MONTAGUE, Act 1, Scene 1, 72

Three civil brawls, bred of an airy word

By thee, old Capulet, and Montague,

Have thrice disturbed the quiet of our streets

And made Verona's ancient citizens 85

Cast by their grave-beseeming ornaments

To wield old partisans, in hands as old,

Cankered with peace, to part your cankered hate.

If ever you disturb our streets again,

Your lives shall pay the forfeit of the peace. 90

For this time all the rest depart away.

You, Capulet, shall go along with me;

And, Montague, come you this afternoon,

To know our farther pleasure in this case,

To old Free-town, our common judgement-place. 95

Once more, on pain of death, all men depart.

Exeunt all but MONTAGUE, LADY MONTAGUE and BENVOLIO.

82–4 *Three ... streets:* three times the peace of Verona's streets has been disturbed by quarrels started when members of your families insulted each other

85–8 *And ... hate:* the old citizens of Verona have had to lay aside their dignity and use their peaceful hands to wield old weapons to break up your hateful brawls

90 *Your ... peace:* you will be executed for having broken the peace

91 *For ... away:* everyone must leave now

Exeunt: more than one character is leaving the stage

97 *Who . . . abroach?* Who opened up this old quarrel again?
98 *by:* near

MONTAGUE

Who set this ancient quarrel new abroach?

Speak, nephew, were you by when it began?

BENVOLIO

Here were the servants of your adversary

99 *adversary:* enemy (Capulet)
100 *ere:* before
101 *In the instant:* at that moment
102 *prepared:* drawn

100 And yours, close fighting ere I did approach.

I drew to part them. In the instant came

The fiery Tybalt, with his sword prepared;

Which, as he breathed defiance to my ears,

He swung about his head and cut the winds,

105 *hurt withal:* the winds were not hurt by Tybalt's wild swings

105 Who nothing hurt withal, hissed him in scorn.

While we were interchanging thrusts and blows,

107 *on part and part:* on either side; some on each side
108 *parted either part:* separated the two sides

Came more and more, and fought on part and part,

Till the Prince came, who parted either part.

LADY MONTAGUE

O where is Romeo? Saw you him today?

110 *fray:* brawl

110 Right glad I am he was not at this fray.

BENVOLIO

Madam, an hour before the worshipped sun

111 *worshipped:* esteemed, honoured
112 *Peered forth:* looked from
113 *drive:* drove
abroad: around, away from home

Peered forth the golden window of the East,

A troubled mind drive me to walk abroad;

Where, underneath the grove of sycamore

115 *westward . . . side:* grows on the west side of the city

115 That westward rooteth from the city side,

So early walking did I see your son.

117 *ware:* aware

Towards him I made. But he was ware of me

118 *stole:* slipped furtively
covert: thicket

And stole into the covert of the wood.

119–23 *I . . . me:* I thought that Romeo, like me, was feeling the need to get away from people. So I avoided him, and didn't find out what was causing his mood

I, measuring his affections by my own,

120 Which then most sought where most might not be found,

Being one too many by my weary self,

Pursued my humour, not pursuing his,

And gladly shunned who gladly fled from me.

MONTAGUE

Many a morning hath he there been seen

125 *augmenting:* adding to

125 With tears augmenting the fresh morning's dew,

Adding to clouds more clouds with his deep sighs.

127 *all so soon:* just

But all so soon as the all-cheering sun

Should in the farthest East begin to draw

129 *Aurora:* goddess of the dawn
130 *heavy:* sad, moody

The shady curtains from Aurora's bed,

130 Away from the light steals home my heavy son

And private in his chamber pens himself,

Shuts up his windows, locks far daylight out,

And makes himself an artificial night.

Black and portentous must this humour prove

Unless good counsel may the cause remove.   135

BENVOLIO

My noble uncle, do you know the cause?

MONTAGUE

I neither know it nor can learn of him.

BENVOLIO

Have you importuned him by any means?

MONTAGUE

Both by myself and many other friends.

But he, his own affections' counsellor,   140

Is to himself — I will not say how true —

But to himself so secret and so close,

So far from sounding and discovery,

As is the bud bit with an envious worm

Ere he can spread his sweet leaves to the air   145

Or dedicate his beauty to the sun.

Could we but learn from whence his sorrows grow,

We would as willingly give cure as know.

Enter ROMEO.

BENVOLIO

See, where he comes. So please you, step aside.

I'll know his grievance, or be much denied.   150

MONTAGUE

I would thou wert so happy by thy stay

To hear true shrift. Come, madam, let's away.

Exeunt MONTAGUE and LADY MONTAGUE.

BENVOLIO

Good morrow, cousin.

ROMEO

                    Is the day so young?

BENVOLIO

But new struck nine.

---

131   *pens:* confines

134–5   *Black ... remove:* Romeo's mood will lead to tragedy unless someone can advise him as to how he can overcome it

138   *importuned him:* pressed him for an explanation

140–2   *he ... close:* Romeo is keeping the secret of his feelings to himself

143   *So ... discovery:* so far from measuring the depth of his feelings and revealing them

144–6   *As ... sun:* Romeo is like a bud eaten by a nasty worm. Until the worm is dealt with, the bud will not flower; likewise, until Romeo's problem is resolved, he will not be his natural self

147–8   *Could ... know:* if only we knew the cause of his sadness; we want to cure it as much as to know the details

149   *So please you:* if you please

150   *I'll ... denied:* it will take a lot to stop me from finding out what is troubling him

151–2   *I ... shrift:* I hope that during your stay you will be lucky enough to get Romeo to confess the truth about his sorrow
152   *shrift:* confession

153   *morrow:* morning

153   *Is ... young?* Romeo is surprised to know that it is still morning

154   *But new:* only just

154	*Sad . . . long:* time is passing slowly for him because of his sadness
155	*hence:* away from here
157	*Not . . . short:* if I had what I want (the love of Rosaline), the hours would seem short; without it, they seem long
161	*Out . . . love:* the girl I love does not love me
162–3	*Alas . . . proof!* it's a pity that love, which looks so gentle, should be so cruel and savage underneath
164–5	*Alas . . . will!* it's a pity that love, which is blind, should see clearly enough to bring about what it wants
164	*view is muffled:* a reference to Cupid, the god of love, who is usually shown with bandages over his eyes
168	*Here's . . . love:* there is a great deal of upset in the city because of the brawl that was caused by hatred, but there is even more upset within me because of the love I feel
169	*brawling . . . hate:* Rosaline, the girl Romeo loves, is niece to his enemy, Capulet. He loves the person he should hate, and his family, servants and friends have been brawling with the Capulets, one of whom he loves
171–4	*heavy . . . it is!* love has so disturbed Romeo's mind that his speech is full of contradictions. Such contradictions ('cold fire, sick health' and so on) are very common in love poems
175	*This . . . this:* I don't enjoy feeling the kind of love I now feel
176	*coz:* cousin
177	*At . . . oppression:* because of the sadness you feel

ROMEO

                   Ay me! Sad hours seem long.

155 Was that my father that went hence so fast?

BENVOLIO

It was. What sadness lengthens Romeo's hours?

ROMEO

Not having that which having makes them short.

BENVOLIO

In love?

ROMEO

Out—

BENVOLIO

160 Of love?

ROMEO

Out of her favour where I am in love.

BENVOLIO

Alas that love, so gentle in his view,

Should be so tyrannous and rough in proof!

ROMEO

Alas that love, whose view is muffled, still

165 Should without eyes see pathways to his will!

Where shall we dine? O me, what fray was here?

Yet tell me not, for I have heard it all.

Here's much to do with hate, but more with love.

Why then, O brawling love, O loving hate,

170 O anything, of nothing first create!

O heavy lightness, serious vanity,

Misshapen chaos of well-seeming forms,

Feather of lead, bright smoke, cold fire, sick health,

Still-waking sleep, that is not what it is!

175 This love feel I, that feel no love in this.

Dost thou not laugh?

BENVOLIO

                No, coz, I rather weep.

ROMEO

Good heart, at what?

BENVOLIO

                At thy good heart's oppression.

ROMEO

Why, such is love's transgression.

Griefs of mine own lie heavy in my breast,

Which thou wilt propagate, to have it pressed   180

With more of thine. This love that thou hast shown

Doth add more grief to too much of mine own.

Love is a smoke made with the fume of sighs;

Being purged, a fire sparkling in lovers' eyes;

Being vexed, a sea nourished with lovers' tears.   185

What is it else? A madness most discreet,

A choking gall and a preserving sweet.

Farewell, my coz.

BENVOLIO

                  Soft! I will go along.

An if you leave me so, you do me wrong.

ROMEO

Tut, I have lost myself. I am not here.   190

This is not Romeo, he's some other where.

BENVOLIO

Tell me in sadness, who is that you love?

ROMEO

What, shall I groan and tell thee?

BENVOLIO

Groan? Why, no. But sadly tell me who.

ROMEO

Bid a sick man in sadness make his will.   195

Ah, word ill urged to one that is so ill!

In sadness, cousin, I do love a woman.

BENVOLIO

I aimed so near when I supposed you loved.

ROMEO

A right good markman. And she's fair I love.

BENVOLIO

A right fair mark, fair coz, is soonest hit.   200

ROMEO

Well, in that hit you miss. She'll not be hit

With Cupid's arrow. She hath Dian's wit,

---

178 *transgression:* fault

179–81 *Griefs … thine:* I have my own share of sadness. You will only add to my sadness if you burden me with your sorrows

180 *propagate:* increase

181–2 *This … own:* the love and kindness you have shown me make my sorrow all the greater

186 *madness most discreet:* love is a madness, but at the same time it allows lovers to see things clearly and accurately. Romeo believes that love consists of opposites

187 *gall:* something bitter

188 *Soft!* wait a moment

189 *An if:* if

190–1 *I have … where:* love has altered Romeo's personality; he is no longer himself

194 *sadly:* seriously

195 *Bid … will:* this is like asking a sick man to make his will on the point of death (i.e. it will only make me miserable)

198 *I … near:* I guessed as much

199 *she's … love:* the woman I love is beautiful

200 *A … hit:* a target easily seen is easiest to hit. Benvolio is telling Romeo that he should have little trouble in winning the love of the girl

201 *in … miss:* you are wrong there

201–2 *She'll … arrow:* she won't fall in love

202 *Dian's wit:* the cleverness of Diana, the goddess of the chastity

203–4 *And ... uncharmed:* and she is able to resist the temptations of love

And, in strong proof of chastity well armed,

From love's weak childish bow she lives uncharmed.

205 *stay:* submit to, be won over by
loving terms: fine words of love
206 *bide:* put up with
assailing eyes: loving glances
207 *ope:* open

205 She will not stay the siege of loving terms,

Nor bide th' encounter of assailing eyes,

Nor ope her lap to saint-seducing gold.

O, she is rich in beauty; only poor

209 *with ... store:* as she will have no children, her beauty will not pass on to the next generation

That, when she dies, with beauty dies her store.

BENVOLIO

210 *still:* always

210 Then she hath sworn that she will still live chaste?

ROMEO

She hath; and in that sparing makes huge waste.

211 *sparing:* economy, miserliness

For beauty, starved with her severity,

Cuts beauty off from all posterity.

She is too fair, too wise, wisely too fair,

215 *To ... despair:* to want to earn heaven through her virtue, while making me commit the sin of despair
216–17 *She ... now:* she has promised not to love any man, and this means that I must go on living in a half-dead state

215 To merit bliss by making me despair.

She hath forsworn to love; and in that vow

Do I live dead that live to tell it now.

BENVOLIO

Be ruled by me — forget to think of her.

ROMEO

O, teach me how I should forget to think!

BENVOLIO

220–1 *By ... beauties:* allow yourself the freedom to look at other beautiful girls

220 By giving liberty unto thine eyes.

Examine other beauties.

ROMEO

'Tis the way

221–2 *'Tis ... more:* looking at other beauties will only make me think about her superior beauty even more
223 *masks:* worn to protect the face from the sun

To call hers, exquisite, in question more.

These happy masks that kiss fair ladies' brows,

Being black, put us in mind they hide the fair.

225 *is strucken:* has been stricken

225 He that is strucken blind cannot forget

The precious treasure of his eyesight lost.

227–9 *Show ... fair?* when I see a beautiful woman this only reminds me of the woman I now love (Rosaline), who is more beautiful than any other

Show me a mistress that is passing fair,

What doth her beauty serve but as a note

Where I may read who passed that passing fair?

230 Farewell. Thou canst not teach me to forget.

BENVOLIO

231 *I'll ... debt:* I'll teach you that lesson or else die in the attempt

I'll pay that doctrine, or else die in debt.

Exeunt.

Key points

This scene has two main divisions. In the first part (lines 1–108), we witness the feud between the Montagues and the Capulets in action. In the second (lines 109–231), we learn of Romeo's feelings for a beautiful girl who refuses to return his love.

Timeline

Sunday	Monday	Tuesday	Wednesday	Thursday

- One of the main themes of the play is the feud between the Montagues and the Capulets. This scene brings us into the heart of that feud. Nobody knows when, how or why this feud between the Montagues and the Capulets began. Despite this, they seem ready to fight each other at every opportunity. As soon as servants of the two households see each other, they start a quarrel.

- Although it looks trivial at this stage, when Sampson bites his thumb at the Montague servants (lines 37–8) he starts off a process that will lead to several deaths before the play ends. In this scene, his insulting gesture leads to a fight in which the hot-headed Tybalt takes part. Tybalt will look for a chance to resume the quarrel as soon as possible.

- This fight also brings Prince Escalus on stage. He is the ruler of Verona and seems to be the only person able to stop the violence. His announcement that those who riot in future will face the death penalty (lines 89–90) is another key moment. This new law has major consequences later in the play.

- This scene also introduces one of the two title characters: Romeo. We learn from his worried parents, Lord and Lady Montague, that Romeo appears sad and depressed. They ask Romeo's cousin and friend Benvolio to try to find out what is wrong with their troubled son so that they can help him.

- The remainder of the scene is devoted to Romeo's frustrated love for a beautiful girl (we later find out that her name is Rosaline). He is obsessed with her but she has sworn never to marry.

- Romeo claims that he cannot stop thinking about Rosaline. His friend Benvolio thinks that if Romeo can be persuaded to turn his attention to other beauties, he will soon forget her.

- Romeo's love woes are also linked to the feud: Romeo is a Montague, while Rosaline is a Capulet.

- Some scenes in *Romeo and Juliet* contain puns and other examples of **wordplay**. The opening exchange between Sampson and Gregory is an example of this feature. These crude characters make a series of jokes based on the different meanings, spellings and sounds of words. We have to assume that Shakespeare's early audiences found these very funny. But more than four hundred years later, it can be easy to miss the joke. Fortunately, actors on stage or screen can use facial expressions and gestures to help us understand. It is worth taking time to read the margin notes given here to get a better grasp of the text of the play.

Useful quotes

> *I will bite my thumb at them; which is disgrace to them if they bear it.*
>
> (Sampson, lines 37–8)

> *If ever you disturb our streets again,*
> *Your lives shall pay the forfeit of the peace.*
>
> (Prince Escalus, lines 89–90)

> *What, drawn, and talk of peace? I hate the word*
> *As I hate hell, all Montagues, and thee.*
>
> (Tybalt, lines 63–4)

> *She hath forsworn to love; and in that vow*
> *Do I live dead that live to tell it now.*
>
> (Romeo, lines 216–17)

? Questions

1 What starts the fight in this scene?

2 Who tries to stop the fight?

3 In what way is Tybalt an important contributor to this scene?

4 What do Capulet's first words (line 68) tell us about him?

5 The attitude of Lady Capulet and Lady Montague to the feud appears to differ from the attitude of their husbands. How is this difference shown?

6 What ends the fight in this scene?

7 What impression does Prince Escalus make in this scene?

8 Why are Romeo's parents and Benvolio so concerned about Romeo?

9 What advice does Benvolio give to Romeo? Do you agree with this advice?

10 Imagine you are Romeo. Write a short letter to Agnes, the agony aunt at *Verona Today* magazine, describing how you feel about Rosaline and asking for advice on what to do.

11 Imagine you are the agony aunt. Write a response to Romeo's request for advice.

12 If you were directing the play, how would you help the audience to know who is a Capulet and who is a Montague? Consider issues such as casting, costume, hair and make-up.

Talking point

The feud in *Romeo and Juliet* involves two families who have grown up hating each other. Can you think of situations in today's world where people on one side hate those on the other side? Think about supporters of rival teams, criminal gangs, groups with religious, cultural or political differences, etc. What is their hatred based on? Why do people like to take sides?

Plot summary

Count (or County) Paris is a young nobleman related to Prince Escalus. He wants permission to marry Capulet's only daughter, Juliet. Capulet encourages him to win the love of Juliet first and then he can marry her in two years' time when she will be sixteen. Capulet will be hosting a great feast that evening and suggests that this will be a chance for Paris to meet and woo Juliet. Everyone who is not a Montague will be welcome at the feast.

Capulet gives a list of names to a servant and asks him to go and invite them to the feast. The servant is not able to read and asks Romeo and Benvolio for their help. Romeo sees that his beloved, Rosaline, who is Capulet's niece, is a guest. He decides to risk going to the house of his deadly enemies in order to see Rosaline.

Compare her face with some that I shall show,
And I will make thee think thy swan a crow.

BENVOLIO, Act 1, Scene 2, 86–7

County: Count (title of rank; a nobleman)

1 *bound:* forced to keep the peace

2 *In penalty alike:* both of us will suffer the same punishment if we do not keep the peace

4 *reckoning:* reputation

6 *suit:* important request (he wants to marry Juliet)

7 *saying o'er:* repeating

9 *change:* passage, or passing

10 *pride:* prime, fullest flowering

11 *Ere:* before
ripe: ready

13 *marred ... made:* suffering bad health by having children when they are too young (or perhaps dying in childbirth)

14 *Earth ... she:* she is the only one of my children left alive

15 *She's ... earth:* all my hopes depend on her

16 *get her heart:* win her love

17–19 *My ... voice:* my say in Juliet's choice of husband is not absolute; if she favours somebody else, I will go along with her wishes

19 *according:* approving, agreeing

20 *an old accustomed feast:* a feast that the Capulets have been hosting for many years

21 *Whereto:* to which

22 *store:* number (of guests)

24 *behold:* observe, watch

25 *Earth-treading ... light:* the ladies at the feast will be like stars – as they walk, or dance, they will reflect light into the sky, and change darkness to brightness

27 *well-apparalled April:* April is the month of new leaves, plants and flowers. Capulet thinks of April as being dressed in foliage

28 *limping winter:* winter is slow to go away

30 *Inherit:* have, receive

31 *And ... be:* and give your love to the girl who most deserves it

32–3 *Which ... none:* when you see more girls than Juliet, it may happen that you will prefer somebody other than her

Verona. Another street.

Enter CAPULET, COUNTY PARIS, and a SERVANT (CLOWN).

CAPULET

But Montague is bound as well as I,

In penalty alike; and 'tis not hard, I think,

For men so old as we to keep the peace.

PARIS

Of honourable reckoning are you both,

5 And pity 'tis you lived at odds so long.

But now, my lord, what say you to my suit?

CAPULET

But saying o'er what I have said before:

My child is yet a stranger in the world;

She hath not seen the change of fourteen years.

10 Let two more summers wither in their pride

Ere we may think her ripe to be a bride.

PARIS

Younger than she are happy mothers made.

CAPULET

And too soon marred are those so early made.

Earth hath swallowed all my hopes but she;

15 She's the hopeful lady of my earth.

But woo her, gentle Paris, get her heart.

My will to her consent is but a part,

And, she agreed, within her scope of choice

Lies my consent and fair according voice.

20 This night I hold an old accustomed feast,

Whereto I have invited many a guest,

Such as I love; and you among the store,

One more, most welcome, makes my number more.

At my poor house look to behold this night

25 Earth-treading stars that make dark heaven light.

Such comfort as do lusty young men feel

When well-apparelled April on the heel

Of limping winter treads, even such delight

Among fresh female buds shall you this night

30 Inherit at my house. Hear all; all see;

And like her most whose merit most shall be;

Which, on more view of many, mine, being one,

May stand in number, though in reckoning none.

Come, go with me. [*to SERVANT*] Go, sirrah, trudge about

Through fair Verona; find those persons out   35

Whose names are written there, and to them say,

My house and welcome on their pleasure stay.

Exeunt CAPULET and PARIS.

SERVANT

Find them out whose names are written here! It is written that the shoemaker should meddle with his yard, and the tailor with his last, the fisher with his   40 pencil, and the painter with his nets. But I am sent to find those persons whose names are here writ, and can never find what names the writing person hath here writ. I must to the learned.

Enter BENVOLIO and ROMEO.

In good time!   45

BENVOLIO

Tut, man, one fire burns out another's burning.

One pain is lessened by another's anguish.

Turn giddy, and be help by backward turning.

One desperate grief cures with another's languish.

Take thou some new infection to thy eye,   50

And the rank poison of the old will die.

ROMEO

Your plaintain leaf is excellent for that.

BENVOLIO

For what, I pray thee?

ROMEO

                        For your broken shin.

BENVOLIO

Why, Romeo, art thou mad?

ROMEO

Not mad, but bound more than a madman is;   55

Shut up in prison, kept without my food,

Whipped and tormented and—

Good-e'en, good fellow.

SERVANT

God gi' good-e'en. I pray, sir, can you read?

ROMEO

Ay, mine own fortune in my misery.   60

34	*sirrah:* a form of address used by a master to a servant
36	*there:* he is giving the servant a piece of paper with the names of those who are to be invited
37	*stay:* wait
38–44	*Find … learned:* I can't invite the people on the list because I can't read and everything is mixed up. I must find somebody who can read
44	*learned:* educated
45	*In good time!* just in time; he is glad to meet Benvolio and Romeo, who will be able to tell him the names on the list
46	*one … burning:* if Romeo falls in love a second time, it will make him forget his first love
47	*another's anguish:* the distress caused by a second one
48	*holp … turning:* helped by turning in a reverse direction
50–1	*Take … die:* a new infection will drive out an old one
52	*plantain:* a herb supposed to prevent small cuts from being infected
55	*bound … is:* insane people were often kept in captivity in Shakespeare's time
58	*e'en:* evening
59	*God … e'en:* (God give you a) good evening (a greeting)
60	*mine … misery:* I can predict a bad future for myself because of my present misery

SERVANT

Perhaps you have learned it without book. But, I pray, can you read any thing you see?

ROMEO

Ay, if I know the letters and the language.

SERVANT

Ye say honestly. Rest you merry.

ROMEO

65   Stay, fellow. I can read.

[*reads*] 'Signor Martino and his wife and daughters. County Anselme and his beauteous sisters. The lady widow of Utruvio. Signor Placentio and his lovely nieces. Mercutio and his brother Valentine. Mine uncle Capulet, his wife, 70   and daughters. My fair niece Rosaline and Livia. Signor Valentio and his cousin Tybalt. Lucio and the lively Helena.' A fair assembly. Whither should they come?

SERVANT

Up.

ROMEO

Whither? To supper?

SERVANT

75   To our house.

ROMEO

Whose house?

SERVANT

My master's.

ROMEO

Indeed I should have asked thee that before.

SERVANT

Now I'll tell you without asking. My master is the great rich 80   Capulet; and if you be not of the house of Montagues, I pray come and crush a cup of wine. Rest you merry.

Exit SERVANT.

BENVOLIO

At this same ancient feast of Capulet's
Sups the fair Rosaline whom thou so loves,
With all the admirèd beauties of Verona.
85   Go thither, and with unattainted eye

---

64 *Ye ... merry:* the servant, thinking Romeo cannot read, thanks him for being honest enough to say so and says goodbye to him

66 *County:* Count

72 *Whither ... come?* Where are they invited to?

81 *crush:* drink down

83 *Rosaline:* Capulet's niece

85 *thither:* there
     unattainted: impartial, unprejudiced

Compare her face with some that I shall show,

And I will make thee think thy swan a crow.

ROMEO

When the devout religion of mine eye

Maintains such falsehood, then turn tears to fires;

And these, who, often drowned, could never die,   90

Transparent heretics, be burnt for liars!

One fairer than my love! The all-seeing sun

Ne'er saw her match since first the world begun.

BENVOLIO

Tut, you saw her fair, none else being by,

Herself poised with herself in either eye.   95

But in that crystal scales let there be weighed

Your lady's love against some other maid

That I will show you shining at this feast,

And she shall scant show well that now seems best.

ROMEO

I'll go along, no such sight to be shown,   100

But to rejoice in splendour of mine own.

Exeunt.

86–7 *Compare . . . crow:* when you see the beautiful girls I will point out to you at the feast, you will consider Rosaline much inferior to them

88–91 *When . . . liars!* if my eyes ever cause me to think Rosaline ugly, may my tears, which often drowned my eyes without destroying them, turn to fires and burn my eyes for being obvious liars

91 *heretics:* those who dispute the teachings of religion (they were often burned to death in Shakespeare's day)

94–9 *Tut . . . best:* using a strange image, Benvolio imagines Romeo's eyes as a pair of scales in which he can weigh the value of two different women. Rosaline seems beautiful to Romeo because he has not weighed her so far against anybody else. When he compares her with the lovely women at the Capulets' feast, she will seem quite ordinary

101 *splendour . . . own:* the beauty of Rosaline

Key points

This scene introduces the issue of Juliet's future and presents Paris as a possible husband for her. They will meet at a great feast due to take place at the Capulets' later in the day.

Timeline

Sunday	Monday	Tuesday	Wednesday	Thursday

- Capulet's opening comments (lines 1–3) suggest that he has little interest in keeping the feud with the Montagues going.

- Capulet would be happy to see Juliet marry Paris. However, both men agree that Juliet has to consent to the marriage first. Capulet would also prefer to delay Juliet's marriage for two years, until she is sixteen.

- A key moment in this scene is the chance encounter between Romeo and Capulet's servant. The servant has the list of guests invited to the Capulets' feast, but he is unable to read and asks Romeo to tell him the names on the list. Romeo reads that Capulet's 'fair niece Rosaline' (line 70) will be a guest. As a Montague, Romeo would never be invited to an event at the Capulets' home, but now he is tempted to go along in disguise.

- Benvolio encourages Romeo to go to the feast, believing that when Romeo sees all the beautiful women there, he will forget Rosaline.

- Although the feast is in the home of the Capulets, and Romeo is a Montague and therefore unwelcome, Romeo decides to go in order to be near Rosaline.

- Rosaline, Capulet's illiterate servant and Benvolio are all part of a pattern woven by fate. Had there been no desire to see Rosaline, no chance meeting with a servant who could not read and no encouragement from Benvolio, Romeo would not decide to gate-crash the Capulets' feast, and therefore would not meet Juliet.

Useful quotes

> 'tis not hard, I think,
> For men so old as we to keep the peace.
>
> (Capulet, lines 2–3)

> At this same ancient feast of Capulet's
> Sups the fair Rosaline whom thou so loves,
> With all the admirèd beauties of Verona.
>
> (Benvolio, lines 82–4)

> Earth hath swallowed all my hopes but she;
> She's the hopeful lady of my earth.
> But woo her, gentle Paris, get her heart.
>
> (Capulet, lines 14–16)

> I'll go along, no such sight to be shown,
> But to rejoice in splendour of mine own.
>
> (Romeo, lines 100–1)

? Questions

1. Why has Paris come to speak with Capulet?

2. What advice does Capulet give Paris?

3. Why is Capulet concerned about Juliet?

4. There is evidence in this scene that Capulet may feel that the time has come to end the feud. Where do we find this evidence?

5. What does Capulet instruct his servant to do?

6. Why does Capulet's servant need Romeo's help?

7. What does Benvolio think of Romeo's attitude to Rosaline?

8. Why does Romeo decide to go to the Capulets' feast? Do you think this is a good reason? Explain your answer.

9. Imagine you were Romeo. Would you go uninvited to a feast at your enemy's house? Give reasons for your answer.

10. Comment on the kind of language used by Romeo in describing his love for Rosaline.

Talking point

Arranged marriages were once quite common, especially among powerful and wealthy families who wanted to unite their properties. How would you feel if your parents or guardian had the right to choose your future husband or wife? Would you prefer to make the decision yourself? Do you think you would make a better choice than they would?

ACT 1 † Scene 3

Lady Capulet and Juliet's Nurse discuss Juliet's age. The Nurse, remembering a moment from Juliet's childhood, says that Juliet is not yet fourteen. Despite this, Lady Capulet is anxious that her daughter should marry Count Paris, whom she will meet at the feast. Lady Capulet, unlike her husband, wants her daughter to marry sooner rather than later, pointing out that some girls in Verona younger than Juliet are already married, and that she herself became Juliet's mother at much the same age as Juliet is now. Juliet is not attracted to the idea of marrying Paris, although she does not turn it down.

> *I'll lay fourteen of my teeth –*
> *And yet, to my teen be it spoken, I have but four*
>
> NURSE, Act 1, Scene 3, 13–14

Verona. The Capulets' house.

Enter LADY CAPULET and NURSE.

LADY CAPULET
Nurse, where's my daughter? Call her forth to me.

NURSE
Now, by my maidenhead at twelve year old,
I bade her come. What, lamb! What, ladybird! —
God forbid! — Where's this girl? What, Juliet!

Enter JULIET.

JULIET
5 How now! Who calls?

NURSE
Your mother.

JULIET
Madam, I am here. What is your will?

LADY CAPULET
This is the matter — Nurse, give leave awhile.
We must talk in secret. — Nurse, come back again.
10 I have remembered me, thou's hear our counsel.
Thou knowest my daughter's of a pretty age.

NURSE
Faith, I can tell her age unto an hour.

LADY CAPULET
She's not fourteen.

NURSE
                     I'll lay fourteen of my teeth —
And yet, to my teen be it spoken, I have but four —
15 She's not fourteen. How long is it now
To Lammastide?

LADY CAPULET
                    A fortnight and odd days.

NURSE
Even or odd, of all days in the year,
Come Lammas Eve at night shall she be fourteen.
Susan and she — God rest all Christian souls! —
20 Were of an age. Well, Susan is with God.

1 *forth:* directly

2–3 *Now ... come:* by my virginity when I was twelve years old, I told her to come here
3 *ladybird:* a term of endearment (like 'lamb'), but it could also mean 'an immoral woman' and the Nurse then apologises (by saying 'God forbid') for using it in reference to Juliet

5 *How now!* an expression of surprise or reproach

8 *give leave awhile:* leave us alone for a while

10 *thou's ... counsel:* you shall hear what we have to say
11 *pretty age:* proper age for marriage

12 *unto an hour:* to the nearest hour

13–15 *I'll ... not fourteen:* I'll bet fourteen of my teeth, although to my sorrow I have to say that I have only four, that she's not fourteen

16 *Lammastide:* harvest time (Lammas Day is 1 August)

16 *odd days:* a few more days

17 *Even or odd:* the Nurse misunderstands Lady Capulet's 'odd days' and tells her that it does not matter whether the days are even or odd in number
18 *Lammas Eve:* 31 July
20 *of an age:* the same age
with God: (the Nurse's daughter, Susan, is) dead

She was too good for me. But, as I said,

On Lammas Eve at night shall she be fourteen.

That shall she, marry! I remember it well.

'Tis since the earthquake now eleven years;

And she was weaned — I never shall forget it —   25

Of all the days of the year, upon that day.

For I had then laid wormwood to my dug,

Sitting in the sun under the dovehouse wall.

My lord and you were then at Mantua.

Nay, I do bear a brain. But, as I said,   30

When it did taste the wormwood on the nipple

Of my dug and felt it bitter, pretty fool,

To see it tetchy and fall out wi' th' dug!

Shake quoth the dovehouse! 'Twas no need, I trow,

To bid me trudge.   35

And since that time it is eleven years.

For then she could stand high-lone. Nay, by th' rood,

She could have run and waddled all about.

For even the day before she broke her brow.

And then my husband — God be with his soul!   40

'A was a merry man — took up the child.

'Yea,' quoth he, 'dost thou fall upon thy face?

Thou wilt fall backward when thou hast more wit.

Wilt thou not, Jule?' And, by my holidam,

The pretty wretch left crying and said, 'Ay'.   45

To see now how a jest shall come about!

I warrant, an I should live a thousand years,

I never should forget it: 'Wilt thou not, Jule?' quoth he,

And, pretty fool, it stinted and said, 'Ay'.

LADY CAPULET

Enough of this. I pray thee hold thy peace.   50

NURSE

Yes, madam. Yet I cannot choose but laugh

To think it should leave crying and say 'Ay'.

And yet, I warrant, it had upon it brow

A bump as big as a young cockerel's stone,

A perilous knock. And it cried bitterly.   55

'Yea,' quoth my husband, 'fallest upon thy face?

Thou wilt fall backward when thou comest to age.

Wilt thou not, Jule?' It stinted, and said, 'Ay'.

23 *marry!* by Mary (an oath)

25 *weaned:* the Nurse had breastfed Juliet for almost three years (until eleven years ago)

27 *I … dug:* I had put wormwood (a bitter plant supposed to kill worms) on my breast

30 *I do … brain:* I still have a good memory

31 *it:* Juliet

33 *tetchy:* fretful

34 *Shake … dovehouse!* the dovehouse began to shake because of the earthquake. The Nurse imagines the dovehouse as a person describing its own movements

34–5 *'Twas … trudge:* there was no need, I can assure you, to send me packing. The Nurse left because of the earthquake and because Juliet no longer needed her

37 *high-lone:* upright without help
by th' rood: by the cross of Christ (an oath)

39 *broke her brow:* cut the skin of her forehead

41 *'A:* he

42 *quoth:* said

43 *wilt:* will
wit: sense, understanding

44 *by my holidam:* by my holiness (an oath)

46 *To … about!* my husband's joke ('jest') now proves true (as Juliet is ready for marriage)

47 *warrant:* guarantee
an: if

49 *stinted:* stopped crying

53 *I warrant:* I assure you
it had … brow: Juliet had on her forehead
54 *stone:* testicle

59	*stint thou:* stop talking
60	*God . . . grace!* may God make you one of his chosen ones
62	*An:* if *once:* some day
66	*How . . . married?* Have you any wish to be married?
69	*thy teat:* the breast that fed you
71	*esteem:* respectable reputation, high rank
73–4	*I . . . a maid:* I became your mother at the same age that you are now
75	*valiant:* worthy, fine
77	*man of wax:* perfect picture of a man, as if he were modelled from wax
82–3	*Read . . . pen:* read his face like it is a book and you will enjoy what you find as he is very handsome
84–5	*every . . . content:* each feature of his face is in harmony with every other feature
85	*content:* satisfaction

JULIET
And stint thou too, I pray thee, Nurse, say I.

NURSE
60 Peace, I have done. God mark thee to his grace!

Thou wast the prettiest babe that e'er I nursed.

An I might live to see thee married once,

I have my wish.

LADY CAPULET
Marry, that 'marry' is the very theme

65 I came to talk of. Tell me, daughter Juliet,

How stands your disposition to be married?

JULIET
It is an honour that I dream not of.

NURSE
An honour! Were not I thine only nurse,

I would say thou hadst sucked wisdom from thy teat.

LADY CAPULET
70 Well, think of marriage now. Younger than you,

Here in Verona, ladies of esteem

Are made already mothers. By my count,

I was your mother much upon these years

That you are now a maid. Thus then in brief:

75 The valiant Paris seeks you for his love.

NURSE
A man, young lady! Lady, such a man

As all the world — why, he's a man of wax.

LADY CAPULET
Verona's summer hath not such a flower.

NURSE
Nay, he's a flower; in faith, a very flower.

LADY CAPULET
80 What say you? Can you love the gentleman?

This night you shall behold him at our feast.

Read o'er the volume of young Paris' face,

And find delight writ there with beauty's pen.

Examine every married lineament,

85 And see how one another lends content.

And what obscured in this fair volume lies

Find written in the margent of his eyes.

This precious book of love, this unbound lover,

To beautify him only lacks a cover.

The fish lives in the sea, and 'tis much pride   90

For fair without the fair within to hide.

That book in many's eyes doth share the glory,

That in gold clasps locks in the golden story.

So shall you share all that he doth possess,

By having him making yourself no less.   95

NURSE

No less? Nay, bigger! Women grow by men.

LADY CAPULET

Speak briefly, can you like of Paris' love?

JULIET

I'll look to like, if looking liking move.

But no more deep will I endart mine eye

Than your consent gives strength to make it fly.   100

Enter SERVINGMAN.

SERVINGMAN

Madam, the guests are come, supper served up, you called, my young lady asked for, the Nurse cursed in the pantry, and everything in extremity. I must hence to wait. I beseech you follow straight.

LADY CAPULET

We follow thee.

Exit SERVINGMAN.

                        Juliet, the County stays.   105

NURSE

Go, girl, seek happy nights to happy days.

Exeunt.

---

87   *margent:* margins, depths

88–9   *unbound . . . cover:* he is 'unbound' by the ties of marriage and 'lacks a cover' because he is without the embraces of his wife

90–1   *The . . . hide:* the beautiful sea is made even more beautiful by hiding beautiful fish within it

92–5   *That book . . . less:* the binding of a book and its contents unite to win praise for it. In the same way, Juliet and Paris will win honour when they unite in marriage and Juliet will not make herself less honourable if she marries Paris

96   *grow:* expand when they become pregnant

97   *like of:* be favourable to

98–100   *I'll . . . fly:* I'll expect to like him, if looking at him can make me like him, but I will make my feelings for him depend on your consent

102–3   *the Nurse . . . pantry:* the Nurse is being cursed in the pantry (kitchen storeroom) because she is not dealing with her household duties (instead she has been talking to Lady Capulet and Juliet)

103   *extremity:* disorder
hence to wait: go from here to serve

104   *I . . . straight:* may I ask you to come immediately

105   *the County stays:* Count Paris is waiting

106   *to:* to follow

Key points

This scene introduces us to the Nurse, who has been Juliet's close companion since Juliet was a baby and who is to play an important part in the coming action.

Timeline

Sunday	Monday	Tuesday	Wednesday	Thursday

- The Nurse gives this scene a strong note of comedy. Her rambling account of Juliet's age (lines 17–58) is very funny, although Lady Capulet and Juliet find it long and tedious.

- Lady Capulet wants to find out what her daughter, Juliet, thinks of marriage in general, and of Paris as a potential husband in particular.

- This scene resembles the opening of the previous scene, where Capulet met with Paris about Juliet as a possible wife for him. Notice a difference between Capulet's attitude to the matter and his wife's. Capulet is not in favour of the early marriage of Juliet, and warns against it. Lady Capulet thinks that Juliet should be prepared to marry immediately.

- Both of Juliet's parents believe that Paris should be Juliet's husband, and her Nurse agrees. Lady Capulet urges Juliet to observe Paris at the feast, to study his face, 'And find delight writ there with beauty's pen' (line 83).

- **Dramatic irony** occurs when the audience knows more than the character(s) on stage. We know from the Prologue that Juliet is destined to meet and fall in love with Romeo. We also know that Romeo is planning to come to the Capulets' feast. Armed with this knowledge, we expect Juliet to find 'delight' in Romeo's face, rather than that of Paris, and therefore find Lady Capulet's remark ironic.

- As the scene closes, it seems that Juliet's life is full of possibilities.

Useful quotes

> *Tell me, daughter Juliet,*
> *How stands your disposition to be married?*
>
> (Lady Capulet, lines 65–6)

> *Speak briefly, can you like of Paris' love?*
>
> (Lady Capulet, line 97)

> *I was your mother much upon these years*
> *That you are now a maid.*
>
> (Lady Capulet, lines 73–4)

> *I'll look to like, if looking liking move.*
> *But no more deep will I endart mine eye*
> *Than your consent gives strength to make it fly.*
>
> (Juliet, lines 98–100)

Questions ?

1 Why does Lady Capulet want to talk to Juliet?

2 What age is Juliet?

3 Suggest why Lady Capulet calls the Nurse back, having just dismissed her (line 9).

4 Is the Nurse an important member of the Capulet household? Give reasons for your answer.

5 The Nurse is a comic character. Her role in this scene makes the audience laugh. How does she do this?

6 In what ways does the Nurse differ from Lady Capulet? In your answer you might discuss the type of language each woman uses and the number of words each needs to say what she means.

7 Make a sketch of the Nurse and Lady Capulet. In your drawings, try to convey the kind of character each is, through her facial expression, costume, hair and so on.

8 On the evidence of this scene, does Juliet have any say in her own future? Explain your answer by referring to the text.

9 Imagine that you are Juliet. Write an entry in your diary in which you discuss how you feel about your mother's news and about the feast later this evening.

10 Using details from this scene, and your imagination, write two or three paragraphs on the Nurse's background. Consider how she might have come to be a member of the Capulets' household and her relationship with Juliet.

Talking point

Lady Capulet points out that she was married and a mother before she was fourteen. History tells us that arranged marriages involving young teenagers were once quite common. Indeed, the practice persists in many cultures; although today such marriages are often linked to poverty: if parents cannot afford to care for all their children, marrying off one (usually a daughter) can help improve the situation for the others. In your opinion, what age is too young to marry?

Plot summary

Romeo and some of his friends, disguised in masks, are about to enter the Capulets' house. Romeo's love for Rosaline has made him miserable and he cannot be persuaded to join in the merriment. Romeo had a dream that has made him uneasy about attending the feast. Mercutio, a relative of Prince Escalus, tries to convince Romeo that dreams are not important: they are merely fantasies that should be quickly forgotten. But nothing that his friends say can reassure Romeo. He is convinced that something terrible is in store for him. He worries that this night may even be his last.

For my mind misgives
Some consequence, yet hanging in the stars,
Shall bitterly begin his fearful date

ROMEO, Act 1, Scene 4, 106–8

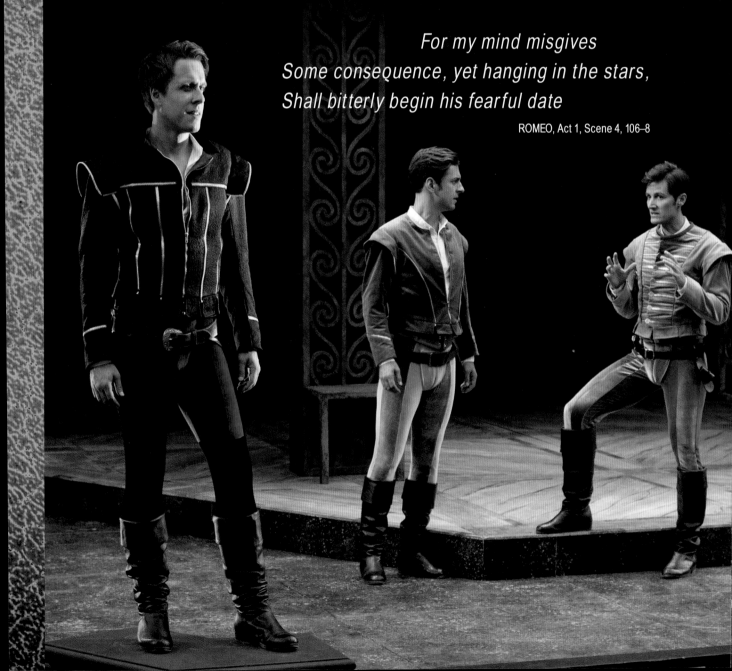

Verona. Outside the Capulets' house, then indoors.

Enter ROMEO, MERCUTIO, BENVOLIO, with five or six other MASKERS, and TORCHBEARERS.

ROMEO

What, shall this speech be spoke for our excuse?

Or shall we on without apology?

BENVOLIO

The date is out of such prolixity.

We'll have no Cupid hoodwinked with a scarf,

Bearing a Tartar's painted bow of lath,   5

Scaring the ladies like a crowkeeper,

Nor no without-book prologue, faintly spoke

After the prompter, for our entrance.

But, let them measure us by what they will,

We'll measure them a measure, and be gone.   10

ROMEO

Give me a torch. I am not for this ambling.

Being but heavy, I will bear the light.

MERCUTIO

Nay, gentle Romeo, we must have you dance.

ROMEO

Not I, believe me. You have dancing shoes

With nimble soles. I have a soul of lead   15

So stakes me to the ground I cannot move.

MERCUTIO

You are a lover. Borrow Cupid's wings

And soar with them above a common bound.

ROMEO

I am too sore empiercèd with his shaft

To soar with his light feathers; and so bound   20

I cannot bound a pitch above dull woe.

Under love's heavy burden do I sink.

MERCUTIO

And, to sink in it, should you burden love —

Too great oppression for a tender thing.

ROMEO

Is love a tender thing? It is too rough,   25

Too rude, too boisterous, and it pricks like thorn.

maskers: they are wearing masks
torchbearers: this indicates that it is dark (i.e. night)

1–2 *What … apology?* Should the speech we have ready be made as an apology for intruding into the feast, or should we go in without apology?

3 *The … prolixity:* these long-winded speeches are now out of fashion

4–10 *We'll … gone:* we won't bother putting on a show featuring Cupid masked with a scarf and carrying a wooden bow shaped like the upper lip, scaring women as a boy scares crows. We won't bother either with a badly delivered speech. Let them judge us as they wish. We'll dance one dance with them and then go

11 *ambling:* dancing

12 *Being … light:* since I am sad, I will carry a lighted torch (a pun based on the different meanings of 'heavy' and 'light')

15 *nimble … lead:* Romeo's friends are happy and can dance with light feet. Romeo is weighed down by his misery (a pun based on the fact that 'sole' and 'soul' sound the same)

18 *a common bound:* the ordinary limits

19–21 *I am … woe:* Cupid's arrow of love has so wounded me that I cannot fly upwards to happiness

24 *oppression:* misfortune

29 *case ... in:* mask to cover my face

30 *visor ... visor:* mask to hide an ugly face

31 *quote:* take notice of, remark on

32 *Here ... me:* to show his own aggression to love, he wears a mask with bushy and overhanging eyebrows and red cheeks

34 *betake ... legs:* dance

35–6 *A ... heels:* I would prefer to carry a torch than to dance, and will leave more light-hearted people to dance on the rush-covered floor

37–8 *For ... on:* I wisely follow the old-fashioned proverb that those who look on will see the best of the game

39 *done:* a pun on 'dun', which means 'dark' or 'sad'

40–3 *dun's ... ears:* keep quiet, as the policeman says when he is going to arrest someone. If you are sad, we'll get you out of your misery, even if you are up to your ears in it

41 *If ... mire:* refers to the old Christmas custom of pulling Dun, a wooden horse, out of the mud

43 *we ... ho!* we're wasting time

46–7 *Take ... wits:* accept the plain meaning of what we say, because you will find five times more sense in that than in all our fine figures of speech (metaphors, similes, etc.)

48–9 *we ... go:* we have good intentions in going to the Capulets' feast, but it is not a wise thing to do

MERCUTIO

If love be rough with you, be rough with love.

Prick love for pricking, and you beat love down.

Give me a case to put my visage in.

30 A visor for a visor! What care I

What curious eye doth quote deformities?

Here are the beetle brows shall blush for me.

BENVOLIO

Come, knock and enter; and no sooner in,

But every man betake him to his legs.

ROMEO

35 A torch for me! Let wantons light of heart

Tickle the senseless rushes with their heels.

For I am proverbed with a grandsire phrase —

I'll be a candle-holder and look on;

The game was ne'er so fair, and I am done.

MERCUTIO

40 Tut, dun's the mouse, the constable's own word!

If thou art Dun, we'll draw thee from the mire

Of — save your reverence — love, wherein thou stickest

Up to the ears. Come, we burn daylight, ho!

ROMEO

Nay, that's not so.

MERCUTIO

I mean, sir, in delay

45 We waste our lights in vain, like lamps by day.

Take our good meaning, for our judgement sits

Five times in that ere once in our five wits.

ROMEO

And we mean well in going to this masque,

But 'tis no wit to go.

MERCUTIO

Why, may one ask?

ROMEO

I dreamt a dream tonight.

MERCUTIO

50 And so did I.

ROMEO

Well, what was yours?

MERCUTIO

                     That dreamers often lie.

ROMEO

In bed asleep, while they do dream things true.

MERCUTIO

O, then I see Queen Mab hath been with you.

She is the fairies' midwife, and she comes

In shape no bigger than an agate stone   55

On the forefinger of an alderman,

Drawn with a team of little atomies

Over men's noses as they lie asleep.

Her chariot is an empty hazelnut,

Made by the joiner squirrel or old grub,   60

Time out o' mind the fairies' coachmakers.

Her wagon spokes made of long spinners' legs;

The cover, of the wings of grasshoppers;

Her traces, of the smallest spider web;

Her collars, of the moonshine's watery beams;   65

Her whip, of cricket's bone; the lash, of film;

Her wagoner, a small grey-coated gnat,

Not half so big as a round little worm

Pricked from the lazy finger of a maid.

And in this state she gallops night by night   70

Through lovers' brains, and then they dream of love;

O'er courtiers' knees, that dream on curtsies straight;

O'er lawyers' fingers, who straight dream on fees;

O'er ladies' lips, who straight on kisses dream,

Which oft the angry Mab with blisters plagues,   75

Because their breaths with sweetmeats tainted are.

Sometime she gallops o'er a courtier's nose,

And then dreams he of smelling out a suit.

And sometime comes she with a tithe-pig's tail

Tickling a parson's nose as 'a lies asleep;   80

Then he dreams of another benefice.

Sometime she driveth o'er a soldier's neck;

And then dreams he of cutting foreign throats,

Of breaches, ambuscados, Spanish blades,

53–4 *Queen Mab ... midwife:* the queen of the fairies has been with you in your dreams and is responsible for your fantasies

55 *In ... stone:* she is no bigger than the figure carved on a ring

56 *alderman:* high-ranking member of the council (who wore a ring of office)

57 *atomies:* tiny figures

60 *Made ... grub:* the squirrel gnaws the nuts and the grub or worm bores holes in them

61 *Time ... coachmakers:* the squirrel and the worm have made coaches for fairies from the earliest times

62 *spinners:* spiders

64 *traces:* reins

65 *collars:* halters

66 *film:* fine thread

67 *wagoner:* driver

70 *in this state:* moving in this dignified way

72 *curtsies straight:* bowing (before their superiors) immediately

75–6 *Which ... are:* she often gives them blisters or sores on their lips because their bad breath has annoyed her

78 *suit:* petition. A courtier who presented a petition to the king or queen on behalf of someone else got a fee for doing so

79 *tithe:* one-tenth of a

81 *benefice:* church appointment

84 *ambuscados:* ambushes
Spanish blades: great Spanish swords, made in Toledo

85 *healths ... deep:* deep drinking
anon: immediately

90–1 *bakes ... bodes:* makes the manes of horses hard
and matted, which when unknotted is a sign of
bad luck

92 *hag:* an evil fairy who causes nightmares

93 *learns ... bear:* teaches them to have children

100 *inconstant:* unreliable

104 *from ourselves:* from what we intend to do

106 *my mind misgives:* I have doubts and fears

107–11 *Some ... death:* destiny has decided that some
chain of events will start at this feast tonight and
end with my early death

112–13 *he ... sail:* Romeo asks God, or providence, to
direct his path

113 *lusty:* merry

114 *Strike, drum:* Benvolio is telling the drummer to
start beating his drum

85 Of healths five fathom deep; and then anon

Drums in his ear, at which he starts and wakes,

And being thus frighted, swears a prayer or two

And sleeps again. This is that very Mab

That plaits the manes of horses in the night

90 And bakes the elf-locks in foul sluttish hairs,

Which once untangled much misfortune bodes.

This is the hag, when maids lie on their backs,

That presses them and learns them first to bear,

Making them women of good carriage.

This is she—

ROMEO

95   Peace, peace, Mercutio, peace!

Thou talkest of nothing.

MERCUTIO

                         True. I talk of dreams;

Which are the children of an idle brain,

Begot of nothing but vain fantasy;

Which is as thin of substance as the air,

100 And more inconstant than the wind, who woos

Even now the frozen bosom of the north

And, being angered, puffs away from thence,

Turning his face to the dew-dropping south.

BENVOLIO

This wind you talk of blows us from ourselves.

105 Supper is done, and we shall come too late.

ROMEO

I fear, too early. For my mind misgives

Some consequence, yet hanging in the stars,

Shall bitterly begin his fearful date

With this night's revels and expire the term

110 Of a despisèd life, closed in my breast,

By some vile forfeit of untimely death.

But he that hath the steerage of my course

Direct my sail! On, lusty gentlemen!

BENVOLIO

Strike, drum.

They march about the stage.

Key points

This scene dwells on Romeo's depressed state. He is reluctant to attend the Capulets' feast because of a dream he has had, and he fears for his future.

Timeline

Sunday	Monday	Tuesday	Wednesday	Thursday

- Romeo isn't much fun. He is wallowing in his misery: 'Under love's heavy burden do I sink' (line 22). He finds love 'too rough, too rude, too boisterous' (lines 25–6) for his delicate feelings. Romeo's friends are in a party mood. They try hard to cheer him up, but fail. In a famous speech (lines 53–95), Mercutio reminds him that dreams are not real and suggests that Romeo is silly to pay attention to them.

- Romeo's words at the end of the scene deal with one of the play's main themes: the influence of fate, or the stars, on the course of human life. Romeo fears that fate has evil things in store for him. He feels that by entering the Capulets' home, he will start something that will cost him his life. We know from the Prologue that he is right to be fearful.

Useful quotes

I talk of dreams;

Which are the children of an idle brain,

Begot of nothing but vain fantasy;

Which is as thin of substance as the air

(Mercutio, lines 96–9)

For my mind misgives

Some consequence, yet hanging in the stars,

Shall bitterly begin his fearful date

With this night's revels

(Romeo, lines 106–9)

Questions ?

1 Contrast the different personalities of Romeo and Mercutio by choosing four adjectives from the following list for each character: happy, depressed, negative, positive, serious, light-hearted, confident, doubtful.

2 How has love (real or imaginary) affected Romeo?

3 Why has Mercutio received an invitation to the Capulets' feast?

4 How do the Montagues plan to attend the feast without being recognised?

5 Why does Romeo think he will die soon?

6 How do members of the audience already know that he will die soon?

7 What does Mercutio think of dreams? Say why you agree or disagree with him.

Talking point

Fate is the idea that some unseen power decides and governs everything that will happen to a person from birth to death. The play's focus on fate encourages us to ask questions about destiny and free will. Are we free to choose our own path in life or has it all been decided in advance for us? Are we fully responsible for our own actions? What do you think?

ACT 1 † Scene 5

Plot summary

The Capulets' feast is in full swing. The servants are busy and Capulet is greeting guests and encouraging them to dance. He talks with an elderly cousin about their younger days. Romeo spots Juliet dancing and falls in love at first sight. Tybalt recognises Romeo's voice and, looking on him as an unwelcome intruder, is prepared to strike him dead. Capulet, who has heard good reports of Romeo, lays the feud aside in the interest of good manners. He is angry with Tybalt for threatening to spoil his party. Tybalt storms off, planning to get revenge on Romeo at the next opportunity.

When Romeo approaches Juliet, she feels as strongly about him as he does about her. Later, when each finds out who the other is, a terrible truth becomes obvious. Romeo realises that his life and happiness are in the hands of the Capulets, the sworn enemies of his family. Juliet wonders why fate has made her love a man whom family loyalty should make her hate. They both feel deeply troubled about the results their love may have.

Is she a Capulet?
O dear account! My life is my foe's debt.
ROMEO, Act 1, Scene 5, 115–16

Verona. The Capulets' house.

SERVINGMEN come forward with napkins.

FIRST SERVINGMAN

Where's Potpan, that he helps not to take away? He shift a trencher? He scrape a trencher!

SECOND SERVINGMAN

When good manners shall lie all in one or two men's hands and they unwashed too, 'tis a foul thing.

FIRST SERVINGMAN

Away with the joint-stools, remove the court-cupboard; 5
look to the plate. Good thou, save me a piece of marchpane; and, as thou loves me, let the porter let in Susan Grindstone and Nell.

Exit SECOND SERVINGMAN.
Anthony, and Potpan!

Enter two more SERVINGMEN.

THIRD SERVINGMAN

Ay, boy, ready. 10

FIRST SERVINGMAN

You are looked for and called for, asked for and sought for, in the Great Chamber.

FOURTH SERVINGMAN

We cannot be here and there too. Cheerly, boys!
Be brisk awhile, and the longer liver take all.

Exeunt THIRD and FOURTH SERVINGMEN.

Enter CAPULET FAMILY, GUESTS and GENTLEWOMEN to the MASKERS.

CAPULET

Welcome, gentlemen! Ladies that have their toes 15
Unplagued with corns will walk a bout with you.
Ah, my mistresses, which of you all
Will now deny to dance? She that makes dainty,
She, I'll swear, hath corns. Am I come near ye now?
Welcome, gentlemen! I have seen the day 20
That I have worn a visor and could tell
A whispering tale in a fair lady's ear,

---

1 *take away:* clear the table
1–2 *He ... trencher!* it seems it is too much to expect the lazy fellow to clear a wooden dish or even to scrape one

4 *foul:* bad, dirty

5 *court-cupboard:* sideboard

6 *plate:* tableware, generally made of silver

7 *marchpane:* marzipan

8 *Susan ... Nell:* these girls will be coming to the servants' party after the Capulets' party has ended

14 *longer ... all:* winner takes all

16 *walk a bout:* have a dance

18 *makes dainty:* is slow to accept the invitation
19 *Am ... now?* Have I said something that makes you take notice?
20 *gentlemen:* this includes Mercutio and his disguised friends
21 *visor:* part of a helmet covering the face

23	*'Tis gone:* those days are over for me
25	*A hall, a hall!* Capulet wants them to clear a space for the dancers
26	*knaves:* servants
28	*unlooked-for sport:* unexpected entertainment
32	*Were . . . mask:* wore a mask
32	*By'r Lady:* by our Lady (an oath)
34	*nuptial:* wedding
35	*Pentecost:* Whit (seven weeks after Easter)
39	*ward:* minor (i.e. a person under twenty-one years of age)
41	*yonder knight:* that nobleman there
42	*teach the torches:* because she is brighter than they are
44	*Ethiop's:* Ethopian's
45	*use:* ordinary life
48	*The measure done:* when this dance is over
49	*hers:* her hand
	rude: guilty, sinful

Such as would please. 'Tis gone, 'tis gone, 'tis gone!

You are welcome, gentlemen! Come, musicians, play.

Music plays, and they dance.

25 A hall, a hall! Give room, and foot it, girls.

More light, you knaves, and turn the tables up;

And quench the fire, the room is grown too hot.

Ah, sirrah, this unlooked-for sport comes well.

Nay, sit, nay, sit, good cousin Capulet,

30 For you and I are past our dancing days.

How long is't now since last yourself and I

Were in a mask?

COUSIN CAPULET
                    By'r Lady, thirty years.

CAPULET

What, man? 'Tis not so much, 'tis not so much.

'Tis since the nuptial of Lucentio,

35 Come Pentecost as quickly as it will,

Some five-and-twenty years; and then we masked.

COUSIN CAPULET

'Tis more, 'tis more. His son is elder, sir.

His son is thirty.

CAPULET
                    Will you tell me that?

His son was but a ward two years ago.

ROMEO

40 [*to SERVINGMAN*] What lady's that, which doth enrich the hand

Of yonder knight?

SERVINGMAN
                    I know not, sir.

ROMEO

O, she doth teach the torches to burn bright!

It seems she hangs upon the cheek of night

As a rich jewel in an Ethiop's ear —

45 Beauty too rich for use, for earth too dear!

So shows a snowy dove trooping with crows

As yonder lady o'er her fellows shows.

The measure done, I'll watch her place of stand

And, touching hers, make blessèd my rude hand.

Did my heart love till now? Forswear it, sight! 50

For I ne'er saw true beauty till this night.

TYBALT

This, by his voice, should be a Montague.

Fetch me my rapier, boy. What, dares the slave

Come hither, covered with an antic face,

To fleer and scorn at our solemnity? 55

Now, by the stock and honour of my kin,

To strike him dead I hold it not a sin.

CAPULET

Why, how now, kinsman? Wherefore storm you so?

TYBALT

Uncle, this is a Montague, our foe.

A villain, that is hither come in spite 60

To scorn at our solemnity this night.

CAPULET

Young Romeo is it?

TYBALT

      'Tis he, that villain Romeo.

CAPULET

Content thee, gentle coz, let him alone.

'A bears him like a portly gentleman.

And, to say truth, Verona brags of him 65

To be a virtuous and well-governed youth.

I would not for the wealth of all the town

Here in my house do him disparagement.

Therefore be patient; take no note of him.

It is my will, the which if thou respect, 70

Show a fair presence and put off these frowns,

An ill-beseeming semblance for a feast.

TYBALT

It fits when such a villain is a guest.

I'll not endure him.

CAPULET

      He shall be endured.

What, goodman boy! I say he shall. Go to! 75

Am I the master here, or you? Go to!

You'll not endure him! God shall mend my soul!

You'll make a mutiny among my guests!

You will set cock-a-hoop! You'll be the man!

50 *Forswear:* deny
53 *rapier:* long, slender sword
54 *hither:* here (to the Capulets' feast) *covered ... face:* hidden behind a weird mask
55 *fleer:* sneer, mock *solemnity:* celebrations
56 *stock ... kin:* my family
57 *hold:* consider
58 *Wherefore:* why
59 *foe:* enemy
60 *villain ... spite:* scoundrel who has come here out of hatred
64 *'A ... gentleman:* he carries himself like a well-mannered gentleman
68 *disparagement:* offence, insult
72 *An ... feast:* Tybalt's frowns do not suit a celebration *semblance:* appearance
73 *It fits:* it is proper for me to frown
74 *I'll ... him:* I won't put up with him
75 *goodman boy:* a 'good man' was less than a gentleman; Capulet is showing contempt for Tybalt *Go to!* an expression of anger and impatience
78 *mutiny:* disturbance
79 *set cock-a-hoop:* show no self-control *the man:* the big fellow, the bully

80 *a shame:* an insult to us

81 *saucy:* cheeky

82 *This . . . you:* your habit of quarrelling may harm you

83 *contrary:* oppose

84–6 Capulet's conversation with Tybalt is interrupted as he speaks to his guests and servants

84 *hearts:* fine friends
princox: impertinent youth, cocky young fellow

87–8 *Patience . . . greeting:* because I have to control myself in response to your anger ('choler'), my body is quivering with rage

89–90 *But . . . gall:* but Romeo's visit will have the worst results

91–104 *If . . . take:* these lines make up a sonnet

91–2 *If . . . shrine:* Romeo thinks he is touching the hand of a saint

96 *mannerly:* proper

97–8 *For . . . kiss:* we saints have hands and do not require kisses – a handshake will be enough. Holy pilgrims greet each other in this way

98 *palmers:* pilgrims who have travelled to the Holy Land and returned with palm leaves

101 *let . . . do:* let our lips meet, as our hands do

102 *They . . . despair:* my lips are praying. Please grant what they are praying for, or my faith, which is my love for you, will turn to despair

103 *Saints . . . sake:* if I am the statue of a saint, as you think I am, I must tell you that statues do not move, although saints may grant what they are asked for

104 *Then . . . take:* then keep still while I kiss you and take the answer to my prayer

---

TYBALT

Why, uncle, 'tis a shame.

CAPULET

80   Go to, go to!

You are a saucy boy. Is't so, indeed?

This trick may chance to scathe you. I know what.

You must contrary me! Marry, 'tis time —

[*to GUESTS*] Well said, my hearts! — You are a princox, go!

85   Be quiet, or — [*to SERVANTS*] More light, more light! —
         for shame!

I'll make you quiet, what! — [*to GUESTS*] Cheerly, my hearts!

TYBALT

Patience perforce with wilful choler meeting

Makes my flesh tremble in their different greeting.

I will withdraw. But this intrusion shall,

90   Now seeming sweet, convert to bitterest gall.

Exit TYBALT.

ROMEO

If I profane with my unworthiest hand

This holy shrine, the gentle sin is this.

My lips, two blushing pilgrims, ready stand

To smooth that rough touch with a tender kiss.

JULIET

95   Good pilgrim, you do wrong your hand too much,

Which mannerly devotion shows in this.

For saints have hands that pilgrims' hands do touch,

And palm to palm is holy palmers' kiss.

ROMEO

Have not saints lips, and holy palmers too?

JULIET

100   Ay, pilgrim, lips that they must use in prayer.

ROMEO

O, then, dear saint, let lips do what hands do!

They pray; grant thou, lest faith turn to despair.

JULIET

Saints do not move, though grant for prayers' sake.

ROMEO

Then move not while my prayer's effect I take.

He kisses her.

Thus from my lips, by thine my sin is purged. 105

JULIET

Then have my lips the sin that they have took.

ROMEO

Sin from thy lips? O trespass sweetly urged!

Give me my sin again.

He kisses her.

JULIET

You kiss by th' book.

NURSE

Madam, your mother craves a word with you.

ROMEO

What is her mother?

NURSE

Marry, bachelor, 110

Her mother is the lady of the house,

And a good lady, and a wise and virtuous.

I nursed her daughter that you talked withal.

I tell you, he that can lay hold of her

Shall have the chinks.

ROMEO [*aside*]

Is she a Capulet? 115

O dear account! My life is my foe's debt.

BENVOLIO

Away, be gone. The sport is at the best.

ROMEO

Ay, so I fear. The more is my unrest.

CAPULET

Nay, gentlemen, prepare not to be gone.

We have a trifling foolish banquet towards. 120

They whisper in his ear.

Is it e'en so? Why then, I thank you all.

I thank you, honest gentlemen. Good night.

More torches here! Come on then, let's to bed.

Ah, sirrah, by my fay, it waxes late.

I'll to my rest. 125

Exeunt all but JULIET and NURSE.

---

105 *Thus … purged:* your lips have cleansed my sins

107–8 *Sin … again:* you have been given my sin and mention this crime in such a charming way, but I must take it away from your lips again. Romeo cleverly uses Juliet's words to kiss her once more

108 *by th' book:* expertly, like an expert; also, you are taking my words literally to take advantage of me

109 *craves:* begs

110 *What:* who

110 *Marry, bachelor:* my goodness, young man

113 *withal:* with

115 *the chinks:* plenty of money

aside: speech to the audience (not heard by other characters on stage)

116 *dear … debt:* what a terrible price to pay; my life is now dependent upon my family's enemy

118 *Ay … unrest:* indeed, I am afraid the worst is yet to happen. My uneasiness is growing

120 *towards:* on the way, ready

121 *Is … so?* Is it true? (we don't know what they told him)
122 *honest:* honourable

124 *by … late:* by my faith, it is growing late
125 *to my rest:* go to bed

126 *What ... gentleman?* Who is that gentleman there?

128 *out of door:* outside

133 *like:* likely

136–9 *My ... enemy:* the one man I love is the son of the one family I hate. I saw him too soon and, without knowing who he was, fell in love with him, and now I cannot do anything about it. It is horribly unlucky for me that the first man I love should be an enemy of my family

138 *Prodigious:* abnormal, likely to prove unlucky

One calls within: a voice is heard calling from off stage

JULIET
Come hither, Nurse. What is yond gentleman?

NURSE
The son and heir of old Tiberio.

JULIET
What's he that now is going out of door?

NURSE
Marry, that, I think, be young Petruchio.

JULIET
130 What's he that follows here, that would not dance?

NURSE
I know not.

JULIET
Go ask his name.

NURSE goes.
                              If he be marrièd,
My grave is like to be my wedding bed.

NURSE returns.

NURSE
His name is Romeo, and a Montague,
135 The only son of your great enemy.

JULIET
My only love, sprung from my only hate!
Too early seen unknown, and known too late!
Prodigious birth of love it is to me
That I must love a loathèd enemy.

NURSE
What's this, what's this?

JULIET
140   A rhyme I learnt even now
Of one I danced withal.

One calls within: 'Juliet'.

NURSE
                              Anon, anon!
Come, let's away. The strangers all are gone.

Exeunt.

Key points

This scene features the first meeting of Romeo and Juliet. For both, it is love at first sight. Tybalt, who wants to attack Romeo for coming to the Capulets' feast, is sent away by Capulet, and vows revenge on Romeo. Thus, the seeds of tragedy for Romeo and Juliet have been sown.

Timeline

Sunday	Monday	Tuesday	Wednesday	Thursday

- Earlier Benvolio told Romeo that Rosaline isn't all that special and that when he compares her with other beauties, she will seem less like a swan and more like a crow (Act 1, Scene 2, line 87). Romeo discovers the truth of this remark in this scene. His first glimpse of Juliet makes him instantly forget his obsession with Rosaline. Romeo sees the dancing Juliet as 'a snowy dove trooping with crows' (line 46). This astonishing change shows that Romeo's love for Rosaline was not real.

- As they fall in love, neither Romeo nor Juliet knows the identity of the other. The Nurse has to tell each of them who the other is. They respond in similar ways.

- Romeo senses that he will have a terrible price to pay, since his life will now depend on his family's enemy: 'My life is my foe's debt' (line 116).

- Juliet is appalled that the one man she loves is the son of the one family she hates: 'My only love, sprung from my only hate' (line 136).

- Fate has placed the two young lovers in a cruel situation, and there is trouble in store for them. Romeo has now reason to feel that his deep unease before going to the feast was justified.

- Another key event is Tybalt's recognition of Romeo, and his angry response to Romeo's presence at the Capulets' feast. Tybalt does not know that Romeo has come to see Rosaline, Capulet's niece. He assumes that Romeo intends to insult the Capulets by mocking their feast (line 55). The rude and aggressive behaviour of Tybalt shows that the feud is very much alive.

- Capulet's defence of Romeo's presence at the feast and his angry dismissal of Tybalt will prove highly significant. Tybalt is quarrelsome, hot-headed and arrogant, and hates all Montagues. He leaves the party full of anger. This anger will be stored up, and later prove disastrous for Romeo (and Tybalt).

- This scene also features use of the **aside**, when Romeo says: 'Is she a Capulet? O dear account! My life is my foe's debt' (lines 115–16). Playwrights use this device to allow one character to say something that the audience can hear but that the other characters on stage do not hear. It is a way of giving the audience 'inside' information. Here, we are given an insight into Romeo's thoughts and his reaction to finding out that Juliet is a Capulet.

Useful quotes

Did my heart love till now? Forswear it, sight!
For I ne'er saw true beauty till this night.

(Romeo, lines 50–1)

I will withdraw. But this intrusion shall,
Now seeming sweet, convert to bitterest gall.

(Tybalt, lines 89–90)

This, by his voice, should be a Montague.
Fetch me my rapier, boy.

(Tybalt, lines 52–3)

Is she a Capulet?
O dear account! My life is my foe's debt.

(Romeo, lines 115–16)

You are a princox, go!

(Capulet, line 84)

My only love, sprung from my only hate!
Too early seen unknown, and known too late!

(Juliet, lines 136–7)

? Questions

1 What does this scene reveal about Romeo's attitude to love?

2 What does Romeo's behaviour tell us about his character?

3 Describe your impression of Juliet in this scene.

4 There are hints about trouble to come for Romeo and Juliet. What are these?

5 Does this scene suggest that the Capulet–Montague feud might easily be ended? Are there any signs that it might soon get worse? Explain your answers.

6 Is Capulet right to become angry with Tybalt? Give reasons for your answer.

7 Write an account of the events of this scene from Capulet's point of view.

8 Imagine you are Tybalt and write a diary entry to record your responses to what happens in this scene. Your entry might begin: 'I was enjoying myself at the family feast when I discovered that Romeo Montague was present . . .' You might like to do the same for other key characters and update these diaries as you work your way through the play. This will help you to understand the point of view of each character.

Talking point

Romeo and Juliet fall in love at first sight. Do you believe that it is possible to fall in love so quickly in real life? Do you think you would recognise your soul-mate in an instant?

ACT 1   Key moments

Scene 1

- Benvolio, Romeo's cousin, tries to stop a fight between the servants of Capulet and those of Montague. Benvolio is attacked by Tybalt, Juliet's cousin. Prince Escalus intervenes, and threatens that those who fight in public in future will suffer the death penalty.
- Romeo is depressed because he is in love with Rosaline but she has rejected him.

Scene 2

- Count Paris asks Capulet for permission to woo his only daughter, Juliet. Capulet agrees.
- Capulet is holding a feast at his house. All are welcome except the Montagues.
- Having discovered that Rosaline will be at the Capulets' feast, Romeo decides to attend.

Scene 3

- Lady Capulet tells Juliet that Paris wants to marry her. Juliet agrees to consider the idea.

Scene 4

- Romeo has had a bad dream. He fears that going to the Capulets' feast will lead to his death.

Scene 5

- Romeo sees Juliet dancing. He is captivated by her beauty. He speaks his thoughts aloud, and Tybalt, recognising his voice, wants to kill him. Tybalt is stopped by Capulet, and leaves the feast in a rage.
- Juliet falls instantly in love with Romeo, and he with her. When they discover that they should be enemies, they know that the feud between their families will be an obstacle to their love and fear that it may prove deadly.

ACT 1   Speaking and listening

1 Select a student to play the part of Romeo. Members of the class interview him, based on what they know about him from Act 1. Possible questions might be about his feelings for Juliet or for Rosaline and why he prefers one over the other. Or, since he does not give details of the dream he has had (Act 1, Scene 4, line 50), you might want to ask why he was so worried about it. Or, maybe you are interested in whether he thinks other characters will approve of his relationship with Juliet. Try to think of at least three questions to ask him.

2 In groups of three, discuss how you would perform either the meeting of the Servant, Romeo and Benvolio in Act 1, Scene 2 (lines 38–101) or the exchange between Lady Capulet, the Nurse and Juliet in Act 1, Scene 3 (lines 5–100). Think about where the actors would be positioned on the stage and how they would move about. Decide how the actors should deliver their various lines, paying special attention to accents, timing, facial expressions and gestures. Read through your chosen scene and see how your ideas work in practice.

Q Revision quiz: plot summary

Use the words and phrases listed in the panel to fill in the blanks in this summary of Act 1:

Benvolio
Capulet
death
disguise
dream
enemy
fate
feast
Juliet
kill
kiss
Mercutio
Montagues
name
peacemaker
Prince Escalus
Prologue
Romeo
Rosaline
sixteen
star-crossed
tragedy
troublemaker
Verona
young

A short _____ introduces the play, which is set in the Italian city of _____. It features two feuding families: the _____ and the Capulets. Their long-standing feud will come to an end when one child from each family falls in love with the other and eventually takes their own life. The play is a _____ as this 'pair of _____-_____ lovers' are destined to die at the end.

In the opening scene the servants of the two households start a fight. Benvolio, a Montague, is a _____ and tries to stop it. Tybalt, a Capulet, is a _____ and tries to make it worse. The heads of the households get involved and it takes the intervention of _____ _____ to stop the violence. He announces that anyone who takes part in further street riots may be sentenced to _____.

Count Paris, an eligible young nobleman, has asked _____ if he can marry his daughter, Juliet. Capulet likes Paris but says that Juliet must consent to the marriage as well. He is worried that she is too _____ to marry and he wants to wait until she is _____ years of age. He advises Paris to win her heart.

The lovesick young Romeo is infatuated with _____, but she is not interested in him. He is miserable and his parents and friends are worried about him. _____ suggests that Romeo should go to the Capulets' _____ as he may find a more suitable girl at the party to fall in love with. He agrees to go because Rosaline will be there.

Romeo has a bad _____ and fears that some terrible _____ awaits him at the feast. _____ dismisses Romeo's belief in dreams and persuades him to go along.

Romeo spots _____ at the feast. She is dancing and he falls in love with her beauty instantly. Although Romeo is in _____, Tybalt recognises his voice and wants to _____ him. Capulet stops Tybalt and sends him away. Tybalt is furious and intends to make _____ pay.

Romeo approaches Juliet. They hold hands and _____. She falls in love with him as well. Later, when they each discover the _____ of the other, they realise that they love their _____ and that there will be trouble ahead.

ACT 2 † Prologue

Plot summary

The Chorus returns to update the audience on what has just happened and what will happen later in the play. Romeo's love for Juliet is replacing his love for Rosaline. The young lovers face obstacles as they are from two feuding families, but their love is strong, and they find a way to be together. Their love, however, brings a mixture of sorrow and pleasure.

Enter CHORUS.

CHORUS

Now old desire doth in his deathbed lie,
And young affection gapes to be his heir.
That fair for which love groaned for and would die,
With tender Juliet matched, is now not fair.
Now Romeo is beloved and loves again,   5
Alike betwitchèd by the charm of looks.
But to his foe supposed he must complain,
And she steal love's sweet bait from fearful hooks.
Being held a foe, he may not have access
To breathe such vows as lovers use to swear,   10
And she as much in love, her means much less
To meet her new belovèd anywhere.
But passion lends them power, time means, to meet,
Tempering extremities with extreme sweet.

Exit.

1–2 *Now . . . heir:* Romeo's love for Rosaline is now dying, and his new love for Juliet is longing to replace it

3–4 *That . . . not fair:* Rosaline no longer seems beautiful in Romeo's eyes, now that he has compared her with Juliet

7 *to . . . complain:* he must speak words of love to one who is supposed to be his enemy

8 *she . . . hooks:* she must behave like a fish trying to take a bait without being caught by the hook

9–12 *Being . . . anywhere:* since Romeo is considered an enemy by Juliet's family, he cannot visit or woo her easily. She has fewer freedoms and will find it even more difficult to meet him

13–14 *passion . . . sweet:* their love is so strong that it will enable them, with the help of time, to find a way of meeting. They will be able to reduce their sufferings by finding happiness in their meetings

Key points

The Chorus returns for a second and final time to give the audience more details of what will happen in the play.

- The first four lines refer to the death of Romeo's love for Rosaline, now that he has met Juliet. Romeo, who believed that there could be no one more beautiful than Rosaline, and who was prepared to die for her, has quickly transferred his admiration and love to Juliet. This observation shows that Romeo's love for Rosaline was not real, and perhaps suggests that Romeo can be somewhat shallow.

- Lines 5 and 6 note the difference between Romeo's two loves: this time, his love is returned. Rosaline rejected Romeo's love, but Juliet shares the same feelings.

- The next six lines focus on the problem that Romeo and Juliet face: he is a Montague and she is a Capulet. As their families are bitter enemies, their relationship is very dangerous. The families do not mix together and so it will be difficult for Romeo and Juliet to meet. As girls (at that time) have very few freedoms, it will be particularly hard for Juliet to find a way to see Romeo.

- The final two lines tell us that their love is so strong and passionate that they will find a way to meet up, but also warn us that the young couple will face extreme difficulties as well as extreme pleasures.

- As with the opening Prologue, the Prologue to Act 2 is in the form of a sonnet, which is a fourteen-line poem made up of three quatrains (groups of four lines) and a rhyming couplet (two lines). It has the same Shakespearean rhyming scheme: *abab cdcd efef gg*.

ACT 2 † Scene 1

When they left the Capulets' feast, Romeo gave his friends the slip. He now turns back and jumps over the wall of the Capulets' orchard to be near Juliet. Benvolio and Mercutio try to find him. They think he is still pining for Rosaline, and comment on the strange things love makes him do. Mercutio, pretending to be a magician, tries to make Romeo appear. 'I conjure thee by Rosaline's bright eyes ... that in thy likeness thou appear to us!' Then, deciding that Romeo doesn't want to be found, Benvolio and Mercutio give up and head home to bed. Benvolio knows Romeo very well and recognises that his friend wants time out: ''tis in vain to seek him here that means not to be found'.

Can I go forward when my heart is here?

ROMEO, Act 2, Scene 1, 1

Verona. Outside the Capulets' walled garden.

Enter ROMEO alone.

ROMEO

Can I go forward when my heart is here?

Turn back, dull earth, and find thy centre out.

Enter BENVOLIO with MERCUTIO. ROMEO withdraws.

BENVOLIO

Romeo! My cousin Romeo! Romeo!

MERCUTIO

He is wise,

And, on my life, hath stolen him home to bed.

BENVOLIO

5 He ran this way and leapt this orchard wall.

Call, good Mercutio.

MERCUTIO

Nay, I'll conjure too.

Romeo! Humours! Madman! Passion! Lover!

Appear thou in the likeness of a sigh.

Speak but one rhyme, and I am satisfied.

10 Cry but 'Ay me!' Pronounce but 'love' and 'dove'.

Speak to my gossip Venus one fair word,

One nickname for her purblind son and heir,

Young Abraham Cupid, he that shot so trim

When King Cophetua loved the beggar maid.

15 He heareth not, he stirreth not, he moveth not.

The ape is dead, and I must conjure him.

I conjure thee by Rosaline's bright eyes,

By her high forehead and her scarlet lip,

By her fine foot, straight leg, and quivering thigh,

20 And the demesnes that there adjacent lie,

That in thy likeness thou appear to us!

BENVOLIO

An if he hear thee, thou wilt anger him.

MERCUTIO

This cannot anger him. 'Twould anger him

To raise a spirit in his mistress' circle

25 Of some strange nature, letting it there stand

---

1 *forward:* away from Juliet

2 *dull earth:* his body
   thy centre: Juliet, the centre of his world

   withdraws: moves to the back or side of the stage, where the other characters do not see him

4 *hath stolen him:* has gone quietly

6 *conjure:* call up spirits by using magic words

11 *my gossip Venus:* my friend, the goddess of love

12 *purblind:* half-blind, dim-sighted

13 *Abraham Cupid:* the rascally god of love
    trim: accurately

14 *When . . . maid:* King Cophetua fell in love with a poor girl, and was therefore the victim of one of Cupid's arrows

16 *The . . . him:* the poor fellow is pretending to be lifeless and I must raise him from the dead

20 *demesnes . . . lie:* the territories that lie near these

24 *circle:* magic circle

25 *Of . . . nature:* not belonging to Romeo

Turn back, dull earth, and find thy centre out.

ROMEO, Act 2, Scene 1, 2

Till she had laid it and conjured it down.

That were some spite. My invocation

Is fair and honest. In his mistress' name,

I conjure only but to raise up him.

BENVOLIO

Come, he hath hid himself among these trees   30

To be consorted with the humorous night.

Blind is his love and best befits the dark.

MERCUTIO

If love be blind, love cannot hit the mark.

Now will he sit under a medlar tree

And wish his mistress were that kind of fruit   35

As maids call medlars when they laugh alone.

O, Romeo, that she were, O that she were

An open-arse and thou a poppering pear!

Romeo, good night. I'll to my truckle-bed.

This field-bed is too cold for me to sleep.   40

Come, shall we go?

BENVOLIO

                    Go, then, for 'tis in vain

To seek him here that means not to be found.

Exeunt BENVOLIO and MERCUTIO.

---

26 *laid it:* put it to rest

27 *were:* would be
spite: vexation
invocation: calling of a spirit

29 *raise up him:* make him appear

31 *consorted . . . night:* associated with the humid (muggy) night

32 *befits:* suits

33 *mark:* target

34 *medlar tree:* fruit tree

38 *open-arse:* name for fruit of the medlar tree
poppering pear: Belgian variety of pear

39 *truckle-bed:* a bed on wheels

40 *field-bed:* bed on the ground

42 *means . . . found:* does not want to be found

Key points

Romeo decides to return to the Capulets to see Juliet and hides from his friends, Benvolio and Mercutio, who look for him and discuss his feelings for Rosaline.

Timeline

Sunday	Monday	Tuesday	Wednesday	Thursday

- Romeo wants to be as near as he can to Juliet. His single comment in this scene reveals that he now thinks of Juliet, and not Rosaline, as the centre of his world.

- A **soliloquy** is a speech in which a character, who is alone on stage, expresses his or her thoughts and feelings aloud. The character speaks the truth as he or she sees it (i.e. soliloquies are never used to deceive the audience). Soliloquies provide the audience with information about a character's state of mind, motives, intentions and outlook. Romeo's opening lines in this scene (lines 1–2) are a soliloquy: he is thinking out loud.

- Mercutio mocks Romeo, whom love has made miserable. Mercutio's language is full of bawdy jokes and double meanings. He has a poor view of love and women, altogether different from Romeo's. He suggests that Romeo's feelings for Rosaline are closer to lust than love. He does not know that Romeo has already moved on from Rosaline and fallen in love with Juliet.

- Remember that Romeo is on the other side of the wall and able to hear what Benvolio and Mercutio are saying. In the theatre, the audience can often see what is happening on both sides of the wall.

? Questions

1 Look back at the Prologue to this Act. What does the Chorus tell us about the situation Romeo and Juliet are now in?

2 At the start of this scene, what does Romeo decide to do?

3 Why does he decide to do this?

4 In line 13, Mercutio makes one of many references to Cupid, god of love, in the play. Why is the figure of Cupid, with his arrows and his blindfold, so appropriate to the play at this stage?

5 What words would you use to describe Mercutio? Choose two from the list and say why: witty, rude, clever, fun-loving, insulting, imaginative, suspicious, nasty, educated.

6 Imagine you are Benvolio. Write a short account of the Capulets' feast in which you guess where Romeo disappeared to.

Talking point

In this scene, the theatre audience must accept that it is late at night and that Romeo is on the other side of a wall, listening to Mercutio and Benvolio, who have no idea that he is there. It is easier to make this set-up appear realistic on film as the director can use real locations, different camera angles, close-up shots, etc. But there are advantages in watching a live performance in the theatre. Can you suggest what these might be? Think in particular about the relationship between the audience and the actors.

ACT 2 ✠ Scene 2

Romeo sees Juliet at her window. He marvels at her beauty, which he celebrates in images of brightness. She expresses her love for Romeo, unaware (at first) that he is there. Her love for him is greater than the feud between their families, but she still has well-founded fears. When she realises that Romeo is in the grounds of her home, she warns him that her family will murder him if they see him. She is overjoyed at his declaration of love, but realises that it is too soon as they have just met. Nevertheless, she goes on to tell Romeo that if he does love her, they should marry the next day. They find it hard to part, even though the Nurse is calling Juliet inside. When they do, it is on the understanding that Juliet will send a messenger to Romeo the next morning. Meanwhile Romeo will go to Friar Laurence, his friend and confessor, to tell him his good news and to seek his advice.

What man are thou that, thus bescreened in night,
So stumblest on my counsel?

JULIET, Act 2, Scene 2, 52–3

Verona. The Capulets' orchard.

ROMEO

[*comes forward*] He jests at scars that never felt a wound.

Enter JULIET above.

But, soft! What light through yonder window breaks?

It is the East, and Juliet is the sun!

Arise, fair sun, and kill the envious moon,

5 Who is already sick and pale with grief

That thou her maid art far more fair than she.

Be not her maid, since she is envious.

Her vestal livery is but sick and green,

And none but fools do wear it. Cast it off.

10 It is my lady. O, it is my love!

O that she knew she were!

She speaks. Yet she says nothing. What of that?

Her eye discourses. I will answer it.

I am too bold. 'Tis not to me she speaks.

15 Two of the fairest stars in all the heaven,

Having some business, do entreat her eyes

To twinkle in their spheres till they return.

What if her eyes were there, they in her head?

The brightness of her cheek would shame those stars

20 As daylight doth a lamp. Her eyes in heaven

Would through the airy region stream so bright

That birds would sing and think it were not night.

See how she leans her cheek upon her hand!

O that I were a glove upon that hand,

That I might touch that cheek!

JULIET

                              Ay me!

ROMEO

25   She speaks.

O, speak again, bright angel! — for thou art

As glorious to this night, being o'er my head,

As is a wingèd messenger of heaven

Unto the white-upturnèd wondering eyes

30 Of mortals that fall back to gaze on him

When he bestrides the lazy, puffing clouds

And sails upon the bosom of the air.

---

1 *He . . . wound:* it is easy for those who have never experienced pain to laugh at it when others experience it. He is referring to what Mercutio has just been saying
above: in the gallery over the stage (the balcony of her bedroom). She cannot yet see or hear Romeo

2 *soft:* wait a moment

7–8 *Be . . . green:* do not be a follower of the moon goddess, who is opposed to marriage. Her virgin clothes are a pale, sickly colour

11 *O . . . were!* I wish she knew that I loved her

13 *discourses:* speaks

16 *business:* mission, purpose
entreat: persuade, prevail upon
17 *spheres:* orbits

18 *there:* in the place left by the two stars
they: the stars

27 *o'er:* over, above (Juliet is on her balcony)

28 *a wingèd messenger:* an angel

29 *white-upturnèd:* looking upwards, so that the whites of the eyes are visible
wondering: admiring, marvelling

31 *bestrides:* straddles like a horse

JULIET

O Romeo, Romeo, wherefore art thou Romeo?

Deny thy father and refuse thy name.

Or, if thou wilt not, be but sworn my love, 35

And I'll no longer be a Capulet.

ROMEO [*aside*]

Shall I hear more, or shall I speak at this?

JULIET

'Tis but thy name that is my enemy.

Thou art thyself, though not a Montague.

What's Montague? It is nor hand nor foot 40

Nor arm nor face nor any other part

Belonging to a man. O, be some other name!

What's in a name? That which we call a rose

By any other name would smell as sweet.

So Romeo would, were he not Romeo called, 45

Retain that dear perfection which he owes

Without that title. Romeo, doff thy name;

And for that name, which is no part of thee,

Take all myself.

ROMEO

        I take thee at thy word.

Call me but love, and I'll be new baptised. 50

Henceforth I never will be Romeo.

JULIET

What man art thou that, thus bescreened in night,

So stumblest on my counsel?

ROMEO

          By a name

I know not how to tell thee who I am.

My name, dear saint, is hateful to myself, 55

Because it is an enemy to thee.

Had I it written, I would tear the word.

JULIET

My ears have not yet drunk a hundred words

Of that tongue's uttering, yet I know the sound.

Art thou not Romeo, and a Montague? 60

ROMEO

Neither, fair maid, if either thee dislike.

---

33 *wherefore art thou:* why are you

34 *refuse:* give up

aside: speech to the audience (not heard by other characters on stage)

38–49 Juliet is still not aware of Romeo's presence

39 *though not:* even if you were not

46 *owes:* owns

47 *title:* name
    doff: take away, get rid of

48 *for that name:* in exchange for your name

51 *Henceforth:* from now on

52 *bescreened:* hidden

53 *stumblest … counsel:* discover by chance what I am saying to myself

57 *tear the word:* rip up the page on which my name is written

61 *if … dislike:* if you do not like either of these names

JULIET

How camest thou hither, tell me, and wherefore?

The orchard walls are high and hard to climb,

And the place death, considering who thou art,

65   If any of my kinsmen find thee here.

ROMEO

With love's light wings did I o'er-perch these walls.

For stony limits cannot hold love out,

And what love can do, that dares love attempt.

Therefore thy kinsmen are no stop to me.

JULIET

70   If they do see thee, they will murder thee.

ROMEO

Alack, there lies more peril in thine eye

Than twenty of their swords! Look thou but sweet,

And I am proof against their enmity.

JULIET

I would not for the world they saw thee here.

ROMEO

75   I have night's cloak to hide me from their eyes.

And but thou love me, let them find me here.

My life were better ended by their hate

Than death proroguèd, wanting of thy love.

JULIET

By whose direction foundest thou out this place?

ROMEO

80   By love, that first did prompt me to inquire.

He lent me counsel, and I lent him eyes.

I am no pilot; yet, wert thou as far

As that vast shore washed with the farthest sea,

I would adventure for such merchandise.

JULIET

85   Thou knowest the mask of night is on my face,

Else would a maiden blush bepaint my cheek

For that which thou hast heard me speak tonight.

Fain would I dwell on form — fain, fain deny

What I have spoke. But farewell compliment!

90   Dost thou love me? I know thou wilt say 'Ay'.

And I will take thy word. Yet, if thou swearest,

---

62 *How ... wherefore?* How did you come to be here, tell me, and why?

64 *death:* deadly (for Montagues)

66 *o'er-perch:* fly over

68 *what love ... attempt:* love will lead us to attempt whatever is possible

71 *Alack:* an expression of regret or sorrow
    peril: danger

73 *proof:* armoured
    enmity: hostility, aggression

76 *but:* unless

78 *proroguèd:* deferred, postponed
    wanting ... love: if I am deprived of your love

81 *counsel:* advice

82–4 *I am ... merchandise:* I'm not a sailor, but if you were at the other end of the world, I'd sail in search of you

88 *Fain ... form:* I would gladly ('fain') keep my behaviour correct and proper

89 *farewell compliment:* Juliet is saying that she loves Romeo so much that she can no longer hide her feelings in polite, reserved language

Thou mayst prove false. At lovers' perjuries,

They say, Jove laughs. O gentle Romeo,

If thou dost love, pronounce it faithfully.

Or if thou thinkst I am too quickly won, 95

I'll frown, and be perverse, and say thee nay,

So thou wilt woo. But else, not for the world.

In truth, fair Montague, I am too fond,

And therefore thou mayst think my 'haviour light.

But trust me, gentleman, I'll prove more true 100

Than those that have more cunning to be strange.

I should have been more strange, I must confess,

But that thou overheardst, ere I was ware,

My true-love passion. Therefore pardon me,

And not impute this yielding to light love, 105

Which the dark night hath so discoverèd.

ROMEO

Lady, by yonder blessèd moon I vow,

That tips with silver all these fruit-tree tops—

JULIET

O, swear not by the moon, th' inconstant moon,

That monthly changes in her circled orb, 110

Lest that thy love prove likewise variable.

ROMEO

What shall I swear by?

JULIET

                Do not swear at all.

Or if thou wilt, swear by thy gracious self,

Which is the god of my idolatry,

And I'll believe thee.

ROMEO

              If my heart's dear love— 115

JULIET

Well, do not swear. Although I joy in thee,

I have no joy of this contract tonight.

It is too rash, too unadvised, too sudden;

Too like the lightning, which doth cease to be

Ere one can say 'It lightens'. Sweet, good night! 120

This bud of love, by summer's ripening breath,

May prove a beauteous flower when next we meet.

---

92   *perjuries:* deliberate lies under oath

93   *Jove:* Jupiter, chief of the Roman gods

96–7   *I'll … world:* I'll pretend I do not love you in order to make you keep on trying to win me. Otherwise I would not behave like that for all the world

98   *fond:* foolishly in love

99   *thou … light:* you may think I am not behaving seriously

101   *strange:* distant, formal

103   *ere … ware:* before I was aware

105   *not … love:* do not think that I am being forward or insincere when I tell you how much I love you

109   *inconstant:* always changing, fickle

110   *her circled orb:* as it orbits the earth

111   *Lest … variable:* in case your love also turns out to be so changeable

114   *of my idolatry:* that I worship

116   *joy in thee:* am happy with you

117   *contract:* exchange of lovers' vows

118   *rash:* impulsive, hasty

121–2   *This … meet:* our love will have grown to maturity by the time we next meet

Good night, good night! As sweet repose and rest
Come to thy heart as that within my breast!

ROMEO

125 O, wilt thou leave me so unsatisfied?

JULIET

What satisfaction canst thou have tonight?

ROMEO

Th' exchange of thy love's faithful vow for mine.

JULIET

I gave thee mine before thou didst request it.

And yet I would it were to give again.

ROMEO

130 Wouldst thou withdraw it? For what purpose, love?

JULIET

But to be frank and give it thee again.

And yet I wish but for the thing I have.

My bounty is as boundless as the sea,

My love as deep. The more I give to thee,

135 The more I have, for both are infinite.

I hear some noise within. Dear love, adieu!

NURSE calls within.

Anon, good Nurse! — Sweet Montague, be true.

Stay but a little, I will come again.

Exit JULIET.

ROMEO

O blessèd, blessèd night! I am afeard,

140 Being in night, all this is but a dream,

Too flattering-sweet to be substantial.

Enter JULIET above.

JULIET

Three words, dear Romeo, and good night indeed.

If that thy bent of love be honourable,

Thy purpose marriage, send me word tomorrow,

145 By one that I'll procure to come to thee,

Where and what time thou wilt perform the rite,

And all my fortunes at thy foot I'll lay

And follow thee my lord throughout the world.

129 *would . . . again:* wish I could give you my promise of love again

131 *frank:* generous

133 *bounty:* generosity, desire to give

134 *as deep:* as deep as the sea

135 *infinite:* without end, everlasting

136 *adieu:* farewell

within: from off stage

137 *Anon:* just a moment
true: faithful, loyal

139 *afeard:* afraid

141 *Too . . . substantial:* too appealing and delicious to be real

143 *thy . . . love:* the inclination of your love

145 *procure:* arrange

146 *rite:* ceremony of marriage

148 *my lord:* as my master

NURSE [*within*]

Madam!

JULIET

I come, anon — But if thou meanest not well, 150

I do beseech thee—

NURSE [*within*]

Madam!

JULIET

By and by, I come —

To cease thy strife and leave me to my grief.

Tomorrow will I send.

ROMEO

So thrive my soul—

JULIET

A thousand times good night!

Exit JULIET.

ROMEO

A thousand times the worse, to want thy light! 155

Love goes toward love as schoolboys from their books;

But love from love, toward school with heavy looks.

Enter JULIET above again.

JULIET

Hist! Romeo, hist! O for a falconer's voice,

To lure this tassel-gentle back again!

Bondage is hoarse and may not speak aloud, 160

Else would I tear the cave where Echo lies

And make her airy tongue more hoarse than mine

With repetition of 'My Romeo'.

ROMEO

It is my soul that calls upon my name.

How silver-sweet sound lovers' tongues by night, 165

Like softest music to attending ears!

JULIET

Romeo!

ROMEO

My nyas?

JULIET

What o'clock tomorrow

Shall I send to thee?

---

150 *anon:* immediately

151 *beseech:* beg

151 *By and by:* straight away

152 *strife:* struggle to win me

153 *thrive:* save. He is swearing on the salvation of his soul

155 *want thy light:* lack the light of your company

159 *tassel-gentle:* male falcon (bird of prey)

160–3 *Bondage ... Romeo:* because I am a prisoner in my father's house, I must whisper Romeo's name. Otherwise, I would shout his name at the top of my voice and make it echo and re-echo

161 *Echo:* in Greek mythology, when Echo was rejected by Narcissus, she pined away in caves until only her voice was left

166 *attending:* listening

167 *nyas:* young hawk that has yet to fly

167–8 *What ... thee?* What time should I send my messenger to you tomorrow?

ROMEO

By the hour of nine.

JULIET

I will not fail. 'Tis twenty years till then.

170   I have forgot why I did call thee back.

ROMEO

Let me stand here till thou remember it.

JULIET

I shall forget, to have thee still stand there,

Remembering how I love thy company.

ROMEO

And I'll still stay, to have thee still forget,

175   Forgetting any other home but this.

JULIET

'Tis almost morning. I would have thee gone.

And yet no farther than a wanton's bird,

That lets it hop a little from his hand,

Like a poor prisoner in his twisted gyves,

180   And with a silken thread plucks it back again,

So loving-jealous of his liberty.

ROMEO

I would I were thy bird.

JULIET

Sweet, so would I.

Yet I should kill thee with much cherishing.

Good night, good night! Parting is such sweet sorrow

185   That I shall say good night till it be morrow.

Exit JULIET.

ROMEO

Sleep dwell upon thine eyes, peace in thy breast!

Would I were sleep and peace, so sweet to rest!

The grey-eyed morn smiles on the frowning night,

Chequering the eastern clouds with streaks of light,

190   And darkness fleckled like a drunkard reels

From forth day's pathway made by Titan's wheels.

Hence will I to my ghostly Friar's close cell,

His help to crave and my dear hap to tell.

Exit.

176   *would . . . gone:* want you to go

177   *wanton's bird:* bird owned by a spoiled child

179   *gyves:* restraints, bindings, chains

181   *So . . . liberty:* the child loves the bird so much that he does not want it to escape from him

190   *fleckled:* marked with spots of light
191   *From forth:* out of the way of
      day's . . . wheels: Titan, sun god and bringer of day, drove across the sky in a chariot
192–3 *Hence . . . tell:* from here I will go to the cell of my confessor to ask his advice and to tell him of my good fortune ('hap')
192   *ghostly:* spiritual
      close: narrow
      cell: small dwelling

Key points

This is by far the most popular scene in the play, and one of the most moving of all love scenes in the theatre.

Timeline

Sunday	Monday	Tuesday	Wednesday	Thursday

- This scene moves the **plot**, which is the story or action of the play, forward considerably. It has some surprising features. As it begins, Romeo and Juliet scarcely know each other. By the time it ends, each has expressed undying love for the other, and they have made plans to get married on the following day.

- Juliet recognises that this exchange of vows is 'too rash, too unadvised, too sudden' (line 118). In other words, they appear to be rushing into marriage without getting to know one another and thinking about it properly. Despite this, she is the one who suggests that they marry on the next day.

- A key point about the kind of marriage Romeo and Juliet are planning is that it is going to be performed in secret, without the knowledge of their parents. This secrecy will lead to serious problems for both of them.

- Note that Romeo's language is full of images and ideas from popular love poetry, whereas Juliet has a more down-to-earth, practical outlook. Romeo sees Juliet as the rising sun, with eyes like stars and with the voice of an angel. When she touches her cheek, he wants to be as close to her as the glove on her hand. But when Juliet speaks, it is about her very real concerns about loving a Montague.

- When Juliet realises that Romeo is in the garden below her bedroom, she points out that her family will kill him if they find him there. Although he is in danger, Romeo continues to speak the language of romance. He says, 'Look thou but sweet, and I am proof against their enmity' (lines 72–3). In other words, Juliet's admiration will protect him. This is not a very practical response to her real concerns for his safety.

- In the opening part of this scene (lines 1–49), although Romeo and Juliet are visible on stage at the same time, they are not talking to each other and so their speeches are soliloquies. This device allows Shakespeare to make their true feelings for each other clear to the audience.

Useful quotes

> Romeo, doff thy name;
> And for that name, which is no part of thee,
> Take all myself.
>
> (Juliet, lines 47–9)

> O blessèd, blessèd night! I am afeard,
> Being in night, all this is but a dream,
> Too flattering-sweet to be substantial.
>
> (Romeo, lines 139–41)

> Do not swear at all.
> Or if thou wilt, swear by thy gracious self,
> Which is the god of my idolatry,
> And I'll believe thee.
>
> (Juliet, lines 112–15)

> If that thy bent of love be honourable,
> Thy purpose marriage, send me word tomorrow,
> By one that I'll procure to come to thee,
> Where and what time thou wilt perform the rite
>
> (Juliet, lines 143–6)

? Questions

1 How do we know that Romeo was listening to Mercutio's words in the previous scene?

2 How does Romeo describe Juliet's beauty?

3 Juliet's soliloquy (lines 33–49) reveals her thoughts and feelings for Romeo. In your own words, write down what she says.

4 In your opinion, why is Juliet worried that Romeo has overheard her say that she loves him?

5 Why does Juliet say that Romeo's life is in danger?

6 How does Romeo respond to this threat?

7 Which of the two, Romeo or Juliet, seems more sensible and practical? In your answer, start by choosing key phrases and sentences typical of Romeo and other sentences and phrases typical of Juliet. Then draw your own conclusions from the different language used by each.

8 In your opinion, why is Juliet anxious to marry Romeo the next day?

9 What arrangements do the couple make for the next day?

10 Think about how you would stage this scene in a theatre. What props and scenery would you need? How would you light the stage? What costumes would Romeo and Juliet wear? You may like to make sketches of your set and costume design.

Talking point

'What's in a name?' Juliet argues that we should not judge a person by his/her name but by the person's own individual qualities. Do you agree? If you met someone with a very unusual name that seems strange or amusing to you, would it affect your attitude towards the person? What about a name that you do not know how to pronounce – would that affect your perception of the person?

ACT 2 ✝ Scene 3

Plot summary

It is dawn and Friar Laurence is gathering plants and noting their positive and negative qualities when Romeo arrives. He is surprised to see Romeo so early in the day. He is even more amazed when he hears that Romeo now loves Juliet instead of Rosaline. Nevertheless, he agrees to perform a marriage ceremony for Romeo and Juliet because he thinks their union will help to end the feud between their families.

Within the infant rind of this weak flower
Poison hath residence, and medicine power.

FRIAR LAURENCE, Act 2, Scene 3, 19–20

Verona. Friar Laurence's cell.

Enter FRIAR LAURENCE alone, with a basket.

FRIAR

Now, ere the sun advance his burning eye

The day to cheer and night's dank dew to dry,

I must up-fill this osier cage of ours

With baleful weeds and precious-juicèd flowers.

5   The earth that's nature's mother is her tomb.

What is her burying grave that is her womb;

And from her womb children of divers kind

We sucking on her natural bosom find,

Many for many virtues excellent,

10   None but for some, and yet all different.

O mickle is the powerful grace that lies

In plants, herbs, stones, and their true qualities.

For nought so vile that on the earth doth live

But to the earth some special good doth give;

15   Nor aught so good, but strained from that fair use,

Revolts from true birth, stumbling on abuse.

Virtue itself turns vice, being misapplied,

And vice sometime's by action dignified.

Within the infant rind of this weak flower

20   Poison hath residence, and medicine power.

For this, being smelt, with that part cheers each part;

Being tasted, slays all senses with the heart.

Two such opposèd kings encamp them still

In man as well as herbs — grace and rude will.

25   And where the worser is predominant,

Full soon the canker death eats up that plant.

Enter ROMEO.

ROMEO

Good morrow, father.

FRIAR

                   Benedicite!

What early tongue so sweet saluteth me?

Young son, it argues a distempered head

30   So soon to bid good morrow to thy bed.

Care keeps his watch in every old man's eye,

And where care lodges, sleep will never lie.

---

1   *ere:* before
    advance: raise
2   *dank:* damp
3   *osier cage:* basket made of willow
4   *baleful:* harmful

7–8   *from . . . find:* we find different plants drawing nutrients from mother earth

9–10   *Many . . . some:* many plants are useful for many purposes, and there are no plants that are not useful for some purpose

11   *mickle . . . grace:* great is the power

12   *true:* natural

13–14   *For . . . give:* there is nothing on earth, even the meanest thing, that does not do some good to the planet

15–16   *Nor . . . abuse:* but when things are used in ways that nature did not intend, they reject the good powers for which they were created

17–18   *Virtue . . . dignified:* when good things are abused the results are bad, and when bad things are properly used the results may be good

20   *Poison . . . power:* both poison and cures are present

21   *with . . . each part:* its smell revives each part of the body

22   *slays . . . heart:* brings the heart to a standstill, and takes away a person's senses

23–6   *Two . . . plant:* human beings, like plants, are influenced by two forces, God's grace and man's evil will. Where evil takes control, disaster will follow

26   *canker:* worm

27   *Benedicite!* God bless you

29   *argues:* suggests
    distempered: sick

31   *keeps his watch:* remains awake
32   *where . . . lie:* sleep will never come to those who worry

But where unbruisèd youth with unstuffed brain

Doth couch his limbs, there golden sleep doth reign.

Therefore thy earliness doth me assure   35

Thou art uproused by some distemperature.

Or if not so, then here I hit it right —

Our Romeo hath not been in bed tonight.

ROMEO

The last is true. The sweeter rest was mine.

FRIAR

God pardon sin! Wast thou with Rosaline?   40

ROMEO

With Rosaline, my ghostly father? No.

I have forgot that name and that name's woe.

FRIAR

That's my good son! But where hast thou been then?

ROMEO

I'll tell thee ere thou ask it me again.

I have been feasting with mine enemy,   45

Where on a sudden one hath wounded me

That's by me wounded. Both our remedies

Within thy help and holy physic lies.

I bear no hatred, blessèd man, for, lo,

My intercession likewise steads my foe.   50

FRIAR

Be plain, good son, and homely in thy drift.

Riddling confession finds but riddling shrift.

ROMEO

Then plainly know my heart's dear love is set

On the fair daughter of rich Capulet.

As mine on hers, so hers is set on mine,   55

And all combined, save what thou must combine

By holy marriage. When, and where, and how

We met, we wooed, and made exchange of vow,

I'll tell thee as we pass. But this I pray,

That thou consent to marry us today.   60

FRIAR

Holy Saint Francis! What a change is here!

Is Rosaline, that thou didst love so dear,

33	*unbruisèd:* unharmed by the world
	unstuffed: not blocked up by worries
34	*couch:* rest
36	*Thou … distemperature:* you had to get up early because of some sickness
37	*hit it right:* have the right explanation
41	*ghostly:* spiritual
42	*woe:* sorrow
46	*on a sudden:* unexpectedly
47–8	*Both … lies:* the cure for our problems lies with you as a priest (because you can marry us)
50	*My … foe:* what I am asking you for also benefits my enemy (Juliet)
51	*homely … drift:* straightforward in what you are telling me
52	*Riddling … shrift:* a confused confession will be followed by a confused absolution ('shrift')
56	*And all combined:* we are united in our feelings for each other
	save: except
59	*pass:* go along
61	*Holy Saint Francis!* Laurence is a Franciscan friar

So soon forsaken? Young men's love then lies

Not truly in their hearts, but in their eyes.

65 Jesu Maria! What a deal of brine

Hath washed thy sallow cheeks for Rosaline!

How much salt water thrown away in waste

To season love, that of it doth not taste!

The sun not yet thy sighs from heaven clears.

70 Thy old groans yet ring in mine ancient ears.

Lo, here upon thy cheek the stain doth sit

Of an old tear that is not washed off yet.

If e'er thou wast thyself, and these woes thine,

Thou and these woes were all for Rosaline.

75 And art thou changed? Pronounce this sentence then:

Women may fall when there's no strength in men.

ROMEO

Thou chid'st me oft for loving Rosaline.

FRIAR

For doting, not for loving, pupil mine.

ROMEO

And bad'st me bury love.

FRIAR

                  Not in a grave,

80 To lay one in, another out to have.

ROMEO

I pray thee chide me not. Her I love now

Doth grace for grace and love for love allow.

The other did not so.

FRIAR

                  O, she knew well

Thy love did read by rote and could not spell.

85 But come, young waverer, come, go with me,

In one respect I'll thy assistant be.

For this alliance may so happy prove

To turn your households' rancour to pure love.

ROMEO

O, let us hence! I stand on sudden haste.

FRIAR

90 Wisely and slow. They stumble that run fast.

Exeunt.

---

65 *brine:* salt tears

66 *sallow:* pale yellow

67–8 *How ... taste!* you tried to preserve your love by salting it with tears, but did not taste its flavour

73 *e'er:* ever

75 *sentence:* wise saying, proverb

77 *chid'st:* criticised, rebuked
oft: often

78 *doting:* loving foolishly, stupidly or excessively

79 *bad'st me:* asked me to

79–80 *Not ... have:* when I asked you to bury love I did not intend that you should bury one foolish love in order to embark on another

81–3 *I pray ... so:* please do not scold me. Juliet, the woman I now love, has exchanged vows of love with me. Rosaline did not do this

84 *Thy ... spell:* your love meant very little to you; you were like a person who could recite a text by heart without knowing what the words meant

86 *In ... be:* for one reason I'll help you

87–8 *For ... love:* your marriage to Juliet may unite the Capulets and Montagues in love rather than in bitterness

89 *stand:* insist

Key points

Friar Laurence, who will play a major part in the lives of Romeo and Juliet as their advisor and helper, is the last of the major characters to appear on stage. In this scene, he consents to marry Romeo and Juliet 'on sudden haste', as Romeo puts it (line 89).

Timeline

Sunday	Monday	Tuesday	Wednesday	Thursday

- Friar Laurence is collecting plants and herbs that can be used as healing medicines as well as poisons. The same flower can contain both: 'Poison hath residence, and medicine power' (line 20). This remark is grimly significant in the light of what will happen later in the play as a result of sleeping drugs and poisons.

- Notice that Friar Laurence compares plants and human beings. Just as plants have good as well as bad qualities (allowing them to hurt or heal), each person is a combination of opposites: God's grace and man's evil desires ('grace and rude will', line 24). In other words, there is a struggle between good and evil inside everyone.

- This scene also emphasises the fickle nature of Romeo's love for Rosaline. Less than one day ago he was lovesick and pining for her; yet now he wants to arrange a speedy marriage to Juliet. Friar Laurence points out to Romeo that he is too quick to fall in and out of love, and remarks that Rosaline was wise to reject his love.

- Despite his doubts about Romeo's impatience and the speed at which things are changing, Friar Laurence agrees to perform a secret marriage ceremony (i.e. without witnesses). He has no idea that this secrecy will have deadly consequences for a number of characters in the play.

- Friar Laurence believes that the marriage will heal the divisions between the Montagues and Capulets. It is ironic that it will be the deaths of Romeo and Juliet, rather than their marriage, that actually reconciles the two families and ends the feud.

Useful quotes

I have been feasting with mine enemy,
Where on a sudden one hath wounded me
That's by me wounded. Both our remedies
Within thy help and holy physic lies.
(Romeo, lines 45–8)

But this I pray,
That thou consent to marry us today.
(Romeo, lines 59–60)

In one respect I'll thy assistant be.
For this alliance may so happy prove
To turn your households' rancour to pure love.
(Friar Laurence, lines 86–8)

O, let us hence! I stand on sudden haste.
(Romeo, line 89)

Wisely and slow. They stumble that run fast.
(Friar Laurence, line 90)

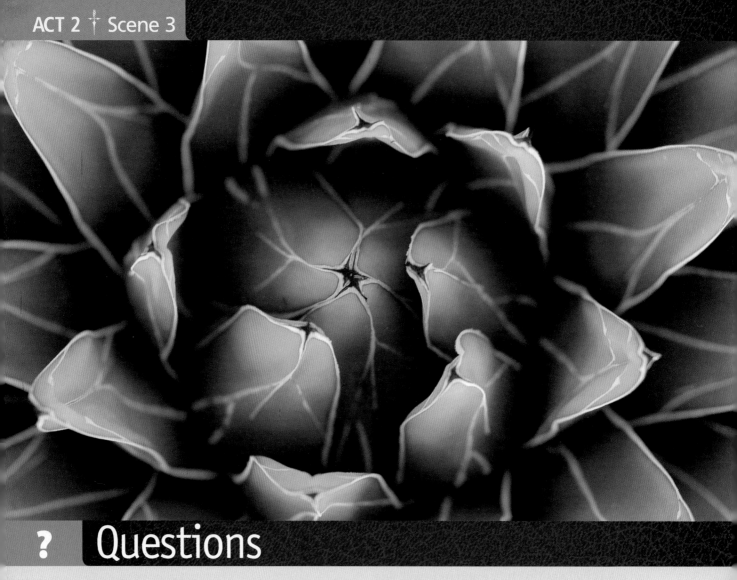

? Questions

1 What does Friar Laurence suggest that we can learn from plants (lines 23–6)?

2 Why is Friar Laurence surprised to see Romeo?

3 Why is Friar Laurence surprised to hear about Romeo's love for Juliet?

4 Describe the relationship between Romeo and Friar Laurence as revealed in this scene.

5 It has been said that Friar Laurence likes to preach and teach. Can you find an example of this in this scene?

6 What is the Friar's reason for agreeing to help Romeo?

7 Do you think Romeo shares the Friar's outlook?

8 Does it surprise you that Friar Laurence agrees so quickly to perform the marriage ceremony of Romeo and Juliet?

9 The final two lines of the scene provide a good summary of the characters of Romeo and Friar Laurence. Explain.

10 Do the Friar's words suggest that he is a wise man? Explain your answer.

Talking point

Getting married is a big decision, but Romeo and Juliet have agreed that they will marry the day after their first meeting. Is this too quick? Should they have given it more thought? In Ireland, couples must give official notice that they intend to marry at least three months before their chosen wedding day. Why might this be a good idea?

ACT 2 † Scene 4

Plot summary

We learn from Benvolio that Tybalt has sent a message to the Montagues, challenging Romeo to a duel. Mercutio thinks that the lovesick Romeo is in no state to fight, and observes that Tybalt is a skilled swordsman. When Romeo arrives, he and Mercutio engage in bawdy banter and wordplay, which continues after the arrival of the Nurse (as Juliet's messenger) and her servant Peter. Then Romeo speaks privately with the Nurse, asking her to arrange for Juliet to visit Friar Laurence, who will hear Juliet's confession and perform their marriage ceremony. The Nurse is also to make sure that Romeo will have access to Juliet's room that night.

This afternoon, sir? Well, she shall be there.

NURSE, Act 2, Scene 4, 166

Verona. A street.

Enter BENVOLIO and MERCUTIO.

MERCUTIO

Where the devil should this Romeo be?

Came he not home tonight?

BENVOLIO

Not to his father's. I spoke with his man.

MERCUTIO

Why, that same pale hard-hearted wench, that Rosaline,

5   Torments him so that he will sure run mad.

BENVOLIO

Tybalt, the kinsman of old Capulet,

Hath sent a letter to his father's house.

MERCUTIO

A challenge, on my life.

BENVOLIO

Romeo will answer it.

MERCUTIO

10   Any man that can write may answer a letter.

BENVOLIO

Nay, he will answer the letter's master, how he dares,

being dared.

MERCUTIO

Alas, poor Romeo, he is already dead — stabbed with a

white wench's black eye; run through the ear with a love

15   song; the very pin of his heart cleft with the blind bow-

boy's butt-shaft. And is he a man to encounter Tybalt?

BENVOLIO

Why, what is Tybalt?

MERCUTIO

More than Prince of Cats, I can tell you. O, he's the

courageous captain of compliments. He fights as you

20   sing pricksong; keeps time, distance, and proportion.

He rests me his minim rests, one, two, and the third in

your bosom. The very butcher of a silk button. A duellist,

a duellist. A gentleman of the very first house, of the first

and second cause. Ah, the immortal *passado*, the *punto*

25   *reverso*, the *hay*!

---

2 *tonight:* last night

3 *man:* servant

4 *wench:* uncomplimentary or offensive term for a woman

6 *kinsman:* Tybalt is Lady Capulet's nephew
7 *his:* Romeo's

9 *answer it:* turn up in person to face the challenge

12 *dared:* challenged

15 *pin:* bullseye
15–16 *cleft . . . butt-shaft:* pierced at the centre by Cupid's arrow
butt-shaft: blunt arrow used for practising archery

18 *Prince of Cats:* a survivor (since some believe that cats have nine lives)
19 *compliments:* good manners, formalities
19–21 *He . . . minim rests:* he is a disciplined fighter. Mercutio explains this by comparing him to a skilled and technically precise musician
20 *pricksong:* written music
22 *butcher . . . button:* he is skilful enough to touch with his sword any button on an opponent's shirt
23 *very first house:* best school of fencing
23–4 *first . . . cause:* the steps leading to a duel
24 *passado:* forward thrust of the sword
24–5 *punto reverso:* backward thrust
25 *hay:* penetrating thrust

BENVOLIO

The what?

MERCUTIO

The pox of such antic, lisping, affecting fantasticoes, these new tuners of accent! 'By Jesu, a very good blade, a very tall man, a very good whore!' Why, is not this a lamentable thing, grandsire, that we should be thus 30 afflicted with these strange flies, these fashion-mongers, these 'pardon-me's', who stand so much on the new form that they cannot sit at ease on the old bench? O, their bones, their bones!

Enter ROMEO.

BENVOLIO

Here comes Romeo, here comes Romeo! 35

MERCUTIO

Without his roe, like a dried herring. O flesh, flesh, how art thou fishified! Now is he for the numbers that Petrarch flowed in. Laura, to his lady, was a kitchen wench — marry, she had a better love to berhyme her — Dido a dowdy, Cleopatra a gypsy, Helen and Hero hildings and 40 harlots. This be a grey eye or so, but not to the purpose. Signor Romeo, *bon jour*. There's a French salutation to your French slop. You gave us the counterfeit fairly last night.

ROMEO

Good morrow to you both. What counterfeit did I give you? 45

MERCUTIO

The slip, sir, the slip. Can you not conceive?

ROMEO

Pardon, good Mercutio. My business was great, and in such a case as mine a man may strain courtesy.

MERCUTIO

That's as much as to say, such a case as yours constrains a man to bow in the hams. 50

ROMEO

Meaning, to curtsy.

MERCUTIO

Thou hast most kindly hit it.

27 *The pox of:* a plague on
27–8 *antic … accent:* those ridiculous fools who speak new kinds of language
29 *tall:* brave
29–31 *is not … flies:* isn't it terrible that we should be bothered by these strange parasites
30 *grandsire:* grandfather. He is mocking Benvolio as a grandfather because he doesn't like to fight

36 *Without his roe:* a pun on the first syllable of Romeo's name: without this, he is only half himself, and sounds miserable: me o! Also, a roe is a deer, which is a pun on Romeo's 'dear' Rosaline
37 *fishified:* made pale and weak like fish meat
37–8 *Now … in:* he is now inclined to write the kind of love poetry that (the fourteenth-century poet) Petrarch wrote for his mistress (Laura)
38–9 *Laura … her:* Laura, who was less beautiful than Rosaline, is more famous because Petrarch was a better poet than Romeo
39–41 *Dido … so:* these great female lovers are unattractive in Romeo's eyes when compared with his own beloved
41 *not … purpose:* of no importance
43 *slop:* loose trousers
43–4 *gave … night:* you really gave us the slip last night. A counterfeit (fake) coin was known as a slip

46 *conceive:* imagine, understand

50 *bow … hams:* bend the legs ungracefully

51 *curtsy:* bow

52 *Thou … it:* you have interpreted my words in a most polite way

53	*exposition:* explanation, description
54	*the . . . courtesy:* the most courteous person you will find
55	*for:* is also the name of a
57	*pump:* light shoe; shoes were often decorated with pinkings or floral patterns
58	*jest:* joke
61	*single-soled:* thin *singleness:* silliness. The dialogue between Romeo and Mercutio has now become silly
62	*My wits faint:* my ability to make clever remarks is deserting me
63	*Swits . . . match:* force your wit (like a horse) into action using whips and spurs, or I'll claim a victory in this contest of wits
64	*if . . . done:* the wild-goose chase is a cross-country horserace in which the leading horse must be followed by the others. If Mercutio allows Romeo to lead him in the battle of wits, he will never catch him
67	*goose:* joke, game
71	*bite not:* spare me
72	*sweeting:* apple

ROMEO

A most courteous exposition.

MERCUTIO

Nay, I am the very pink of courtesy.

ROMEO

55 Pink for flower.

MERCUTIO

Right.

ROMEO

Why, then is my pump well-flowered.

MERCUTIO

Sure wit, follow me this jest now till thou hast worn out thy pump, that, when the single sole of it is worn, the jest

60 may remain, after the wearing, solely singular.

ROMEO

O single-soled jest, solely singular for the singleness!

MERCUTIO

Come between us, good Benvolio! My wits faint.

ROMEO

Swits and spurs, swits and spurs, or I'll cry a match.

MERCUTIO

Nay, if our wits run the wild-goose chase, I am done. For

65 thou hast more of the wild goose in one of thy wits than, I am sure, I have in my whole five. Was I with you there for the goose?

ROMEO

Thou wast never with me for anything when thou wast not there for the goose.

MERCUTIO

70 I will bite thee by the ear for that jest.

ROMEO

Nay, good goose, bite not.

MERCUTIO

Thy wit is a very bitter sweeting; it is a most sharp sauce.

ROMEO

And is it not, then, well served in to a sweet goose?

MERCUTIO

O, here's a wit of cheverel, that stretches from an inch narrow to an ell broad! 75

74–5 *here's … broad:* your wit is like a piece of kid leather, able to stretch from one inch to forty-five inches

ROMEO

I stretch it out for that word 'broad', which, added to the goose, proves thee far and wide a broad goose.

MERCUTIO

Why, is not this better now than groaning for love? Now art thou sociable. Now art thou Romeo. Now art thou what thou art, by art as well as by nature. For this 80 drivelling love is like a great natural that runs lolling up and down to hide his bauble in a hole.

79 *sociable:* a person who enjoys the company of others (instead of wanting to be alone to pine over Rosaline)
80 *by art:* through learning
81 *natural:* idiot
82 *bauble:* fancy stick carried by a professional fool

BENVOLIO

Stop there, stop there!

MERCUTIO

Thou desirest me to stop in my tale against the hair.

84 *the hair:* my wish or inclination

BENVOLIO

Thou wouldst else have made thy tale large. 85

85 *else:* otherwise
large: long

MERCUTIO

O, thou art deceived! I would have made it short; for I was come to the whole depth of my tale, and meant indeed to occupy the argument no longer.

88 *occupy the argument:* discuss the matter

ROMEO

Here's goodly gear!

Enter NURSE and PETER.

A sail, a sail! 90

89 *goodly gear:* rubbish, or something to be mocked at. It may refer either to Mercutio's talk or to the Nurse and Peter

90 *A sail, a sail!* this may suggest that the Nurse is over-dressed

MERCUTIO

Two, two. A shirt and a smock.

91 *shirt:* man
smock: woman

NURSE

Peter!

PETER

Anon.

93 *Anon:* immediately, at your service

NURSE

My fan, Peter.

MERCUTIO

Good Peter, to hide her face. For her fan's the fairer face. 95

95 *the fairer face:* nicer than her face

96 *God ye good-morrow:* (God give you a) good morning (a greeting)

97 *God ye good-e'en:* (God give you a) good evening (a greeting)

99 *bawdy:* dirty, obscene

100 *upon . . . noon:* at twelve

101 *Out upon you!* an expression of annoyance

102–3 *One . . . mar:* although Mercutio is made in God's image, he will ruin this image through sin

104 *troth:* faith
'a: he

109 *for fault of:* in the absence of. Romeo is mocking the expression 'for want of a better'

113 *confidence:* she means 'conference' or talk

114 *endite:* Benvolio, mocking the Nurse's misuse of 'confidence', deliberately uses 'endite' when he means 'invite'

115 *bawd:* prostitute
So ho! a huntsman's cry on sighting a quarry, such as a hare

117–18 *No . . . spent:* normally a lenten pie was a meatless dish consumed during Lent (when meat was forbidden). Mercutio's hare-pie may be made of old, stale hare-meat

118 *hoar:* mouldy, rotten; also grey-haired
spent: used up

NURSE

God ye good-morrow, gentlemen.

MERCUTIO

God ye good-e'en, fair gentlewoman.

NURSE

Is it good-e'en?

MERCUTIO

'Tis no less, I tell ye. For the bawdy hand of the dial is now
100   upon the prick of noon.

NURSE

Out upon you! What a man are you!

ROMEO

One, gentlewoman, that God hath made for himself to
mar.

NURSE

By my troth, it is well said. 'For himself to mar', quoth 'a?
105   Gentlemen, can any of you tell me where I may find the
young Romeo?

ROMEO

I can tell you. But young Romeo will be older when you
have found him than he was when you sought him. I am
the youngest of that name, for fault of a worse.

NURSE

110   You say well.

MERCUTIO

Yea, is the worst well? Very well took, i' faith, wisely,
wisely!

NURSE

If you be he, sir, I desire some confidence with you.

BENVOLIO

She will endite him to some supper.

MERCUTIO

115   A bawd, a bawd, a bawd! So ho!

ROMEO

What hast thou found?

MERCUTIO

No hare, sir; unless a hare, sir, in a lenten pie, that is
something stale and hoar ere it be spent.

He walks by them and sings.

> An old hare hoar,
>
> And an old hare hoar, 120
>
> Is very good meat in Lent
>
> But a hare that is hoar
>
> Is too much for a score
>
> When it hoars ere it be spent.

Romeo, will you come to your father's? We'll to dinner 125
thither.

ROMEO

I will follow you.

MERCUTIO

Farewell, ancient lady. Farewell.

[*sings*] Lady, lady, lady.

Exeunt MERCUTIO and BENVOLIO.

NURSE

I pray you, sir, what saucy merchant was this that was so 130
full of his ropery?

ROMEO

A gentleman, Nurse, that loves to hear himself talk and
will speak more in a minute than he will stand to in a
month.

NURSE

An 'a speak anything against me, I'll take him down, an 135
'a were lustier than he is, and twenty such Jacks; and
if I cannot, I'll find those that shall. Scurvy knave! I am
none of his flirt-gills. I am none of his skains-mates.
[*to PETER*] And thou must stand by too, and suffer every
knave to use me at his pleasure? 140

PETER

I saw no man use you at his pleasure. If I had, my weapon
should quickly have been out. I warrant you, I dare draw
as soon as another man, if I see occasion in a good quarrel,
and the law on my side.

NURSE

Now, afore God, I am so vexed, that every part about me 145
quivers. Scurvy knave! [*to ROMEO*] Pray you, sir, a word;
and as I told you, my young lady bid me inquire you out.

119–24 *An … spent:* Mercutio continues punning on 'hare', 'hoar' and 'whore'

123 *Is … score:* is not worth paying for

125–6 *to dinner thither:* have dinner there

130 *saucy merchant:* an insolent individual (she is referring to Mercutio)
131 *ropery:* rascally talk

133 *stand to:* put up with

135 *an 'a:* if he
take him down: humble him
136 *Jacks:* people of bad reputation and behaviour
137 *Scurvy knave!* vile, deceitful fellow
138 *flirt-gills:* immoral women; the Nurse is saying that she is respectable
skains-mates: cut throats (a 'skain' is a knife)
139–40 *And … pleasure?* And must you stand quietly by and permit every rogue to make fun of me?

142 *warrant:* assure

145 *afore:* before
vexed: annoyed

146 *inquire:* seek

149 *lead ... paradise:* seduce her

150 *gross:* wicked

152 *deal double with:* deceive

153 *weak:* poor

154 *commend me:* give my best wishes
protest: swear

158 *mark:* listen to

159–60 *I ... offer:* the Nurse thinks that Romeo wants to
send a declaration of love to Juliet

161 *shrift:* confession

163 *shrived:* absolved, have her sins forgiven
163–4 *Here ... penny:* Romeo offers the Nurse money,
which she takes after a token refusal

167 *stay:* wait

169 *tackled stair:* rope-ladder

170 *high ... joy:* highest peak of my happiness
high top-gallant: highest platform or sails of a ship
171 *my convoy:* the means of bringing me (to Juliet's
bedroom)
172 *Be ... pains:* if you prove trustworthy, I'll reward
you

What she bid me say, I will keep to myself. But first let
me tell ye, if ye should lead her in a fool's paradise, as
150   they say, it were a very gross kind of behaviour, as they
say. For the gentlewoman is young; and, therefore, if you
should deal double with her, truly it were an ill thing to
be offered to any gentlewoman, and very weak dealing.

ROMEO

Nurse, commend me to thy lady and mistress. I protest
155   unto thee —

NURSE

Good heart, and i' faith I will tell her as much. Lord, Lord!
She will be a joyful woman.

ROMEO

What wilt thou tell her, Nurse? Thou dost not mark me.

NURSE

I will tell her, sir, that you do protest, which, as I take it, is
a gentlemanlike offer.

ROMEO

160   Bid her devise
Some means to come to shrift this afternoon,
And there she shall at Friar Laurence' cell
Be shrived and married. Here is for thy pains.

NURSE

No, truly, sir. Not a penny.

ROMEO

165   Go to! I say you shall.

NURSE

This afternoon, sir? Well, she shall be there.

ROMEO

And stay, good Nurse, behind the abbey wall.
Within this hour my man shall be with thee
And bring thee cords made like a tackled stair,
170   Which to the high top-gallant of my joy
Must be my convoy in the secret night.
Farewell. Be trusty, and I'll quit thy pains.
Farewell. Commend me to thy mistress.

NURSE

Now God in heaven bless thee! Hark you, sir.

ROMEO

What sayest thou, my dear Nurse?   175

NURSE

Is your man secret? Did you ne'er hear say,

Two may keep counsel, putting one away?

ROMEO

Warrant thee, my man's as true as steel.

NURSE

Well, sir, my mistress is the sweetest lady. Lord, Lord!
when 'twas a little prating thing — O there is a   180
nobleman in town, one Paris, that would fain lay knife
aboard. But she, good soul, had as lief see a toad, a
very toad, as see him. I anger her sometimes, and tell
her that Paris is the properer man. But, I'll warrant you,
when I say so, she looks as pale as any clout in the   185
versal world. Doth not rosemary and Romeo begin
both with a letter?

ROMEO

Ay, Nurse. What of that? Both with an 'R'.

NURSE

Ah, mocker! That's the dog's name. 'R' is for the — No, I
know it begins with some other letter; and she hath the   190
prettiest sentGentious of it, of you and rosemary, that it
would do you good to hear it.

ROMEO

Commend me to thy lady.

Exit ROMEO.

NURSE

Ay, a thousand times. Peter!

PETER

Anon.   195

NURSE

Before and apace.

Exeunt.

174 *Hark you:* listen

176–7 *Is … away?* Can your servant be trusted? Did you never hear the saying 'two can keep a secret, but not three'?

178 *Warrant:* I guarantee

180 *'twas:* she was
     prating: babbling, chattering
181–2 *fain … aboard:* desire to make a claim for her
182 *had as lief:* would like just as well to

184 *properer:* more attractive

185–6 *clout … world:* cloth in the whole world. Compare 'as pale as a sheet'
     versal: universal, whole
186–7 *begin … letter:* start with the same letter. The Nurse cannot read or write

189 *dog's name:* the letter 'R' sounded like the growling of a dog, and was called the dog's letter

191 *prettiest … it:* Juliet is fond of repeating sayings that mention rosemary and Romeo

196 *apace:* quickly

Key points

This scene is mainly comic, the touches of comedy being provided by Mercutio and the Nurse. A sinister note is sounded towards the beginning, as we learn that Tybalt has challenged Romeo to a duel.

Timeline

Sunday	Monday	Tuesday	Wednesday	Thursday

- The key moment in this scene is Benvolio's comment to Mercutio that Tybalt has challenged Romeo to a duel. He has sent the challenge in a letter delivered to Romeo's house. Tybalt is still angry at Romeo for attending the Capulets' feast and wants to punish him (Act 1, Scene 5, lines 89–90).

- There is irony in Mercutio's remark that Romeo 'is already dead – stabbed with a white wench's black eye' (lines 13–14). Mercutio thinks that Romeo is still in love with Rosaline, and (unlike the audience) knows nothing about his intended marriage to Juliet. Another layer of irony will be completed in a few days when Romeo brings about his own death.

- Notice that his friends have little confidence in Romeo's fitness to fight Tybalt, who is an angrier and more aggressive person as well as a very skilled fighter.

- When Romeo arrives he engages in witty banter with Mercutio. It is clear that Romeo is in better form than he has been in recent times and Mercutio is happy to see this. Their conversation reveals the good friendship between these two men.

- This scene gives scope to the two principal comic characters of the play, the Nurse and Mercutio. Mercutio dominates the first part of the scene, while the Nurse dominates the second as she tries to be ladylike and takes great offence at Mercutio's smutty jokes.

- Both of these characters provide interesting contrasts with Romeo. What Romeo says about Mercutio – he 'loves to hear himself talk' (line 132) – can also be said of the Nurse, who prefers to talk rather than listen. While Romeo has an idealistic and romantic view of love, both the Nurse and Mercutio tend to see it in purely physical terms. Mercutio's wit is coarse and crude, as is the Nurse's. Their view of love, based on sexual activity, contrasts with Romeo's more pure or spiritual view.

- There are some comic moments around the Nurse's choice of words and her failure to get to the point. Then, having got rid of Benvolio and Mercutio, and warned Romeo that he is not to mess Juliet about, she finally gets down to the plans for the marriage.

Useful quotes

> But young Romeo will be older when you have found him than he was when you sought him. I am the youngest of that name, for fault of a worse.
>
> (Romeo, lines 106–9)

> Bid her devise
> Some means to come to shrift this afternoon,
> And there she shall at Friar Laurence' cell
> Be shrived and married.
>
> (Romeo, lines 160–3)

> A gentleman, Nurse, that loves to hear himself talk and will speak more in a minute than he will stand to in a month.
>
> (Romeo, lines 132–4)

> Within this hour my man shall be with thee
> And bring thee cords made like a tackled stair,
> Which to the high top-gallant of my joy
> Must be my convoy in the secret night.
>
> (Romeo, lines 168–71)

Questions ?

1 What impression of Tybalt does this scene convey?

2 Do you think Tybalt can justify his challenge to Romeo?

3 In Shakespeare's plays, many of the characters' names provide clues to their personalities. Mercutio's name suggests 'mercurial' (quickly changing from one state to another) and reminds us of Mercury, messenger of the gods, who is a playful, eloquent and lively trickster. Consider Mercutio from this point of view.

4 Benvolio's name means 'good will' – is this appropriate, in your view? Give reasons for your answer.

5 Consider the Nurse's role as a comic character in this scene. Think about how she might walk and talk on stage. Is there a sense that she may be putting on airs and graces and pretending that she is more ladylike than she actually is?

6 What warning does the Nurse give Romeo about Juliet?

7 What message does Romeo give the Nurse for Juliet?

8 What does the Nurse tell Romeo about Paris?

9 Imagine you are Tybalt. Write the letter that you sent to Romeo's house (lines 6–7).

10 Imagine you are Benvolio. Make a diary entry on the events you witness in this scene.

Talking point

Romeo and Juliet feel that they have no choice but to marry in secret. Are secrets about major life events ever a good idea? Would you feel hurt if a close friend or family member got married without telling you? Or do you think it is the private business of the couple and up to them whether they tell anyone else?

ACT 2 † Scene 5

Plot summary

Juliet is at home, waiting impatiently for the return of the Nurse, who has been away much longer than expected. When the Nurse arrives, she delays giving Romeo's message to Juliet. Instead, she complains about her tiredness, caused by her errand on behalf of the two lovers. Finally, she tells Juliet to meet Romeo at Friar Laurence's cell and be married that afternoon. In the meantime, the Nurse will fetch the rope-ladder that is to give Romeo access to Juliet's bedroom.

Is thy news good or bad? Answer to that.

JULIET, Act 2, Scene 5, 35

Verona. The Capulets' orchard.

JULIET

The clock struck nine when I did send the Nurse.

In half an hour she promised to return.

Perchance she cannot meet him. That's not so.

O, she is lame! Love's heralds should be thoughts,

Which ten times faster glides than the sun's beams   5

Driving back shadows over louring hills.

Therefore do nimble-pinioned doves draw love,

And therefore hath the wind-swift Cupid wings.

Now is the sun upon the highmost hill

Of this day's journey, and from nine till twelve   10

Is three long hours, yet she is not come.

Had she affections and warm youthful blood,

She would be as swift in motion as a ball.

My words would bandy her to my sweet love,

And his to me.   15

But old folks, many feign as they were dead —

Unwieldy, slow, heavy and pale as lead.

Enter NURSE and PETER.

O God, she comes! O honey Nurse, what news?

Hast thou met with him? Send thy man away.

NURSE

Peter, stay at the gate.   20

Exit PETER.

JULIET

Now, good sweet nurse — O Lord, why lookest thou sad?

Though news be sad, yet tell them merrily.

If good, thou shamest the music of sweet news

By playing it to me with so sour a face.

NURSE

I am aweary. Give me leave awhile   25

Fie, how my bones ache! What a jaunt have I!

JULIET

I would thou hadst my bones, and I thy news.

Nay, come, I pray thee speak. Good, good Nurse, speak.

3   *Perchance:* perhaps, maybe

4   *lame:* unsatisfactory, flawed
    heralds: messengers

6   *louring:* dark, gloomy

7   *pinioned:* winged
    draw love: draw the chariot of Venus, goddess of love

9   *highmost:* highest

12   *affections:* passionate feelings

14   *bandy:* speed, rush

16   *old … dead:* old people act as if they were only half-alive

20   *stay:* wait

25   *aweary:* tired

26   *Fie:* an exclamation of disgust
    jaunt: tiring walk

NURSE

Jesu, what haste! Can you not stay awhile?

30 Do you not see that I am out of breath?

JULIET

How art thou out of breath when thou hast breath

To say to me that thou art out of breath?

The excuse that thou dost make in this delay

Is longer than the tale thou dost excuse.

35 Is thy news good or bad? Answer to that.

Say either, and I'll stay the circumstance.

Let me be satisfied, is't good or bad?

NURSE

Well, you have made a simple choice. You know not
how to choose a man. Romeo? No, not he. Though

40 his face be better than any man's, yet his leg excels all
men's; and for a hand and a foot and a body, though they
be not to be talked on, yet they are past compare. He is
not the flower of courtesy, but, I'll warrant him, as gentle
as a lamb. Go thy ways, wench. Serve God. What, have

45 you dined at home?

JULIET

No, no. But all this did I know before.

What says he of our marriage? What of that?

NURSE

Lord, how my head aches! What a head have I!

It beats as it would fall in twenty pieces.

50 My back a't'other side — ah, my back, my back!

Beshrew your heart for sending me about

To catch my death with jauncing up and down!

JULIET

I'faith, I am sorry that thou art not well.

Sweet, sweet, sweet Nurse, tell me, what says my love?

NURSE

55 Your love says, like an honest gentleman, and a courteous,
and a kind, and a handsome, and, I warrant, a virtuous —
Where is your mother?

36 *stay the circumstance:* wait for the details

38 *simple:* foolish

42 *be not ... on:* are not worth discussing

44 *Go ... wench:* off you go, girl

51 *Beshrew:* confound, curse

52 *jauncing:* jaunting, walking

55 *honest:* honourable

JULIET

Where is my mother? Why, she is within.

Where should she be? How oddly thou repliest!

'Your love says, like an honest gentleman,   60

"Where is your mother?"'

NURSE

                                   O God's Lady dear!

Are you so hot? Marry come up, I trow.

Is this the poultice for my aching bones?

Henceforward do your messages yourself.

JULIET

Here's such a coil! Come, what says Romeo?   65

NURSE

Have you got leave to go to shrift today?

JULIET

I have.

NURSE

Then hie you hence to Friar Laurence' cell.

There stays a husband to make you a wife.

Now comes the wanton blood up in your cheeks.   70

They'll be in scarlet straight at any news.

Hie you to church. I must another way,

To fetch a ladder, by the which your love

Must climb a bird's nest soon when it is dark.

I am the drudge, and toil in your delight.   75

But you shall bear the burden soon at night.

Go. I'll to dinner. Hie you to the cell.

JULIET

Hie to high fortune! Honest Nurse, farewell.

Exeunt.

58 *within:* inside

61 *God's Lady:* the Virgin Mary

62 *hot:* eager, impatient
    Marry . . . trow: an expression of impatience
63 *poultice:* hot preparation applied to the skin to soothe aches
64 *Henceforward:* from now on

65 *coil:* trouble, fuss

66 *shrift:* confession

68 *hie you hence:* go quickly from here

70 *comes . . . cheeks:* you are blushing

71 *in scarlet straight:* bright red instantly

72 *Hie:* hurry
    another way: go in another direction

74 *a bird's nest:* to your room

75 *I . . . delight:* I am the slave working for your pleasure

Key points

This scene adds little to the action of the play, except that arrangements for the marriage ceremony have been completed. However, it provides a further opportunity for the Nurse to reveal her talent for comedy.

Timeline

Sunday	Monday	Tuesday	Wednesday	Thursday

- Juliet's impatience to be married to Romeo is at the heart of this scene. The Nurse increases Juliet's anxiety by using some comic delaying tactics: she cannot tell her news because her bones ache, because she is out of breath, her head aches, and so does her back, because she needs a poultice for her back, and until she finds out where Juliet's mother is.

- This behaviour on the part of the Nurse provides excellent comic entertainment on the stage, and gives an ideal opportunity for the person playing the part to improvise using gestures, facial expressions, etc.

- The Nurse's delaying tactics increase the dramatic tension, and we experience some of Juliet's relief when she finally hears that Romeo is waiting to marry her at Friar Laurence's cell.

Useful quotes

The clock struck nine when I did send the Nurse.
In half an hour she promised to return.

(Juliet, lines 1–2)

Then hie you hence to Friar Laurence' cell.
There stays a husband to make you a wife.

(Nurse, lines 68–9)

O God, she comes! O honey Nurse, what news?
Hast thou met with him?

(Juliet, lines 18–19)

Hie you to church. I must another way,
To fetch a ladder, by the which your love
Must climb a bird's nest soon when it is dark.

(Nurse, lines 72–4)

Questions ?

1 How is Juliet feeling at the start of this scene?

2 What makes this scene so funny? It may help to act out the scene with a partner before writing your answer to this question.

3 How does Juliet react when she finally hears the news she has been waiting for?

4 What does this scene tell us about the Nurse's position in the Capulet household?

5 On the evidence of this scene, do you think that Juliet trusts the Nurse? Explain your answer.

6 Does this scene tell us anything about the Nurse's feelings for Juliet?

7 Imagine you are Juliet and write an account of this scene from her point of view.

8 Now imagine you are the Nurse and write an account of this scene from her point of view.

Talking point

The Nurse is employed by Capulet but obviously has a strong emotional bond with Juliet. She has chosen to act as Juliet's go-between with Romeo rather than to inform Capulet or Lady Capulet about the young couple's marriage plans. In your opinion, is this the right decision? Was it her duty to tell Juliet's parents what is happening? Should a person's loyalty always be to his/her employer?

ACT 2 † Scene 6

Plot summary

Before performing the marriage ceremony, Friar Laurence preaches to Romeo about the dangers of sudden and intense love. When Juliet runs in, it is clear to the Friar that she loves Romeo as much as he loves her. He advises Romeo and Juliet to love moderately if they want their love to last. He then leads them off to be married.

Ah, Juliet, if the measure of thy joy
Be heaped like mine, and that thy skill be more
To blazon it, then sweeten with thy breath
This neighbour air

ROMEO, Act 2, Scene 6, 24–7

Verona. Friar Laurence's cell.

Enter FRIAR LAURENCE and ROMEO.

FRIAR

So smile the heavens upon this holy act

That after-hours with sorrow chide us not!

ROMEO

Amen, amen! But come what sorrow can,

It cannot countervail the exchange of joy

That one short minute gives me in her sight.   5

Do thou but close our hands with holy words,

Then love-devouring death do what he dare —

It is enough I may but call her mine.

FRIAR

These violent delights have violent ends

And in their triumph die, like fire and powder,   10

Which as they kiss consume. The sweetest honey

Is loathsome in his own deliciousness

And in the taste confounds the appetite.

Therefore love moderately. Long love doth so.

Too swift arrives as tardy as too slow.   15

Enter JULIET somewhat fast. She embraces ROMEO.

Here comes the lady. O, so light a foot

Will ne'er wear out the everlasting flint.

A lover may bestride the gossamers

That idles in the wanton summer air,

And yet not fall. So light is vanity.   20

JULIET

Good even to my ghostly confessor.

FRIAR

Romeo shall thank thee, daughter, for us both.

JULIET

As much to him, else is his thanks too much.

ROMEO

Ah, Juliet, if the measure of thy joy

Be heaped like mine, and that thy skill be more   25

To blazon it, then sweeten with thy breath

This neighbour air, and let rich music's tongue

1–2 *So . . . not!* may the heavens smile on this marriage, and may we not be punished on account of it in the future

3–5 *come . . . sight:* whatever sorrow may come, it cannot equal the happiness I derive from a minute of Juliet's company

6 *close:* join (in marriage)

9 *violent:* extreme, intense

10 *powder:* gunpowder

11 *consume:* destroy

11–13 *The . . . appetite:* the sweetest things at last become disgusting because of their very sweetness and ruin the appetite for them

14–15 *love moderately . . . slow:* the Friar warns him to avoid extremes in love

16–20 *O . . . fall:* love gives Juliet the power to move almost without touching the ground

17 *flint:* stone floor

18 *gossamers:* fine cobwebs

19 *wanton:* playful

20 *So . . . vanity:* even the delights experienced by Romeo and Juliet are passing things

21 *even:* evening
ghostly: spiritual

23 *As . . . too much:* I must kiss him in return, or I shall have been overpaid

24–9 *if . . . encounter:* if your happiness is as great as mine, and if you can describe it better than I can, then let us hear your sweet voice reveal the happiness we receive from each other

Unfold the imagined happiness that both

Receive in either by this dear encounter.

JULIET

30 Conceit, more rich in matter than in words,

Brags of his substance, not of ornament.

They are but beggars that can count their worth.

But my true love is grown to such excess

I cannot sum up some of half my wealth.

FRIAR

35 Come, come with me, and we will make short work.

For, by your leaves, you shall not stay alone

Till Holy Church incorporate two in one.

Exeunt.

30–1 *Conceit ... ornament:* I prefer to express the deeper meaning of our happiness, and not just its outward appearance

32–4 *They ... wealth:* poor people can count their wealth easily, but I am so rich in your love for me that I cannot add it up

37 *incorporate:* join

Key points

The happiness of Romeo and Juliet is complete. Each receives blissful contentment from the other (lines 28–9). However, this will be the last scene in which they enjoy such happiness and good fortune.

Timeline

Sunday	Monday	Tuesday	Wednesday	Thursday

- Friar Laurence is uneasy about the ceremony he is going to perform. Although he prays that the heavens may smile on the marriage, he is also concerned that Romeo, Juliet and he may be punished on account of it (lines 1–2).

- Friar Laurence casts further doubt on the Romeo–Juliet relationship when he tells Romeo that 'These violent delights have violent ends' (line 9). This sentence seems to sum up the kind of love that Romeo and Juliet feel for each other. It also recalls a fear earlier expressed by Juliet that their exchange of vows was 'too rash, too unadvised, too sudden' (Act 2, Scene 2, line 118).

- In the middle of all this joy, Friar Laurence reminds us that nothing lasts, nothing ever remains the same: 'So light is vanity' (line 20). Even the great moments that Romeo and Juliet enjoy can only ever be temporary.

- Romeo and Juliet, however, are caught up in the excitement of the present moment. They are happy and in love. Friar Laurence recognises this and, overcoming his doubts, leads them off to be married.

Useful quotes

> *So smile the heavens upon this holy act*
> *That after-hours with sorrow chide us not!*
>
> (Friar Laurence, lines 1–2)

> *Therefore love moderately. Long love doth so.*
> *Too swift arrives as tardy as too slow.*
>
> (Friar Laurence, lines 14–15)

> *Then love-devouring death do what he dare –*
> *It is enough I may but call her mine.*
>
> (Romeo, lines 7–8)

> *But my true love is grown to such excess*
> *I cannot sum up some of half my wealth.*
>
> (Juliet, lines 33–4)

Questions ?

1 What is worrying Friar Laurence at the start of this scene?

2 Do members of the audience know more than Friar Laurence knows? Explain your answer.

3 What advice does Friar Laurence give Romeo about the best way to love? Do you agree with this advice?

4 How does Juliet enter the Friar's cell? What does this suggest about her mood?

5 Explain the Friar's determination to 'make short work' (line 35) of the marriage ceremony.

6 We do not see the actual marriage ceremony on stage. Imagine you are Friar Laurence and write a diary entry on marrying Romeo and Juliet and how they behaved as they made their vows.

Talking point

Romeo likes to live in the moment. He seeks instant gratification of his desires. He claims that if he holds Juliet for a minute now, then he will be able to endure any sorrow that comes in the future (lines 3–5). Is this a good way to approach life? Discuss the pros and cons of such an attitude.

ACT 2 ⸸ Key moments

Scene 1

- Romeo leaves the Capulets' house and hides from his friends. They eventually give up their search for him.

Scene 2

- Romeo sees Juliet at her window, and hears her declare that she loves him. They exchange expressions of love. Juliet asks Romeo to send a message telling her when and where they can be married.

Scene 3

- Romeo visits Friar Laurence to tell him he wants to marry Juliet, who loves him, without delay. Friar Laurence agrees to conduct the marriage, hoping it will end the feud between the Capulets and the Montagues.

Scene 4

- Benvolio tells Mercutio that Tybalt has challenged Romeo to a duel.
- Romeo tells the Nurse to ask Juliet to meet him that afternoon at Friar Laurence's cell.

Scene 5

- The Nurse, after much delay, tells Juliet to go to Friar Laurence's cell, where she and Romeo are to be married.

Scene 6

- Friar Laurence worries that Romeo's sudden love for Juliet may not end well. However, Juliet arrives and the marriage ceremony goes ahead in secret.

ACT 2 ⸸ Speaking and listening

1 Select a student to play the part of the Nurse. Then other members of the class should interview the Nurse about her attitude to Romeo and to his marriage to Juliet. They might ask her why she is willing to play the role of go-between and what her views are on a secret marriage. They might also question her on why she is keeping such vital information from her employers, the Capulets.

2 Working in pairs, one member should spend a few minutes looking back over Romeo's speeches in this Act and the other over Juliet's. Each person should choose and recite a short speech that indicates the nature of their character. You should be able to say what characteristics the speech reveals. When you have agreed on suitable speeches, merge with another pair. As a group, listen to and discuss each person's chosen speech.

Revision quiz: plot summary

Use the words and phrases listed in the panel to fill in the blanks in this summary of Act 2:

afternoon

beauty

Benvolio

cell

duel

feast

feud

Friar

impatiently

Juliet

kill

Laurence

long

love

marry

Mercutio

messenger

Nurse

plants

Romeo

Rosaline

secret

swordsman

Tybalt

words

As they leave the Capulets' feast, Romeo jumps over a wall and returns to the house to be near to _____. Benvolio and _____ cannot find him. Juliet appears at her bedroom window and Romeo admires her _____. He listens as she declares her _____ for him.

Juliet is shocked to see Romeo in her garden and warns him that her family will _____ him if they find him there. _____ does not care; all that matters to him is his love for Juliet and being close to her. They declare their love for each other and agree to _____ the next day. The _____ calls Juliet to come inside, but she finds it hard to leave Romeo. She agrees to send a _____ to him the next morning.

Friar _____ is gathering _____ at dawn when Romeo arrives to ask him to conduct his marriage ceremony. The Friar is surprised that Romeo no longer loves _____ and now wants to marry Juliet. He agrees to marry them in the hope that it will end the _____ between their two families.

Meanwhile, _____ has sent a letter to Romeo's home, challenging Romeo to a _____. He is still angry about Romeo's presence at the Capulets' _____. Mercutio and _____ worry that the lovesick Romeo will be no match for Tybalt, who is a skilled _____.

Juliet has sent the Nurse to find Romeo. Romeo tells her to make sure that Juliet goes in the _____ to Friar Laurence's _____, where they will be married. The Nurse returns to Juliet, who has been waiting _____ for news. The Nurse takes a _____ time to tell Juliet what she wants to hear.

Romeo and Juliet meet at _____ Laurence's cell. They are very happy and say that _____ cannot express their love. Despite his uneasiness, the Friar marries them in _____.

ACT 3 ✝ Scene 1

Plot summary

Benvolio wants to stay out of the way of the Capulets, but Mercutio jokes that Benvolio really wants a fight. In contrast, Tybalt is determined not to let the feud between the Capulets and the Montagues die. He insults Romeo and challenges him to a duel. But Romeo refuses to fight with Tybalt, for a reason he cannot publicly explain (his secret marriage to Tybalt's cousin Juliet). Mercutio wants to defend Romeo's honour and so he challenges Tybalt. As they fight, Romeo tries to stop them, but his intervention distracts Mercutio, who is then caught off-guard by a sly sword-thrust from Tybalt. At first, no one appreciates the horror of what is happening. Romeo thinks Mercutio can be only slightly hurt, but he is wrong. Before he dies, Mercutio, who is neither a Montague nor a Capulet, curses both the families. Romeo loses self-control and, when Tybalt returns, Romeo kills him. Benvolio persuades Romeo to leave the scene. The Prince arrives and Benvolio explains what happened. Lady Capulet wants Romeo to pay with his life, but the Prince decides that Romeo should be banished from Verona.

I am for you.
TYBALT, Act 3, Scene 1, 78

Climax/crisis Scene (handwritten)

Verona. A public place.

turning point for Romeo (handwritten)

Enter MERCUTIO, BENVOLIO and their MEN.

BENVOLIO

I pray thee, good Mercutio, let's retire.

The day is hot, the Capels abroad.

And if we meet we shall not 'scape a brawl,

For now, these hot days, is the mad blood stirring.

Pathetic fallacy and builds tension (handwritten)

1 *retire:* go home, go inside

2 *Capels abroad:* Capulets are on the street

3 *'scape:* escape

MERCUTIO

Thou art like one of these fellows that, when he enters the confines of a tavern, claps me his sword upon the table and says 'God send me no need of thee', and by the operation of the second cup draws him on the drawer, when indeed there is no need.

5

5–9 *that … need:* who lay their swords aside in a pub, telling everyone that they do not want to use them, but when the alcohol begins to work on them they draw their swords on the barman ('drawer')

BENVOLIO

Am I like such a fellow?

10

MERCUTIO

Come, come, thou art as hot a Jack in thy mood as any in Italy; and as soon moved to be moody, and as soon moody to be moved.

11 *as hot a Jack:* as hot-tempered a fellow. 'Jack' means 'knave'

12 *moved to be moody:* made angry

13 *moody to be moved:* angry at being provoked

BENVOLIO

And what to?

MERCUTIO

Nay, an there were two such, we should have none shortly, for one would kill the other. Thou! Why, thou wilt quarrel with a man that hath a hair more or a hair less in his beard than thou hast. Thou wilt quarrel with a man for cracking nuts, having no other reason but because thou hast hazel eyes. What eye but such an eye would spy out such a quarrel? Thy head is as full of quarrels as an egg is full of meat; and yet thy head hath been beaten as addle as an egg for quarrelling. Thou hast quarrelled with a man for coughing in the street, because he hath wakened thy dog that hath lain asleep in the sun. Didst thou not fall out with a tailor for wearing his new doublet before Easter; with another for tying his new shoes with old riband? And yet thou wilt tutor me from quarrelling!

15

20

25

15 *an … such:* if there were two like you. Mercutio is about to have fun at Benvolio's expense by pretending he is quarrelsome, when in fact he is quite the opposite

22 *meat:* food

22 *addle:* rotten; or confused, scrambled

26 *doublet:* jacket

27 *Easter:* Easter was the time when new clothes were worn

28 *riband:* ribbon
tutor me from: advise me against

BENVOLIO

An I were so apt to quarrel as thou art, any man should buy the fee simple of my life for an hour and a quarter.

30

29–30 *An … quarter:* if I were as argumentative as you, anybody could afford to take full ownership of my life because I would be dead within an hour and a quarter

31 *simple:* stupid (a pun on 'fee-simple')

33 *By my heel:* an expression of contempt to intensify the milder swearing of Benvolio ('By my head')

37 *blow:* strike (in fencing). Mercutio is provoking Tybalt

38–9 *apt ... occasion:* ready to strike, if you give me an excuse

41 *thou ... Romeo:* you are often in Romeo's company

42–5 *Consort ... consort:* Mercutio takes the word 'consort' as an insult, presuming that it means a hired musician, and thus feels that he is being challenged by Tybalt

45 *Zounds:* God's wounds (an oath)

46–9 *We ... us:* Benvolio wants to avoid a public quarrel, and suggests three ways of doing this: to continue their business elsewhere, to discuss their differences calmly or to go their separate ways

52 *my man:* the man I am looking for (Romeo)

MERCUTIO

The fee-simple? O simple!

Enter TYBALT and OTHERS.

BENVOLIO

By my head, here come the Capulets.

MERCUTIO

By my heel, I care not.

funny tense [handwritten note]

TYBALT

Follow me close, for I will speak to them.

35   Gentlemen, good-e'en. A word with one of you.

MERCUTIO

And but one word with one of us? Couple it with something. Make it a word and a blow.

TYBALT

You shall find me apt enough to that, sir, an you will give me occasion.

MERCUTIO

40   Could you not take some occasion without giving?

TYBALT

Mercutio, thou consortest with Romeo.

MERCUTIO

Consort? What, does thou make us minstrels? An thou make minstrels of us, look to hear nothing but discords. Here's my fiddlestick. Here's that shall make you dance.

45   Zounds, consort!

BENVOLIO

We talk here in the public haunt of men.

Either withdraw unto some private place,

Or reason coldly of your grievances,

Or else depart. Here all eyes gaze on us.

MERCUTIO

50   Men's eyes were made to look, and let them gaze. I will not budge for no man's pleasure, I.

Enter ROMEO.

TYBALT

Well, peace be with you, sir. Here comes my man.

MERCUTIO

But I'll be hanged, sir, if he wear your livery.

Marry, go before to field, he'll be your follower!

Your worship in that sense may call him 'man'. 55

TYBALT

Romeo, the love I bear thee can afford

No better term than this: thou art a villain.

ROMEO

Tybalt, the reason that I have to love thee

Doth much excuse the appertaining rage

To such a greeting. Villain am I none. 60

Therefore farewell, I see thou knowest me not.

Dramatic Irony

TYBALT

Boy, this shall not excuse the injuries

That thou hast done me. Therefore turn and draw.

ROMEO

I do protest I never injured thee,

But love thee better than thou canst devise 65

Till thou shalt know the reason of my love.

And so, good Capulet, which name I tender

As dearly as my own, be satisfied.

MERCUTIO

O calm, dishonourable, vile submission!

Alla stoccata carries it away. 70

[*draws his weapon*] Tybalt, you ratcatcher, will you walk?

TYBALT

What wouldst thou have with me?

No longer in poetry to show hes lost composure

MERCUTIO

Good King of Cats, nothing but one of your nine lives.

That I mean to make bold withal, and, as you shall use

me hereafter, dry-beat the rest of the eight. Will you pluck 75

your sword out of his pilcher by the ears? Make haste, lest

mine be about your ears ere it be out.

TYBALT

[*draws his weapon*] I am for you.

ROMEO

Gentle Mercutio, put thy rapier up.

53–5 *I'll … 'man':* Mercutio deliberately misinterprets Tybalt's 'man' as meaning 'manservant' and tells him that Romeo is no servant of his, although if he goes to the duelling-field Romeo will follow him and in that sense be his man or follower

57 *a villain:* this is the ultimate insult, almost certain to provoke a duel

58–60 *Tybalt … greeting:* Romeo is giving an obscure hint that love (for Juliet) is his reason for not showing the anger expected at Tybalt's insult

62 *Boy:* an insulting expression

65 *devise:* imagine

66 *reason:* i.e. Romeo's marriage to Juliet

67 *tender:* value, regard

70 *Alla stoccata:* Mercutio's nickname for Tybalt (a 'stoccata' is a sword-thrust)
carries it away: gets away with it

71 *ratcatcher:* Mercutio sees Tybalt as a cat
walk: walk off with me to fight a duel

74–7 *That … out:* I also intend, depending on how you behave towards me from now on, to cudgel the rest of your eight lives. Now will you draw your sword by the hilt (handle) from its scabbard (cover)? Hurry, or else my sword will be at your ears before your sword is even drawn

MERCUTIO

80   Come, sir, your *passado*!

They fight.

ROMEO

Draw, Benvolio. Beat down their weapons.

Gentlemen, for shame, forbear this outrage!

Tybalt, Mercutio, the Prince expressly hath

Forbid bandying in Verona streets.

85   Hold, Tybalt! Good Mercutio!

TYBALT under ROMEO's arm thrusts MERCUTIO.

A FOLLOWER

Away, Tybalt!

Exit TYBALT with his followers.

MERCUTIO

I am hurt.

A plague a' both your houses! I am sped.

Is he gone and hath nothing?

BENVOLIO

90   What, art thou hurt?

MERCUTIO

Ay, ay, a scratch, a scratch. Marry, 'tis enough.

Where is my page? Go, villain, fetch a surgeon.

Exit PAGE.

ROMEO

Courage, man. The hurt cannot be much.

MERCUTIO

No, 'tis not so deep as a well, nor so wide as a church door.

95   But 'tis enough. 'Twill serve. Ask for me tomorrow, and

you shall find me a grave man. I am peppered, I warrant,

for this world. A plague a' both your houses! Zounds,

a dog, a rat, a mouse, a cat, to scratch a man to death!

A braggart, a rogue, a villain, that fight by the book of

100   arithmetic! Why the devil came you between us? I was

hurt under your arm.

ROMEO

I thought all for the best.

MERCUTIO

Help me into some house, Benvolio,

Or I shall faint. A plague a' both your houses!

They have made worms' meat of me.   105

I have it, and soundly too. Your houses!

Exit BENVOLIO helping MERCUTIO.

ROMEO

This gentleman, the Prince's near ally,

My very friend, hath got his mortal hurt

In my behalf — my reputation stained

With Tybalt's slander — Tybalt, that an hour   110

Hath been my cousin. O sweet Juliet,

Thy beauty hath made me effeminate

And in my temper softened valour's steel!

Enter BENVOLIO.

BENVOLIO

O Romeo, Romeo, brave Mercutio's dead!

That gallant spirit hath aspired the clouds,   115

Which too untimely here did scorn the earth.

ROMEO

This day's black fate on more days doth depend.

This but begins the woe others must end.

Enter TYBALT.

BENVOLIO

Here comes the furious Tybalt back again.

ROMEO

Alive in triumph, and Mercutio slain?   120

Away to heaven respective lenity,

And fire-eyed fury be my conduct now!

Now, Tybalt, take the 'villain' back again

That late thou gavest me. For Mercutio's soul

Is but a little way above our heads.   125

Staying for thine to keep him company.

Either thou or I, or both, must go with him.

TYBALT

Thou, wretched boy, that didst consort him here,

Shalt with him hence.

107 *ally:* relative. Mercutio is related to Prince Escalus

108–9 *My . . . behalf:* my true friend, has received this deadly injury because he tried to defend my honour

111 *cousin:* relative. Tybalt became a relative of Romeo's an hour earlier when Romeo married Juliet

112 *effeminate:* unmanly

113 *And . . . steel:* and toned down my bravery

115 *aspired:* climbed, ascended to

116 *untimely:* soon
scorn: show contempt for

117–18 *This . . . end:* today's bad luck will overshadow all that is to follow. Today's misery will reach its conclusion in the days to come

120 *slain:* killed

121 *respective lenity:* respectful gentleness. Romeo is probably saying that he will not show any more respect to the Prince's ban on street-fighting

122 *conduct:* guide

126 *Staying for thine:* waiting for yours

128 *consort:* keep company with

129 *Shalt . . . hence:* you will leave this earth to join Mercutio

129 *This ... that:* my sword will decide whether you or I will join Mercutio in death

131 *up:* angry, agitated
132 *amazed:* dazed
doom thee: sentence you to
133 *taken:* arrested

134 *fool:* laughing-stock, dupe

ROMEO

                 This shall determine that.

They fight. TYBALT falls.

BENVOLIO

130 Romeo, away, be gone!

The citizens are up, and Tybalt slain.

Stand not amazed. The Prince will doom thee death

If thou art taken. Hence, be gone, away!

ROMEO *He realises he is not in control of his fate*

O, I am fortune's fool!

BENVOLIO

             Why dost thou stay?

Exit ROMEO.

Enter CITIZENS.

CITIZEN

135 Which way ran he that killed Mercutio?

Tybalt, that murderer, which way ran he?

BENVOLIO

There lies that Tybalt.

CITIZEN

            Up, sir, go with me.

138 *charge thee:* order you

I charge thee in the Prince's name, obey.

Enter PRINCE, MONTAGUE, CAPULET, LADY MONTAGUE, LADY CAPULET and all.

PRINCE

Where are the vile beginners of this fray?

BENVOLIO

140 *discover:* reveal

140 O noble Prince, I can discover all

141 *unlucky manage:* unfortunate course

The unlucky manage of this fatal brawl.

There lies the man, slain by young Romeo,

143 *slew:* killed

That slew thy kinsman, brave Mercutio.

LADY CAPULET

Tybalt, my cousin! O my brother's child!

145 O Prince! O cousin! Husband! O, the blood is spilled

Of my dear kinsman! Prince, as thou art true,

For blood of ours shed blood of Montague.

O cousin, cousin!

PRINCE

Benvolio, who began this bloody fray?

BENVOLIO

Tybalt, here slain, whom Romeo's hand did slay.   150

Romeo, that spoke him fair, bid him bethink

How nice the quarrel was, and urged withal

Your high displeasure. All this — utterèd

Your gentle breath, calm look, knees humbly bowed —

Could not take truce with the unruly spleen   155

Of Tybalt deaf to peace, but that he tilts

With piercing steel at bold Mercutio's breast;

Who, all as hot, turns deadly point to point,

And, with a martial scorn, with one hand beats

Cold death aside and with the other sends   160

It back to Tybalt, whose dexterity

Retorts it. Romeo, he cries aloud,

'Hold, friends! Friends, part!' and swifter than his tongue

His agile arm beats down their fatal points,

And 'twixt them rushes; underneath whose arm   165

An envious thrust from Tybalt hit the life

Of stout Mercutio, and then Tybalt fled.

But by and by comes back to Romeo,

Who had but newly entertained revenge,

And to't they go like lightning. For, ere I   170

Could draw to part them, was stout Tybalt slain.

And as he fell, did Romeo turn and fly.

This is the truth, or let Benvolio die.

LADY CAPULET

He is a kinsman to the Montague.

Affection makes him false. He speaks not true.   175

Some twenty of them fought in this black strife,

And all those twenty could but kill one life.

I beg for justice, which thou, Prince, must give.

Romeo slew Tybalt. Romeo must not live.

PRINCE

Romeo slew him. He slew Mercutio.   180

Who now the price of his dear blood doth owe?

MONTAGUE

Not Romeo, Prince, he was Mercutio's friend;

His fault concludes but what the law should end,

The life of Tybalt.

151 *him fair:* courteously to him
bethink: consider

152 *nice:* unimportant, trivial

152–3 *urged ... displeasure:* pointed out that you disapproved of street-fighting

155 *take ... spleen:* calm the uncontrolled temper

156 *tilts:* thrusts

158 *point:* sword-point

159–61 *with a ... Tybalt:* with a warlike contempt, Mercutio fights with a dagger in one hand, with which he deflects blows, and a sword in the other, with which he attacks Tybalt

161–2 *dexterity retorts it:* skill turns it back

165 *'twixt:* between

166 *envious:* malicious, nasty

167 *stout:* brave

168 *by and by:* very soon

169 *Who ... revenge:* who had just allowed the thought of revenge into his mind

175 *Affection ... false:* his friendship with Romeo makes him tell lies on his behalf

181 *Who ... owe?* Who is now going to pay for killing him (Mercutio)?

183 *His ... end:* in the end, the law would have condemned Tybalt to death for killing Mercutio, so Romeo merely did what the law would have done

PRINCE

And for that offence

185   Immediately we do exile him hence.

I have an interest in your hate's proceeding,

My blood for your rude brawls doth lie a-bleeding.

But I'll amerce you with so strong a fine

That you shall all repent the loss of mine.

190   I will be deaf to pleading and excuses.

Nor tears nor prayers shall purchase out abuses.

Therefore use none. Let Romeo hence in haste,

Else, when he is found, that hour is his last.

Bear hence this body, and attend our will.

195   Mercy but murders, pardoning those that kill.

Exeunt.

187   *My blood:* a person related to me (Mercutio)

188   *amerce:* punish

191   *purchase out abuses:* get rid of the penalty

195   *Mercy ... kill:* if the Prince is merciful to murderers, he will be associated with murder and will encourage more people to commit this crime

Key points

On the day of his marriage, when he is at his happiest, Romeo's fortunes take a disastrous turn for the worse.

Timeline

Sunday	Monday	Tuesday	Wednesday	Thursday

- Up to this point, the play has been mainly comic in tone. Much of it has been taken up with crude jokes and puns. We have had the coarse, double-meaning talk of the Nurse and of Romeo and his friends, particularly Mercutio. Also, the feuding families have been obeying the Prince's order, given in Act 1, Scene 1, to avoid conflict. Everything changes in this scene, and the change is brought about by the actions of Tybalt.

- In the previous scene, Friar Laurence prayed that the secret marriage of Romeo and Juliet would not bring them sorrow. In this scene, we find that the Friar's prayer does not get a favourable answer. Indeed, the secrecy of the marriage contributes to the deaths of Mercutio and Tybalt and the resulting banishment of Romeo.

- This scene shows how fate strikes against Romeo. For example, if Mercutio and Tybalt had been aware of the marriage, they probably would have acted differently. Romeo has married Tybalt's cousin and is now Tybalt's relative. If Tybalt knew this, he would see Romeo in a new light and not want to get involved in a duel with him. If the party-loving Mercutio knew that Romeo had just married, it seems likely that he would want to celebrate with Romeo rather than have a fight.

- Romeo does know that he is now related to Tybalt, and as a result refuses to fight him. He does not want to tell Tybalt that he is married, but does all he can to suggest that his relationship with Tybalt is now a friendly one. He tells Tybalt of 'the reason that I have to love thee' (line 58), and gives a stronger hint by refusing to fight him.

- Mercutio is shocked by Romeo's passive behaviour, which he describes as 'dishonourable, vile submission' (line 69). He feels that he must defend Romeo's honour and issues his own challenge to Tybalt, which is met with a mild response: 'What wouldst thou have with me?' (line 72). If Mercutio had controlled his anger at this point, peace might have prevailed. Instead, he offers a second challenge, which Romeo tries to prevent, but Tybalt accepts. Mercutio's mistaken judgement of Romeo's refusal to fight, delivered in ignorance of the truth, brings death to Mercutio himself.

- Mercutio's pun on 'grave' marks the moment in the play when comedy turns to tragedy: 'Ask for me tomorrow, and you shall find me a grave man' (lines 95–6).

- Fate has decided that Mercutio's death will quickly be followed by Tybalt's. Romeo is now so angry that he feels he must abandon his gentle approach. When Tybalt returns to provoke him, Romeo kills him.

- At this point, Romeo knows that fate will punish him, whether he is innocent or guilty of Tybalt's death. The Prince's order at the beginning of the play has come back to haunt him: 'If ever you disturb our streets again, your lives shall pay the forfeit of the peace' (Act 1, Scene 1, lines 89–90). The Prince does not sentence Romeo to death, but to banishment. However, Romeo's banishment is to have disastrous results for him as well as for Juliet.

Useful quotes

I do protest I never injured thee,
But love thee better than thou canst devise
(Romeo, lines 64–5)

O calm, dishonourable, vile submission!
(Mercutio, line 69)

A plague a' both your houses! I am sped.
(Mercutio, line 88)

Away to heaven respective lenity,
And fire-eyed fury be my conduct now!
(Romeo, lines 121–2)

Romeo slew Tybalt. Romeo must not live.
(Lady Capulet, line 179)

Let Romeo hence in haste,
Else, when he is found, that hour is his last.
(Prince Escalus, lines 192–3)

Come, sir, your **passado***!*

MERCUTIO, Act 3, Scene 1, 80

? Questions

1 Benvolio seems nervous at the start of this scene. What is he worried about?

2 Why does Mercutio claim that Benvolio really enjoys a fight?

3 How does Benvolio respond to this accusation?

4 Who is Tybalt looking for?

5 In what ways does Mercutio try to provoke Tybalt?

6 Explain Romeo's attitude to Tybalt.

7 Why does Mercutio fight Tybalt?

8 Romeo's bad luck is a feature of this scene. Explain.

9 Where does Mercutio place the blame for what has happened to him?

10 Why does Romeo fight Tybalt?

11 Can Romeo be blamed for any of the events in this scene? If not, where does the blame lie?

12 Is Benvolio's account of the fighting (lines 150–73) an accurate one?

13 Explain Lady Capulet's attitude to Romeo (line 179).

14 Is the Prince's verdict on Romeo a fair one? Do you think it has been affected by the fact that Mercutio was related to him? Explain your answer.

Talking point

Lady Capulet remarks: 'Romeo slew Tybalt. Romeo must not live' (line 179). She believes in 'an eye for an eye' as fair punishment. How should wrongdoers be punished? Should the sentence be the same as the crime? Should the victim's family members have a say in how the criminal is punished?

ACT 3 † Scene 2

Plot summary

Juliet is eagerly waiting for Romeo to join her. The Nurse brings her the bad news. At first the Nurse torments her by seeming to suggest that it is Romeo who has died. When Juliet learns of Tybalt's death and Romeo's banishment, the shocking reality of the Capulet–Montague feud dawns on her: her husband has killed her cousin, and she sees an end to her happiness as Romeo's wife. She is angry at Romeo's actions. When the Nurse agrees with her, however, Juliet's loyalty to Romeo is restored. The Nurse promises to bring Romeo to her from Friar Laurence's cell, where he is hiding.

What devil art thou that dost torment me thus?

JULIET, Act 3, Scene 2, 43

Verona. The Capulets' orchard.

Enter JULIET alone.

JULIET ~soliloquy

Gallop apace, you fiery-footed steeds,

Towards Phoebus' lodging! Such a waggoner

As Phaëton would whip you to the West

And bring in cloudy night immediately.

5   Spread thy close curtain, love-performing night,

That runaway's eyes may wink, and Romeo

Leap to these arms untalked of and unseen.

Lovers can see to do their amorous rites

By their own beauties; or, if love be blind,

10   It best agrees with night. Come, civil night,

Thou sober-suited matron, all in black,

And learn me how to lose a winning match,

Played for a pair of stainless maidenhoods.

Hood my unmanned blood, bating in my cheeks,

15   With thy black mantle till strange love grow bold,

Think true love acted simple modesty.

Come, night. Come, Romeo. Come, thou day in night;

For thou wilt lie upon the wings of night

Whiter than new snow up on a raven's back.

20   Come, gentle night. Come, loving, black-browed night.

Give me my Romeo, and when he shall die,

Take him and cut him out in little stars,

And he will make the face of heaven so fine

That all the world will be in love with night

25   And pay no worship to the garish sun.

O I have bought the mansion of a love,

But not possessed it; and though I am sold,

Not yet enjoyed. So tedious is this day

As is the night before some festival

30   To an impatient child that hath new robes

And may not wear them.

Enter NURSE, wringing her hands, with the ladder of cords.

                 O here comes my Nurse,

And she brings news; and every tongue that speaks

But Romeo's name speaks heavenly eloquence.

Now, Nurse, what news? What, hast thou there the cords

That Romeo bid thee fetch?

1–2 *Gallop ... lodging!* Juliet is asking the horses of the sun-god Phoebus to take the sun quickly beneath the horizon so that the day may end

2–3 *waggoner as Phaëton:* reckless driver

5 *close:* covering

6 *runaway's ... wink:* the eyes of the sun may close and bring on darkness

8–9 *Lovers ... beauties:* the beauty of lovers provides enough light for them to perform loving acts

10 *agrees with:* suits, matches
    civil: serious, solemn

12 *learn ... match:* teach me how to surrender to Romeo in order to gain him at the same time

13 *stainless maidenhoods:* innocent lovers

14 *Hood ... cheeks:* hide my blushes

15 *till ... bold:* until I get used to this love, which is new to me

16 *Think ... modesty:* think of physical love as a chaste and holy thing

25 *garish:* too bright

30 *robes:* clothes

34 *cords:* rope-ladder

NURSE

Ay, ay, the cords.   35

She throws them down.

JULIET

Ay me! What news? Why dost thou wring thy hands?

NURSE

Ah, weraday! He's dead, he's dead, he's dead!

We are undone, lady, we are undone!

Alack the day! He's gone, he's killed, he's dead!

JULIET

Can heaven be so envious?

NURSE

Romeo can,   40

Though heaven cannot. O Romeo, Romeo!   *Dramatic Irony*

Who ever would have thought it? Romeo!

JULIET

What devil art thou that dost torment me thus?

This torture should be roared in dismal hell.

Hath Romeo slain himself? Say thou but 'Ay'.   45

And that bare vowel 'I' shall poison more

Than the death-darting eye of cockatrice

I am not I, if there be such an 'I'

Or those eyes shut that make thee answer 'Ay'.

If he be slain, say 'Ay'; or if not, 'No'.   50

Brief sounds determine of my weal or woe.

NURSE

I saw the wound. I saw it with mine eyes —

God save the mark! — here on his manly breast.

A piteous corpse, a bloody piteous corpse;

Pale, pale as ashes, all bedaubed in blood   55

All in gore-blood. I swounded at the sight.

JULIET

O, break, my heart! Poor bankrupt, break at once!

To prison, eyes; ne'er look on liberty!

Vile earth, to earth resign; end motion here,

And thou and Romeo press one heavy bier!   60

NURSE

O Tybalt, Tybalt, the best friend I had!

O courteous Tybalt, honest gentleman!

That ever I should live to see thee dead!

---

37 *weraday:* alas

38 *undone:* ruined, destroyed

39 *Alack:* an expression of regret

40 *envious:* full of spite, jealous

40 *Romeo can:* i.e. Romeo was full of hatred when he killed Tybalt

47 *cockatrice:* a mythical animal whose glance could kill

49 *those eyes shut:* if the eyes of Romeo are closed in death

51 *Brief … woe:* single syllables will decide whether I am to be happy or sad

53 *God … mark!* an exclamation excusing the mention of unpleasant things
54 *piteous:* deserving pity
55 *bedaubed:* smeared, spattered

56 *gore-blood:* congealed blood
swounded: swooned, fainted

59 *Vile … here:* give my body up to the grave; stop my feelings now
60 *And … bier!* my body and Romeo's will share the same coffin
bier: a stretcher on which a corpse is carried to the grave

JULIET

What storm is this that blows so contrary?

65 Is Romeo slaughtered, and is Tybalt dead,

My dearest cousin and my dearer lord?

Then, dreadful trumpet, sound the general doom!

For who is living, if those two are gone?

NURSE

Tybalt is gone, and Romeo banishèd;

70 Romeo that killed him, he is banishèd.

JULIET

O God! Did Romeo's hand shed Tybalt's blood?

NURSE

It did, it did! Alas the day, it did!

JULIET

O serpent heart, hid with a flowering face!

Did ever dragon keep so fair a cave?

Beautiful tyrant! Fiend angelical!

Dove-feathered raven! Wolvish-ravening lamb!

Despisèd substance of divinest show!

Just opposite to what thou justly seemest —

A damnèd saint, an honourable villain!

80 O nature, what hadst thou to do in hell

When thou didst bower the spirit of a fiend

In mortal paradise of such sweet flesh?

Was ever book containing such vile matter

So fairly bound? O, that deceit should dwell

In such a gorgeous palace!

NURSE

85   There's no trust,

No faith, no honesty in men; all perjured,

All forsworn, all naught, all dissemblers.

Ah, where's my man? Give me some aqua vitae.

These griefs, these woes, these sorrows make me old.

Shame come to Romeo!

JULIET

90   Blistered be thy tongue

For such a wish! He was not born to shame.

Upon his brow shame is ashamed to sit.

For 'tis a throne where honour may be crowned

---

64 *so contrary:* in opposite directions

66 *lord:* husband (Romeo)

67 *dreadful ... doom:* may the end of the world come

73–85 *O ... palace!* Juliet is saying that Romeo is the opposite to what he seems, that he is pleasant on the outside but evil underneath

73 *serpent ... face:* the serpent who tempted Eve in the Garden of Eden was often shown by artists as having an attractive human face surrounded by flowers

74 *dragon ... cave:* the task of the dragon was to guard treasure in a cave

75 *Fiend angelical!* a devil disguised as an angel

76 *Wolvish-ravening lamb!* a wolf who devours sheep

77 *show:* appearance

80–2 *O ... flesh?* How could nature have put an evil spirit into the fair body of Romeo?

86 *perjured:* lied under oath

87 *forsworn:* falsely swearing
   naught: evil, wicked
   dissemblers: tricksters, hypocrites

88 *aqua vitae:* a strong drink

oxymorons she sounds like romo

Sole monarch of the universal earth.

O, what a beast was I to chide at him!   95

NURSE

Will you speak well of him that killed your cousin?

JULIET

Shall I speak ill of him that is my husband?

Ah, poor my lord, what tongue shall smooth thy name,

When I, thy three-hours wife, have mangled it?

But wherefore, villain, didst thou kill my cousin?   100

That villain cousin would have killed my husband.

Back, foolish tears, back to your native spring!

Your tributary drops belong to woe,

Which you, mistaking, offer up to joy.

My husband lives, that Tybalt would have slain;   105

And Tybalt's dead, that would have slain my husband.

All this is comfort. Wherefore weep I then?

Some word there was, worser than Tybalt's death,

That murdered me. I would forget it fain.

But O, it presses to my memory   110

Like damnèd guilty deeds to sinners' minds!

'Tybalt is dead, and Romeo — banishèd.'

That 'banishèd', that one word 'banishèd',

Hath slain ten thousand Tybalts. Tybalt's death

Was woe enough, if it had ended there;   115

Or, if sour woe delights in fellowship

And needly will be ranked with other griefs,

Why followed not, when she said 'Tybalt's dead',

Thy father, or thy mother, nay, or both,

Which modern lamentation might have moved?   120

But with a rearward following Tybalt's death,

'Romeo is banishèd' — to speak that word

All slain, all dead. 'Romeo is banishèd!' —

Is father, mother, Tybalt, Romeo, Juliet,

There is no end, no limit, measure, bound,   125

In that word's death. No words can that woe sound.

Where is my father and my mother, Nurse?

NURSE

Weeping and wailing over Tybalt's corpse.

Will you go to them? I will bring you thither.

[handwritten marginal note: True love]

---

95 *chide at:* criticise

98 *smooth thy name:* speak well of you

100 *wherefore:* why

102 *native spring:* original source

103 *tributary ... woe:* tears of praise should be tears of sorrow

105 *that:* whom

108 *worser:* that upset me more

109 *murdered:* wounded
would ... fain: would be glad to forget it

116 *delights in fellowship:* loves company

117 *And ... with:* and insists on being alongside

118–20 *Why ... moved?* Why could the news of Tybalt's death not have been followed by the news that one or both of my parents had also died, which might have seemed more natural and caused moderate ('modern') grieving?

121 *But ... following:* rather than the piece of news coming after

125 *bound:* boundary

126 *No ... sound:* words cannot express that sorrow

129 *thither:* there

JULIET

130 Wash they his wounds with tears. Mine shall be spent,

When theirs are dry, for Romeo's banishment.

Take up those cords. Poor ropes, you are beguiled,

Both you and I, for Romeo is exiled.

He made you for a highway to my bed,

135 But I, a maid, die maiden-widowèd.

Come, cords. Come, Nurse. I'll to my wedding bed,

And death, not Romeo, take my maidenhead!

NURSE

Hie to your chamber. I'll find Romeo

To comfort you. I wot well where he is.

140 Hark ye, your Romeo will be here at night.

I'll to him. He is hid at Laurence' cell.

JULIET

O, find him! Give this ring to my true knight

And bid him come to take his last farewell.

Exeunt.

132 *beguiled:* deceived

135 *maid:* virgin

137 *death ... maidenhead:* death will be my husband instead of Romeo

138 *Hie:* go

139 *wot:* know

140 *Hark ye:* listen to me

141 *to:* go to

Key points

The first effects of the disasters of the previous scene begin to be felt when Juliet's joyful anticipation of Romeo's arrival is shattered by the Nurse's bad news. Juliet falls into despair over Romeo's banishment.

Timeline

Sunday	Monday	Tuesday	Wednesday	Thursday

- It is typical of the Nurse that she confuses Juliet about the nature of the bad news. She refuses to confirm the identity of the person who has died and continues to talk about his wounds. Juliet assumes that it must be Romeo. Then the Nurse mentions Tybalt, making Juliet think that both Tybalt and Romeo are dead. Having put Juliet through severe torment, she finally comes to the point: Tybalt is dead, killed by Romeo, who has been banished.

- Juliet's first response is to engage in a wild and confused rant, in which Romeo features as a man whose beautiful appearance hides the evil inside him, like a splendidly bound book containing horrible stories. Juliet changes her tune entirely when the Nurse agrees with her. Juliet then calls down a curse on the Nurse and regrets her first reaction.

- The Nurse compensates for the torment she has visited upon Juliet by offering to see to it that Romeo comes to her at night.

- Juliet experiences some extreme changes of emotion in this scene, but by the end she reaches new levels of maturity.

Useful quotes

> Come, gentle night. Come, loving, black-browed night.
> Give me my Romeo, and when he shall die,
> Take him and cut him out in little stars
>
> (Juliet, lines 20–2)

> There's no trust,
> No faith, no honesty in men; all perjured,
> All forsworn, all naught, all dissemblers.
>
> (Nurse, lines 85–7)

> What storm is this that blows so contrary?
> Is Romeo slaughtered, and is Tybalt dead,
> My dearest cousin and my dearer lord?
>
> (Juliet, lines 64–6)

> O, find him! Give this ring to my true knight
> And bid him come to take his last farewell.
>
> (Juliet, lines 142–3)

Questions ?

1 How is Juliet feeling at the start of this scene?

2 What is the Nurse carrying when she comes on stage? Why is this needed?

3 What mood is the Nurse in?

4 What does Juliet assume when the Nurse says 'he's dead' (line 37)?

5 What is the Nurse describing in lines 52–6?

6 Suggest a reason for the Nurse's delay in telling Juliet that Tybalt, not Romeo, is dead.

7 Read lines 73–85 carefully. What point do they make?

8 What feelings does the Nurse express about Romeo in this scene?

9 What effect does the Nurse's view of Romeo have on Juliet?

10 How does the future look to Juliet now that she knows that Romeo is to be banished from Verona?

11 What comfort does the Nurse offer Juliet? What does this imply about the Nurse's true attitude to what has happened to Romeo and Tybalt?

12 Why does Juliet send her ring to Romeo?

Talking point

Imagine that you found yourself in the awful situation where your partner has just killed your cousin. Would your loyalties be divided? Would you stand by your partner? Or do you think family ties are stronger? Would it depend on the circumstances?

ACT 3 ✝ Scene 3

Plot summary

When Friar Laurence brings him the news of his banishment, Romeo falls into deep despair. He considers a sentence of banishment worse than a sentence of death, since life outside Verona would be meaningless for him. When the Nurse informs him of Juliet's troubled state, Romeo becomes suicidal and has to be prevented from stabbing himself. Friar Laurence tries to explain to Romeo that he is fortunate in many important respects: Juliet is alive; Tybalt who tried to kill him is dead; and he has merely been exiled, not sentenced to death. He advises Romeo to go to Juliet to console her, and then to go into exile in Mantua. He hopes that the news of the marriage of Romeo and Juliet can be made public after a suitable interval. Friar Laurence promises to send Romeo news from Verona from time to time.

Do not say 'banishment'.

ROMEO, Act 3, Scene 3, 14

Verona. Friar Laurence's cell.

Enter FRIAR LAURENCE.

FRIAR
Romeo, come forth. Come forth, thou fearful man.
Affliction is enamoured of thy parts,
And thou art wedded to calamity.

Enter ROMEO.

ROMEO
Father, what news? What is the Prince's doom?
What sorrow craves acquaintance at my hand   5
That I yet know not?

FRIAR
               Too familiar
Is my dear son with such sour company.
I bring thee tidings of the Prince's doom.

ROMEO
What less than doomsday is the Prince's doom?

FRIAR
A gentler judgement vanished from his lips: 10
Not body's death, but body's banishment.

ROMEO
Ha, banishment? Be merciful, say 'death',
For exile hath more terror in his look,
Much more than death. Do not say 'banishment'.

FRIAR
Hence from Verona art thou banishèd.   15
Be patient, for the world is broad and wide.

ROMEO
There is no world without Verona walls,
But purgatory, torture, hell itself.
Hence banishèd is banished from the world,
And world's exile is death. Then 'banishèd'   20
Is death mistermed. Calling death 'banishèd',
Thou cuttest my head off with a golden axe
And smilest upon the stroke that murders me.

FRIAR
O deadly sin! O rude unthankfulness!
Thy fault our law calls death. But the kind Prince,   25
Taking thy part, hath rushed aside the law,

---

1   *fearful:* full of fear as well as causing fear

2–3   *Affliction … calamity:* misery is attracted to you and you are married to disaster

4   *doom:* verdict, judgement

5–6   *What … not?* What bad news am I going to hear?

6–7   *Too … company:* you are well used to sorrow

8   *tidings:* news

9   *doomsday:* death

10–11   *A … banishment:* the Prince was entitled to sentence you to death, but he chose to impose the lighter sentence of banishment

16   *Be patient:* compose yourself

17   *without:* outside

18   *purgatory:* place of suffering for dead sinners

19–20   *Hence … death:* to be banished from Verona is to be banished from the world (since Verona is my world), and to be banished from the world means death

21   *mistermed:* wrongly named

24–7   *O … banishment:* by not being grateful to the Prince you are committing the deadly sin of ingratitude. The Prince has, for your sake, ignored the fact that the law demands death as a penalty for your crime, and given you a milder sentence

And turned that black word 'death' to banishment.

This is dear mercy, and thou seest it not.

ROMEO

'Tis torture, and not mercy. Heaven is here,

30 Where Juliet lives. And every cat and dog

And little mouse, every unworthy thing,

Live here in heaven and may look on her.

But Romeo may not. More validity,

More honourable state, more courtship lives

35 In carrion flies than Romeo. They may seize

On the white wonder of dear Juliet's hand

And steal immortal blessing from her lips,

Who, even in pure and vestal modesty,

Still blush, as thinking their own kisses sin.

40 This may flies do, when I from this must fly.

And sayest thou yet that exile is not death?

But Romeo may not, he is banishèd.

Flies may do this but I from this must fly:

They are free men, but I am banishèd.

45 Hadst thou no poison mixed, no sharp-ground knife,

No sudden mean of death, though ne'er so mean,

But 'banishèd' to kill me — 'banishèd'?

O Friar, the damnèd use that word in hell.

Howling attends it! How hast thou the heart,

50 Being a divine, a ghostly confessor,

A sin-absolver, and my friend professed,

To mangle me with that word 'banishèd'?

FRIAR

Thou fond mad man, hear me a little speak.

ROMEO

O, thou wilt speak again of banishment.

FRIAR

55 I'll give thee armour to keep off that word —

Adversity's sweet milk, philosophy,

To comfort thee, though thou art banishèd.

ROMEO

Yet 'banishèd'? Hang up philosophy!

Unless philosophy can make a Juliet,

60 Displant a town, reverse a Prince's doom,

It helps not, it prevails not. Talk no more.

33 *validity:* value

34 *courtship:* civilised, mannerly behaviour

35 *carrion flies:* flies on corpses

38 *vestal modesty:* chastity

41 *sayest thou yet:* do you still claim

45–6 *poison . . . death:* means of suicide (for Romeo)

48–9 *the damnèd . . . it:* the damned souls in hell howl at the thought that they have been banished

50 *divine:* clergyman
ghostly: spiritual

51 *my friend professed:* claiming to be my friend

52 *mangle:* injure, hurt

53 *fond:* foolish

56 *Adversity's . . . philosophy:* philosophy helps people to bear disappointment

58 *Hang up:* hang

60 *Displant:* transplant, uproot

61 *prevails:* persuades, convinces

FRIAR

O, then I see that madmen have no ears.

ROMEO

How should they, when that wise men have no eyes?

FRIAR

Let me dispute with thee of thy estate.

64 *dispute … estate:* calmly discuss your present circumstances with you

ROMEO

Thou canst not speak of that thou dost not feel.   65

Wert thou as young as I, Juliet thy love,

An hour but married, Tybalt murderèd,

Doting like me, and like me banishèd,

Then mightst thou speak; then mightst thou tear thy hair,

And fall upon the ground, as I do now,   70

Taking the measure of an unmade grave.

Knock.

71 *Taking … grave:* as he speaks, Romeo lies on the stage, measuring with his body the length of the grave in which he will be buried

FRIAR

Arise. One knocks. Good Romeo, hide thyself.

72 *Arise:* get up

ROMEO

Not I; unless the breath of heartsick groans

Mist-like infold me from the search of eyes.

Knock.

73–4 *heartsick … eyes:* my sad sighs hide me like a mist so that I cannot be seen

FRIAR

Hark, how they knock! — Who's there? — Romeo, arise.   75

Thou wilt be taken. — Stay awhile! — Stand up.

Knock.

Run to my study. — By and by! — God's will,

What simpleness is this! — I come, I come!

Knock.

Who knocks so hard? Whence come you?

What's your will?   80

76 *taken:* captured
Stay: wait

78 *simpleness:* stupidity

79–80 *Whence … will?* From where have you come? What do you want?

NURSE

Let me come in, and you shall know my errand.

I come from Lady Juliet.

FRIAR

                    Welcome, then.

Enter NURSE.

NURSE

O holy Friar! O, tell me, holy Friar,

Where is my lady's lord, where's Romeo?

FRIAR

85   There on the ground, with his own tears made drunk.

NURSE

O, he is even in my mistress' case,

Just in her case! O woeful sympathy!

Piteous predicament! Even so lies she,

Blubbering and weeping, weeping and blubbering.

90   Stand up, stand up! Stand, an you be a man.

For Juliet's sake, for her sake, rise and stand!

Why should you fall into so deep an O?

He rises.

ROMEO

Nurse—

NURSE

          Ah sir! Ah sir! Well, death's the end of all.

ROMEO

Spakest thou of Juliet? How is it with her?

95   Doth she not think me an old murderer,

Now I have stained the childhood of our joy

With blood removed but little from her own?

Where is she? And how doth she? And what says

My concealed lady to our cancelled love?

NURSE

100   O, she says nothing, sir, but weeps and weeps,

And now falls on her bed, and then starts up,

And Tybalt calls, and then on Romeo cries,

And then down falls again.

ROMEO

             As if that name,

Shot from the deadly level of a gun,

105   Did murder her; as that name's cursèd hand

Murdered her kinsman. O, tell me, Friar, tell me,

In what vile part of this anatomy

Doth my name lodge? Tell me, that I may sack

The hateful mansion.

He offers to stab himself; the NURSE snatches the dagger away.

---

86 *even … case:* in the same condition as Juliet

90 *an:* if

92 *O:* cry of sorrow

93 *death's … all:* at least you're not dead

95 *old:* experienced

97 *blood … own:* the blood of her close relative

99 *concealed lady:* secret wife
    cancelled: made invalid by what has happened

102 *on:* against

104 *level:* aim

107 *anatomy:* human body

108–9 *sack … mansion:* destroy the body that I hate. Romeo is talking of suicide

FRIAR

Hold thy desperate hand.

Art thou a man? Thy form cries out thou art.   110

Thy tears are womanish. Thy wild acts denote

The unreasonable fury of a beast.

Unseemly woman in a seeming man!

And ill-beseeming beast in seeming both!

Thou hast amazed me. By my holy order,   115

I thought thy disposition better tempered.

Hast thou slain Tybalt? Wilt thou slay thyself?

And slay thy lady that in thy life lives,

By doing damnèd hate upon thyself?

Why railest thou on thy birth, the heaven and earth?   120

Since birth and heaven and earth, all three do meet

In thee at once; which thou at once wouldst lose.

Fie, fie, thou shamest thy shape, thy love, thy wit,

Which, like a usurer, aboundest in all,

And usest none in that true use indeed   125

Which should bedeck thy shape, thy love, thy wit.

Thy noble shape is but a form of wax,

Digressing from the valour of a man;

Thy dear love sworn but hollow perjury,

Killing that love which thou hast vowed to cherish;   130

Thy wit, that ornament to shape and love,

Misshapen in the conduct of them both,

Like powder in a skilless soldier's flask

Is set afire by thine own ignorance,

And thou dismembered with thine own defence.   135

What, rouse thee, man! Thy Juliet is alive,

For whose dear sake thou wast but lately dead.

There art thou happy. Tybalt would kill thee,

But thou slewest Tybalt. There are thou happy.

The law, that threatened death, becomes thy friend   140

And turns it to exile. There art thou happy.

A pack of blessings light upon thy back.

Happiness courts thee in her best array.

But, like a mishavèd and sullen wench,

Thou pouts upon thy fortune and thy love.   145

Take heed, take heed, for such die miserable.

Go, get thee to thy love, as was decreed,

---

110 *form:* shape, physique

113–14 *Unseemly . . . both!* according to the Friar, Romeo looks like a man and behaves like a woman (because he weeps), which is unnatural

115 *my holy order:* the order he belongs to (founded by St Francis)

116 *thy . . . tempered:* you were better balanced

119 *damnèd:* sinful

120 *railest . . . birth:* do you curse your birth

123 *wit:* intelligence

124–6 *Which . . . wit:* you possess beauty, love and intelligence, but make bad use of these

126 *bedeck:* decorate, do honour to

127–8 *Thy . . . man:* your body is only a wax model if it lacks manly qualities

129–30 *Thy . . . cherish:* you lied when you made your marriage vows if you kill yourself now and destroy the love you said you would hold dear

131–2 *Thy . . . both:* your intelligence has not guided you properly

133 *powder:* gunpowder

135 *dismembered . . . defence:* blown up by your own weapons
136 *rouse thee:* wake up

138 *happy:* lucky
would: wanted to

143 *array:* clothes

144 *mishavèd:* misbehaved

145 *Thou . . . fortune:* you make disagreeable faces at your good fortune

147 *decreed:* planned, agreed to

148 *Ascend her chamber:* climb up to her room

149–50 *look . . . Mantua:* leave Verona before the guards ('Watch') take up their positions and prevent you leaving for Mantua

152 *blaze:* announce
friends: families, households

155 *lamentation:* sorrow; grief

156 *before:* first (ahead of Romeo)

157 *And . . . bed:* and ask her to encourage everyone in the house to have an early night
158 *apt unto:* inclined to do

161 *counsel:* advice
what learning is: the Nurse is admiring the Friar's wisdom and knowledge

162 *chide:* scold (Romeo for his actions)

166 *comfort:* happiness

167 *And . . . state:* your fortunes depend on what happens now

170 *Sojourn:* remain, stay
your man: servant (i.e. Balthasar; see Act 5, Scene 1, line 12)

172 *hap . . . here:* happenings in Verona that will benefit you

174–5 *But . . . thee:* if the thought of seeing Juliet did not delight me so much, I would regret parting from you so suddenly

Ascend her chamber. Hence and comfort her.
But look thou stay not till the Watch be set,
150 For then thou canst not pass to Mantua,
Where thou shalt live till we can find a time
To blaze your marriage, reconcile your friends,
Beg pardon of the Prince, and call thee back
With twenty hundred thousand times more joy
155 Than thou wentest forth in lamentation.
Go before, Nurse. Commend me to thy lady,
And bid her hasten all the house to bed.
Which heavy sorrow makes them apt unto.
Romeo is coming.

NURSE
160 O Lord, I could have stayed here all the night
To hear good counsel. O, what learning is! —
My lord, I'll tell my lady you will come.

ROMEO
Do so, and bid my sweet prepare to chide.

The Nurse begins to go in, but turns back again.

NURSE
Here, sir, a ring she bid me give you, sir.
165 Hie you, make haste, for it grows very late.

Exit NURSE.

ROMEO
How well my comfort is revived by this!

FRIAR
Go hence. Good night. And here stands all your state:
Either be gone before the Watch is set,
Or by the break of day disguised from hence.
170 Sojourn in Mantua. I'll find out your man,
And he shall signify from time to time
Every good hap to you that chances here.
Give me thy hand. 'Tis late. Farewell. Good night.

ROMEO
But that a joy past joy calls out on me,
175 It were a grief so brief to part with thee.
Farewell.

Exeunt.

Key points

The theme of this scene is Romeo's banishment, which makes him feel suicidal. Just as the Nurse has offered to help Juliet to overcome her distress at the news of the sentence of banishment, Friar Laurence takes on a similar role in relation to Romeo.

Timeline

Sunday	Monday	Tuesday	Wednesday	Thursday

- Friar Laurence thinks he is bringing good news to Romeo when he tells him that the Prince, who was entitled by law to sentence him to death, showed him mercy by reducing the death sentence to one of banishment from Verona.

- Romeo is outraged and makes it clear that, as far as he is concerned, banishment is a sentence worse than death. He argues that Verona is the world, that exile from Verona is exile from the world, and exile from the world is death. Thus, the sentence of banishment amounts to 'torture, and not mercy' (line 29).

- Juliet, as we learned in the previous scene, feels the same as Romeo does about his banishment.

- When Romeo offers to end his life, the Nurse intervenes to stop him. Then Friar Laurence, in a powerful speech that might remind you of a sermon, shows Romeo the error of his ways. He points out the things Romeo should be grateful for. He tells Romeo to visit Juliet at her home and console her and then to go into exile in Mantua until a suitable time comes to announce his marriage and beg the Prince's pardon.

- The Friar's intervention, and the ring that Juliet sent with the Nurse to assure Romeo of her love for him, turn Romeo's mood from despair to joy: 'How well my comfort is revived by this!' (line 166).

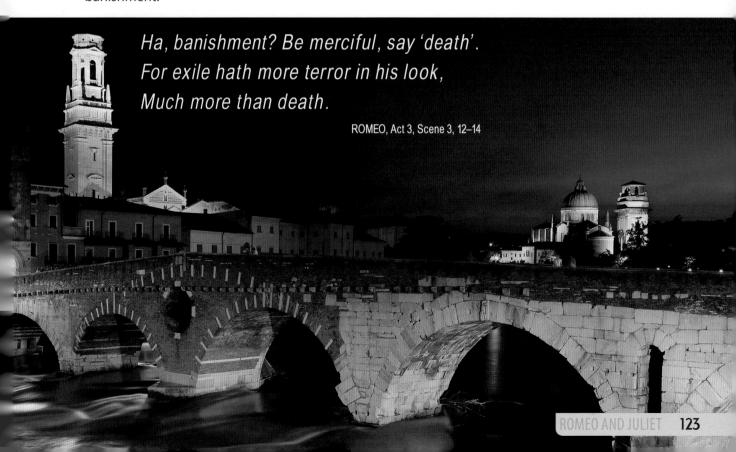

Ha, banishment? Be merciful, say 'death'.
For exile hath more terror in his look,
Much more than death.

ROMEO, Act 3, Scene 3, 12–14

Useful quotes

> Affliction is enamoured of thy parts,
> And thou art wedded to calamity.
>
> (Friar Laurence, lines 2–3)

> What, rouse thee, man! Thy Juliet is alive,
> For whose dear sake thou wast but lately dead.
> There art thou happy.
>
> (Friar Laurence, lines 136–8)

> There is no world without Verona's walls,
> But purgatory, torture, hell itself.
>
> (Romeo, lines 17–18)

> O Lord, I could have stayed here all the night
> To hear good counsel. O, what learning is!
>
> (Nurse, lines 160–1)

? Questions

1 Where is Romeo hiding?

2 Friar Laurence tells Romeo that he is 'wedded to calamity' (line 3). What does this mean? Is it true?

3 What does Romeo expect the Prince's sentence to be?

4 How does Friar Laurence expect Romeo to react to the news of his banishment?

5 Why does Romeo think of life outside Verona as 'torture, hell itself' (line 18)?

6 What does Friar Laurence think of Romeo's attitude?

7 Why has the Nurse come to the Friar's cell?

8 How does Romeo expect Juliet to have reacted to the news that he killed Tybalt?

9 Why does Romeo attempt to kill himself?

10 Set out, in your own words, the main points of Friar Laurence's speech to Romeo (lines 109–59). What is the Friar trying to achieve? Is Romeo convinced?

11 What does the Nurse think of the Friar's words?

12 Romeo is feeling joyful by the end of this scene. What has brought about this dramatic change of mood? Are you surprised at how quickly Romeo has turned from a negative to a positive state of mind, from despair to joy?

Talking point

Friar Laurence helps Romeo to see the positive side of his banishment. Do you tend to see the positive or the negative first in a situation? Is it better to be an optimist and look on the bright side? Should we always try to view problems as opportunities? Is this a difficult thing to do? Are some people better at this than others?

Plot summary

Capulet tells Paris that Juliet is mourning the death of Tybalt, and cannot see him. Unaware of her marriage to Romeo, he decides that Juliet must marry Paris as soon as possible. He sends Lady Capulet to inform Juliet that she is to marry Paris in three days' time. He hopes that this will cheer up Juliet. Paris is delighted with Capulet's change of heart.

These times of woe afford no time to woo.

PARIS, Act 3, Scene 4, 8

Verona. The Capulets' house.

Enter OLD CAPULET, LADY CAPULET and PARIS.

CAPULET
Things have fallen out, sir, so unluckily
That we have had no time to move our daughter.
Look you, she loved her kinsman Tybalt dearly,
And so did I. Well, we were born to die.
5   'Tis very late. She'll not come down tonight.
I promise you, but for your company,
I would have been abed an hour ago.

PARIS
These times of woe afford no time to woo.
Madam, good night. Commend me to your daughter.

LADY CAPULET
10   I will, and know her mind early tomorrow.
Tonight she's mewed up to her heaviness.

PARIS offers to go in and CAPULET calls him again.

CAPULET
Sir Paris, I will make a desperate tender   *Change of attitude*
Of my child's love. I think she will be ruled
In all respects by me. Nay more, I doubt it not.
15   Wife, go you to her ere you go to bed.
Acquaint her here of my son Paris' love,
And bid her — mark you me? — on Wednesday next —
But soft! What day is this?

PARIS
                                        Monday, my lord,

CAPULET
Monday! Ha, ha! Well, Wednesday is too soon,
20   A' Thursday let it be. A' Thursday, tell her,
She shall be married to this noble earl.
Will you be ready? Do you like this haste?
We'll keep no great ado — a friend or two.
For hark you, Tybalt being slain so late,
25   It may be thought we held him carelessly,
Being our kinsman, if we revel much.
Therefore we'll have some half a dozen friends,
And there an end. But what say you to Thursday?   *builds tension*

---

1 *fallen out:* happened

2 *move:* persuade

6 *promise:* assure

7 *abed:* in bed

10 *know her mind:* find out what she is thinking

11 *mewed ... heaviness:* imprisoned by her grief

12 *desperate tender:* bold offer, reckless offer

15 *ere:* before

16 *Acquaint her:* inform her, let her know
    son: Capulet wants Paris to be his son-in-law
17 *mark you:* do you hear

18 *soft:* wait

20 *A':* on

23 *keep ... ado:* make no great fuss

24 *late:* recently

25 *held him carelessly:* had little regard for him

26 *revel:* celebrate

28 *And ... end:* and that will be all

PARIS

My lord, I would that Thursday were tomorrow.

CAPULET

Well get you gone. A' Thursday be it, then.   30

[*to LADY CAPULET*] Go you to Juliet ere you go to bed.

Prepare her, wife, against this wedding day,

Farewell, my lord. — Light to my chamber, ho! —

Afore me, it is so very late that we

May call it early by and by. Good night.   35

Exeunt.

29	*would:* wish
32	*against:* in anticipation of
33	*Light … ho!* he is talking to a servant
34–5	*Afore … by:* I declare, it is so late that we can call it morning immediately

Key points

Juliet's parents are unaware of her marriage. They think that Juliet is depressed over Tybalt's death, and Capulet offers her to Paris in marriage on the following Thursday.

Timeline

Sunday	Monday	Tuesday	Wednesday	Thursday

- The key point in this scene is Capulet's 'desperate tender' (line 12) of Juliet's love to Paris, unaware that she is married to Romeo. This decision is destined to lead to further complications in the lives of Romeo and Juliet. Capulet's 'desperate tender' to Paris makes his marriage to Juliet an urgent issue in the play. But for this, the Friar would not be driven to his desperate remedy of giving Juliet a sleeping drug, and Romeo might wait in Mantua until the Friar could find time to make the marriage public. Thus, what looks like a trivial incident – Capulet calling Paris back as he is leaving and promising Juliet to him in marriage – leads to the tragic events that follow.

- Capulet's decision marks a reversal in his attitude to Juliet getting married. Previously his position was that it was best to wait until she was sixteen, and that she should have a say in who she marries. He is confident, however, that she will accept his decision and marry Paris.

- Juliet's parents believe that marriage to Paris will revive Juliet's spirits. They assume that she is grieving over Tybalt's death. They do not realise that the real cause of her sorrow is Romeo's banishment, and that their actions will make her situation much worse.

- Paris is delighted at Capulet's change of heart. For him, marriage to Juliet cannot come soon enough.

Useful quotes

> These times of woe afford no time to woo.
> Madam, good night. Commend me to your daughter.
>
> (Paris, lines 8–9)

> Wednesday is too soon,
> A' Thursday let it be. A' Thursday, tell her,
> She shall be married to this noble earl.
>
> (Capulet, lines 19–21)

> Sir Paris, I will make a desperate tender
> Of my child's love. I think she will be ruled
> In all respects by me.
>
> (Capulet, lines 12–14)

> Go you to Juliet ere you go to bed.
> Prepare her, wife, against [in time for] this wedding day.
>
> (Capulet, lines 31–2)

? Questions

1 How does Capulet explain Juliet's depressed mood and failure to come down and see the visiting Paris?

2 Do you think Paris is a patient man? Give a reason for your answer.

3 What is Capulet's 'desperate tender' (line 12)?

4 How does Paris respond to this news?

5 Do you pity Paris in this scene, knowing what you know and what he does not? Explain your answer.

6 Compare what Capulet says to Paris in this scene (lines 12–14) with what he told Paris earlier in the play (Act 1, Scene 2, lines 16–19). What do you think has caused this change?

7 What do we learn here about the attitude of Juliet's parents to their daughter?

8 Imagine you are Paris. Write a short letter to Juliet telling her how you feel about her becoming your wife.

Talking point

Parents have to have full authority over their younger children to keep them safe and help them learn what is right and what is wrong, but at what age should they start to let go? If parents still have full responsibility for their child's welfare does that mean that they are entitled to complete authority over the child? Does a child need to learn how to be independent to make a successful transition to adulthood?

ACT 3 ✝ Scene 5

Juliet and Romeo are in her bedroom, saying their farewells as Romeo prepares to go into exile in Mantua. They are reluctant to part, but realise that it is too dangerous for Romeo to stay in Verona. They fear for their future. As Romeo leaves by the rope-ladder, Juliet's mother arrives. Finding Juliet in tears, she tells her that her grief for Tybalt is too much. She considers sending an agent to Mantua to poison Romeo in revenge for Tybalt's death.

Lady Capulet informs Juliet that she is to marry Paris. Juliet refuses. Capulet responds with vile abuse, telling Juliet that he will disown her if she does not marry Paris. Her mother is surprised by Capulet's reaction, but still refuses to help Juliet. Juliet appeals to the Nurse for advice. The Nurse advises Juliet to commit bigamy by forgetting Romeo and marrying Paris. Juliet is appalled, and realises that she can no longer trust the Nurse. As a last resort she decides to ask Friar Laurence to help her. She pretends that she is going to see him to seek forgiveness for having upset her parents.

Look, love, what envious streaks
Do lace the severing clouds in yonder East.

ROMEO, Act 3, Scene 5, 7–8

(handwritten) They spent the night together

Verona. The Capulets' orchard.

Enter ROMEO and JULIET aloft, at the window.

(handwritten) Key scene for

JULIET

(handwritten) ① Juliet doesn't want Romeo to [...]

Wilt thou be gone? It is not yet near day. *(handwritten) but sees the dawn light*

It was the nightingale, and not the lark,

That pierced the fearful hollow of thine ear.

Nightly she sings on yond pomegranate tree.

5   Believe me, love, it was the nightingale.

ROMEO

(handwritten) ② R. is practical (Role reversal)

It was the lark, the herald of the morn;

No nightingale. Look, love, what envious streaks

Do lace the severing clouds in yonder East.

Night's candles are burnt out, and jocund day

10   Stands tiptoe on the misty mountain tops.

I must be gone and live, or stay and die.

JULIET

Yond light is not daylight; I know it, I.

It is some meteor that the sun exhales,

To be to thee this night a torchbearer

15   And light thee on thy way to Mantua.

Therefore stay yet. Thou needest not to be gone.

ROMEO

Let me be ta'en, let me be put to death.

I am content, so thou wilt have it so.

I'll say yon grey is not the morning's eye;

20   'Tis but the pale reflex of Cynthia's brow.

Nor that is not the lark whose notes do beat

The vaulty heaven so high above our heads.

I have more care to stay than will to go.

Come, death, and welcome! Juliet wills it so.

25   How is't, my soul? Let's talk. It is not day.

JULIET

It is, it is! Hie hence, be gone, away!

It is the lark that sings so out of tune,

Straining harsh discords and unpleasing sharps.

Some say the lark makes sweet division.

30   This doth not so, for she divideth us.

Some say the lark and loathèd toad change eyes.

Glossary (left column):

aloft: on the upper stage

4   *yond:* yonder

6   *herald ... morn:* messenger to tell us that it is morning
7   *envious:* malicious, spiteful
8   *Do ... East:* dawn is breaking; as the dawn clouds drift apart, they will separate Romeo and Juliet
9   *Night's candles:* the stars
     jocund: cheerful
10   *Stands tiptoe on:* is peeking over
11   *be ... live:* go if I am to live

13   *exhales:* gives out

17   *ta'en:* taken, arrested
18   *so:* if
19   *yon grey:* that lightening sky
20   *'Tis ... brow:* it is only a pale reflection of moonlight
     Cynthia: another name for the moon goddess, Diana
21   *beat:* echo in
23   *care:* desire

26   *Hie hence:* go from here

28   *Straining ... sharps:* making unnatural efforts and so singing out of tune
29   *division:* a series of musical notes

31   *loathèd:* hateful
     change: exchange

O, now I would they had changed voices too,

Since arm from arm that voice doth us affray,

Hunting thee hence with hunt's-up to the day.

O, now be gone! More light and light it grows.   35

ROMEO

More light and light: more dark and dark our woes.

Enter NURSE hastily.

NURSE

Madam!

JULIET

Nurse?

NURSE

Your lady mother is coming to your chamber.

The day is broke. Be wary. Look about.   40

Exit NURSE.

JULIET

Then, window, let day in, and let life out.

ROMEO

Farewell, farewell! One kiss, and I'll descend.

He goes down the ladder of cords.

JULIET

Art thou gone so, love-lord, aye husband-friend?

I must hear from thee every day in the hour,

For in a minute there are many days.   45

O by this count I shall be much in years

Ere I again behold my Romeo!

ROMEO

Farewell!

I will omit no opportunity

That may convey my greetings, love, to thee.   50

JULIET

O, thinkst thou we shall ever meet again?

ROMEO

I doubt it not; and all these woes shall serve

For sweet discourses in our time to come.

32 *I . . . too:* I wish that the lark and the toad had also swapped voices (an unpleasant croaking like the toad's would suit my mood better than the lark's beautiful voice)

33 *arm . . . affray:* their song frightens us out of our embraces

34 *Hunting thee hence:* chasing you away from here
    hunt's-up: a song used to get hunters up in the morning

40 *wary:* careful

43 *love-lord . . . friend:* Romeo is her lover, husband and friend

46 *much in years:* very old

47 *behold:* see

49–50 *I . . . thee:* I will not miss any chance to send you my greetings

53 *sweet discourses:* happy conversations

54 *ill-divining:* she foresees disaster or evil

55 *Methinks:* I think

JULIET

O God, I have an ill-divining soul!

55 Methinks I see thee, now thou art so low,

As one dead in the bottom of a tomb.

Either my eyesight fails, or thou lookest pale.

ROMEO

And trust me, love, in my eye so do you.

Dry sorrow drinks our blood. Adieu, adieu!

59 *Dry ... blood:* our sighs have exhausted our blood supply, and that is why we look pale; each sigh was believed to drain the heart of one drop of blood

Exit ROMEO.

JULIET

60 O fortune, fortune! All men call thee fickle.

60 *fickle:* changeable

If thou art fickle, what dost thou with him

That is renowned for faith? Be fickle, fortune,

62 *renowned for faith:* known for his faithfulness
Be fickle, fortune: Juliet is making the point that fortune changed in banishing Romeo, and now she hopes it will change again by sending him back to her

For then I hope thou wilt not keep him long

But send him back.

She goes down from the window.

Enter LADY CAPULET.

LADY CAPULET

Ho, daughter! Are you up?

JULIET

65 Who is't that calls? It is my lady mother.

66-7 *Is ... hither?* Is she very late going to bed, or is she up early? What unusual purpose brings her here?

Is she not down so late, or up so early?

What unaccustomed cause procures her hither?

LADY CAPULET

Why, how now, Juliet?

68 *how now:* what's the matter

JULIET

Madam, I am not well.

LADY CAPULET

Evermore weeping for your cousin's death?

69 *Evermore:* always

70 What, wilt thou wash him from his grave with tears?

71 *An if:* even if

An if thou couldst, thou couldst not make him live.

72 *have done:* finish, stop it
72-3 *Some ... wit:* moderate grief shows great love, but too much grief always shows lack of intelligence

Therefore have done. Some grief shows much of love;

But much of grief shows still some want of wit.

JULIET

Yet let me weep for such a feeling loss.

74 *feeling loss:* loss I feel deeply

LADY CAPULET

So shall you feel the loss, but not the friend   75

Which you weep for.

JULIET

                    Feeling so the loss,

I cannot choose but ever weep the friend.

LADY CAPULET

Well, girl, thou weepest not so much for his death

As that the villain lives which slaughtered him.

JULIET

What villain, madam?

LADY CAPULET

                  That same villain, Romeo.   80

JULIET [*aside*]

Villain and he be many miles asunder.

[*to her mother*] God pardon! I do, with all my heart.

And yet no man like he doth grieve my heart.

LADY CAPULET

That is because the traitor murderer lives.

JULIET

Ay, madam, from the reach of these my hands.   85

Would none but I might venge my cousin's death!

LADY CAPULET

We will have vengeance for it, fear thou not.

Then weep no more. I'll send to one in Mantua,

Where that same banished runagate doth live,

Shall give him such an unaccustomed dram   90

That he shall soon keep Tybalt company.

And then I hope thou wilt be satisfied.

JULIET

Indeed I never shall be satisfied

With Romeo, till I behold him — dead —

Is my poor heart so for a kinsman vexed.   95

Madam, if you could find out but a man

To bear a poison, I would temper it —

That Romeo should, upon receipt thereof,

Soon sleep in quiet. O, how my heart abhors

---

75 *friend:* relative

77 *friend:* lover

81 *Villain ... asunder:* there is a great difference between Romeo and a villain

83 *like he:* as much as he. Juliet's comment has a double meaning – one meaning for herself, the other for her mother

85 *from ... hands:* out of my reach. Juliet wants to get her hands on Romeo, so that nobody can punish him for Tybalt's death, but she wants her mother to think that she will use her hands to punish Tybalt's killer

86 *venge:* avenge, get revenge for

89 *runagate:* runaway, fugitive

90 *Shall ... dram:* who shall give him the kind of dose [of poison] he is not used to

94 *dead:* this can refer back to Romeo ('him') or forward to Juliet ('poor heart')

95 *vexed:* tormented

97 *bear:* bring, deliver
    temper: mix

99 *sleep in quiet:* two meanings: (a) die and (b) fall into a harmless, pleasant sleep

100 To hear him named and cannot come to him,

To wreak the love I bore my cousin

Upon his body that slaughtered him!

LADY CAPULET

Find thou the means, and I'll find such a man.

But now I'll tell thee joyful tidings, girl.

JULIET

105 And joy comes well in such a needy time.

What are they, I beseech your ladyship?

LADY CAPULET

Well, well, thou hast a careful father, child:

One who, to put thee from thy heaviness,

Hath sorted out a sudden day of joy

110 That thou expects not nor I looked not for.

JULIET

Madam, in happy time! What day is that?

LADY CAPULET

Marry, my child, early next Thursday morn

The gallant, young, and noble gentleman,

The County Paris, at Saint Peter's Church,

115 Shall happily make thee there a joyful bride.

JULIET

Now by Saint Peter's Church and Peter too,

He shall not make me there a joyful bride!

I wonder at this haste, that I must wed

Ere he that should be husband comes to woo.

120 I pray you tell my lord and father, madam,

I will not marry yet; and when I do, I swear

It shall be Romeo, whom you know I hate,   *Dramatic Irony*

Rather than Paris. These are news indeed!

LADY CAPULET

Here comes your father. Tell him so yourself,

125 And see how he will take it at your hands.

Enter CAPULET and NURSE.

CAPULET

When the sun sets the air doth drizzle dew,

But for the sunset of my brother's son

It rains downright.

---

101 *wreak:* pay

101–2 *wreak ... him:* two meanings: (a) take vengeance on Romeo for killing Tybalt and (b) bestow the love I had for Tybalt on Romeo

104 *joyful tidings:* happy news

106 *they:* the happy news
       beseech: ask

107 *careful:* one who takes care of you

108 *heaviness:* sadness

109 *sorted out:* arranged

110 *I ... for:* I did not ask for

111 *in happy time:* what a suitable time you have chosen to give me good news

112 *Marry:* an exclamation meaning 'By the Virgin Mary'

113 *gallant:* fine, charming

118–19 *I wonder ... woo:* Juliet is understandably surprised that she is being forced to rush into a marriage with a man who has not yet come to court her

126 *the air ... dew:* Capulet sees Juliet in tears, and thinks she is weeping for Tybalt

127 *the sunset of my brother's son:* the death of Tybalt. Tybalt was not the son of Capulet's brother, but of his brother-in-law, the brother of Capulet's wife. See Act 3, Scene 1, line 144

How now? A conduit, girl? What, still in tears?

Evermore showering? In one little body   130

Thou counterfeitest a bark, a sea, a wind.

For still thy eyes, which I may call the sea,

Do ebb and flow with tears. The bark thy body is,

Sailing in this salt flood. The winds, thy sighs,

Who, raging with thy tears and they with them,   135

Without a sudden calm will overset

Thy tempest-tossèd body. How now, wife?

Have you delivered to her our decree?

LADY CAPULET

Ay, sir. But she will none, she gives you thanks.

I would the fool were married to her grave!   140

CAPULET

Soft! Take me with you, take me with you, wife.

How? Will she none? Doth she not give us thanks?

Is she not proud? Doth she not count her blest,

Unworthy as she is, that we have wrought

So worthy a gentleman to be her bride?   145

JULIET

Not proud you have, but thankful, that you have.

Proud can I never be of what I hate,

But thankful even for hate that is meant love.

CAPULET

How, how, how, how, chopped logic? What is this?

'Proud' — and 'I thank you' — and 'I thank you not' —   150

And yet 'not proud'? Mistress minion you,

Thank me no thankings, nor proud me no prouds,

But fettle your fine joints against Thursday next

To go with Paris to Saint Peter's Church,

Or I will drag thee on a hurdle thither.   155

Out, you green-sickness carrion! Out, you baggage!

Your tallow-face!

LADY CAPULET

                  Fie, fie! What, are you mad?

JULIET

Good father, I beseech you on my knees,

Hear me with patience but to speak a word.

129 *conduit:* fountain; he is referring to Juliet's tears

131 *Thou counterfeitest:* you are imitating
bark: ship

136 *Without:* unless there is
overset: capsize

138 *decree:* decision that Juliet will marry Paris

139–40 *But ... grave!* she will have nothing to do with Paris, thank you very much. I wish the foolish girl were dead

141 *Take ... you:* explain your meaning to me. I don't understand

144–5 *Unworthy ... bride:* notice the offensive contrast drawn by Capulet between the 'unworthy' Juliet and the 'worthy' Paris
144 *wrought:* brought it about
145 *bride:* bridegroom

148 *thankful ... love:* grateful for the hatred you are showing me, since it is meant by you to be love

149 *How:* what
chopped logic: misleading and confusing arguments

151 *minion:* minx, brat

153 *fettle:* get ready. To fettle is to groom a horse
against: in preparation for
155 *hurdle:* sledge (a 'hurdle' was a frame on which traitors were dragged to execution)
thither: to the church
156 *Out ... carrion!* away with you, you sickly, pale-faced corpse
baggage: worthless wretch
157 *tallow:* animal fat used for making candles and soap

157 *are you mad:* she is amazed at her husband's fit of rage, and may be saying that he has gone too far

get thee to church a'Thursday,
Or never after look me in the face

CAPULET, Act 3, Scene 5, 161–2

CAPULET

Hang thee, young baggage! Disobedient wretch!　　　160

I tell thee what — get thee to church a' Thursday,

Or never after look me in the face.

Speak not, reply not, do not answer me!

My fingers itch. Wife, we scarce thought us blest

That God had lent us but this only child.　　　165

But now I see this one is one too much,

And that we have a curse in having her.

Out on her, hilding!

NURSE
　　　　　　　　　　God in heaven bless her!

You are to blame, my lord, to rate her so.

CAPULET

And why, my Lady Wisdom? Hold your tongue,　　　170

Good Prudence. Smatter with your gossips, go!

NURSE

I speak no treason.

CAPULET
　　　　　　　　　　O, God-i-good-e'en!

NURSE

May not one speak?

CAPULET
　　　　　　　　　　Peace, you mumbling fool!

Utter your gravity o'er a gossip's bowl,

For here we need it not.

LADY CAPULET
　　　　　　　　　　You are too hot.　　　175

CAPULET

God's bread! It makes me mad.

Day, night; hour, tide, time; work, play;

Alone, in company; still my care hath been

To have her matched. And having now provided

A gentleman of noble parentage,　　　180

Of fair demesnes, youthful, and nobly trained,

Stuffed, as they say, with honourable parts,

Proportioned as one's thought would wish a man —

And then to have a wretched puling fool,

164　*My fingers itch:* he is tempted to strike Juliet

164–7　*we scarce ... her:* we thought we were unfortunate in having only one child, but this child is one too many, and we now feel cursed in having her

168　*hilding:* worthless creature, good for nothing

169　*rate:* rebuke, chastise

171　*Smatter ... gossips:* keep your nonsensical talk for the people you like to gossip with

172　*God-i-good-e'en:* good evening to you; for God's sake, go away

174　*Utter ... bowl:* speak your words of wisdom when you are eating with your companions

175　*too hot:* too excited and bad tempered

176　*God's bread!* the consecrated host (an oath)

177　*tide:* season

178　*still:* always

179　*matched:* married

181　*demesnes:* landed estates

182　*parts:* qualities

184　*puling:* whinging

185 A whining mammet, in her fortune's tender,

To answer 'I'll not wed, I cannot love;

I am too young, I pray you, pardon me'!

But, an you will not wed, I'll pardon you!

Graze where you will, you shall not house with me.

190 Look to't, think on't. I do not use to jest.

Thursday is near. Lay hand on heart. Advise.

An you be mine, I'll give you to my friend.

An you be not, hang, beg, starve, die in the streets,

For, by my soul, I'll ne'er acknowledge thee,

195 Nor what is mine shall never do thee good.

Trust to't. Bethink you. I'll not be forsworn.

Exit CAPULET.

JULIET
Is there no pity sitting in the clouds

That sees into the bottom of my grief?

O sweet my mother, cast me not away!

200 Delay this marriage for a month, a week.

Or, if you do not, make the bridal bed

In that dim monument where Tybalt lies.

LADY CAPULET
Talk not to me, for I'll not speak a word.

Do as thou wilt, for I have done with thee.

Exit LADY CAPULET.

JULIET
205 O God! — O Nurse, how shall this be prevented?

My husband is on earth, my faith in heaven.

How shall that faith return again to earth

Unless that husband send it me from heaven

By leaving earth? Comfort me, counsel me.

210 Alack, alack, that heaven should practise stratagems

Upon so soft a subject as myself!

What sayest thou? Hast thou not a word of joy?

Some comfort, Nurse.

NURSE
                    Faith, here it is.

Romeo is banished; and all the world to nothing,

215 That he dares ne'er come back to challenge you.

Or if he do, it needs must be by stealth.

Then, since the case so stands as now it doth,

I think it best you married with the County.

O, he's a lovely gentleman!

Romeo's a dishclout to him. An eagle, madam,   220

Hath not so green, so quick, so fair an eye

As Paris hath. Beshrew my very heart,

I think you are happy in this second match.

For it excels your first; or if it did not,

Your first is dead — or 'twere as good he were   225

As living here and you no use of him.

JULIET

Speakest thou from thy heart?

NURSE

And from my soul too. Else beshrew them both.

JULIET

Amen!

NURSE

What?   230

JULIET

Well, thou hast comforted me marvellous much.

Go in; and tell my lady I am gone,

Having displeased my father, to Laurence' cell,

To make confession and to be absolved.

NURSE   *soliloquy*

Marry, I will; and this is wisely done.   235

Exit NURSE.

JULIET

Ancient damnation! O most wicked fiend!

Is it more sin to wish me thus forsworn,

Or to dispraise my lord with that same tongue

Which she hath praised him with above compare

So many thousand times? Go, counsellor!   240

Thou and my bosom henceforth shall be twain.

I'll to the Friar to know his remedy.

If all else fail, myself have power to die.

Exit.

---

218 *the County:* Paris

220 *dishclout to him:* dishcloth when compared with him

222 *Beshrew:* curse

223 *happy:* fortunate

224 *excels:* is better than

225 *Your . . . were:* Romeo is dead, or as good as dead

228 *Else . . . both:* otherwise, a curse on both (my heart and soul)

231 *thou . . . much:* you have been a great comfort to me. Juliet is being sarcastic

236–41 *Ancient . . . twain:* the Nurse is a damned old woman and a devil. I wonder if her greater sin is asking me to be untrue to my marriage vows ('forsworn'), or criticising Romeo, whom she used to praise so much. I will no longer trust her with my thoughts and confidences ('bosom')

241 *twain:* separated

242 *I'll to:* I'll go to
remedy: solution to my dilemma

Key points

Although Capulet and Lady Capulet think they are acting in Juliet's best interests in trying to marry her to the eligible Paris, they are making her situation even more desperate.

Timeline

Sunday	Monday	Tuesday	Wednesday	Thursday

- As Romeo leaves Juliet, she fears they will never meet again, and imagines she sees him now 'dead in the bottom of a tomb' (line 56). We know that she is right to be fearful.

- Thinking that Juliet is still grieving over Tybalt's death, Lady Capulet offers what she believes will be good news. For Juliet, the news could not be worse: she is to marry Paris on Thursday. Juliet protests strongly. Lady Capulet passes her over to her father, who angrily dismisses her protests, threatening to have nothing more to do with her if she refuses to marry Paris.

- When Juliet looks to her Nurse for help, all she gets is advice to forget Romeo and marry Paris. She feels utter contempt for the Nurse and her suggestion that she commit bigamy (the offence of marrying one person while still married to another), but pretends she finds it comforting.

- Juliet resorts to another piece of deception. She lets the Nurse believe that she is now sorry for having displeased her parents, and that she is going to Friar Laurence to confess her sin of disobedience and ask for forgiveness. Her real purpose in going to Friar Laurence is to get his advice on how to avoid a marriage to Paris. This visit will eventually result in tragedy for Romeo and Juliet.

- Juliet, in the final line of the scene, makes a disturbing comment: 'If all else fail, myself have power to die' (line 243). She cannot know that fate has decided that she will soon exercise this power.

Useful quotes

O God, I have an ill-divining soul!
Methinks I see thee, now thou art so low,
As one dead in the bottom of a tomb.

(Juliet, lines 54–6)

Well girl, thou weepest not so much for his death
As that the villain lives which slaughtered him.

(Lady Capulet, lines 78–9)

Marry, my child, early next Thursday morn
The gallant, young, and noble gentleman,
The County Paris, at Saint Peter's Church,
Shall happily make thee there a joyful bride.

(Lady Capulet, lines 112–15)

I will not marry yet; and when I do, I swear
It shall be Romeo, whom you know I hate,
Rather than Paris.

(Juliet, lines 121–3)

I think it best you married with the County.
O, he's a lovely gentleman!
Romeo's a dishclout to him.

(Nurse, lines 218–20)

Thou and my bosom henceforth shall be twain.
I'll to the Friar to know his remedy.
If all else fail, myself have power to die.

(Juliet, lines 241–3)

Questions ?

1 At the start of this scene, Juliet tries to delay Romeo's departure. What changes her mind?

2 How is Romeo feeling as he leaves Juliet?

3 What does Lady Capulet believe is the reason for Juliet's tears?

4 What plans does Lady Capulet have for Romeo?

5 How does Juliet handle her mother's comments on Romeo?

6 In this scene, Juliet suffers greatly. What are the causes of her suffering?

7 Why is Capulet so angry with Juliet?

8 As the scene proceeds, Juliet becomes more and more isolated. Explain how this happens.

9 Does the Nurse deserve Juliet's condemnation (line 236) at the end?

10 Lack of awareness of the truth plays an important part in this scene. Explain.

11 Imagine that Juliet decides to write a letter to Friar Laurence at the end of this scene, instead of visiting him. Compose the kind of letter you think she would write.

12 Compose a dialogue between Capulet and Lady Capulet dealing with Juliet's attitudes as expressed in this scene.

Talking point

Parents usually think they know what is best for their children. Why is this? Are they usually right? Do you think it is difficult for parents to pull back and let their children make their own decisions and, perhaps, their own mistakes?

ACT 3 † Key moments

Scene 1

- Tybalt still wants revenge on Romeo, and challenges him to a duel. Romeo refuses.
- Mercutio, angry with Romeo for refusing to fight, challenges Tybalt, who wounds him fatally.
- Romeo kills Tybalt to avenge the killing of Mercutio, and then goes into hiding.
- Prince Escalus decides to banish Romeo from Verona.

Scene 2

- The Nurse informs Juliet that Romeo has killed Tybalt.
- Juliet derives some comfort from the fact that Tybalt started the fight, intending to kill Romeo.
- The Nurse offers to bring Romeo, who is hiding in Friar Laurence's cell, to Juliet.

Scene 3

- Romeo considers banishment from Verona a worse sentence than death. He offers to stab himself, but the Nurse snatches the dagger away. Friar Laurence points out the many things for which Romeo should be grateful. Romeo is cheered by the thought of briefly spending time with Juliet.

Scene 4

- Capulet promises Paris that he will order Juliet to marry him in three days' time, and tells Lady Capulet to inform Juliet of his wedding plans for her.

Scene 5

- As the dawn breaks, Juliet advises Romeo to leave before he is captured.
- Lady Capulet, who thinks Juliet is mourning for Tybalt, wants to have Romeo poisoned.
- Juliet refuses to marry Paris. Her father threatens to throw her out of her home.
- The Nurse advises Juliet to marry Paris and forget Romeo.
- Juliet decides to seek the help of Friar Laurence.

ACT 3 † Speaking and listening

1 Select two students to play the Prince and Benvolio and another five students to be a judging panel. The members of the class question Benvolio in order to find out exactly how Mercutio and Tybalt were killed. The judging panel of five students then assess Benvolio's evidence and decide who is to blame. The Prince, who has decided to banish Romeo as a punishment for killing Tybalt, is then asked to explain his verdict.

2 In groups of four, assign the parts of Juliet, Lady Capulet, Capulet and the Nurse. Imagine that the play has been paused at Act 3, Scene 5, line 141, and set up a freeze-frame of this moment. Think about what each character is thinking and feeling at that exact moment of the play and try to convey that through your frozen facial expression and body language. Agree an adjective for each character that describes their inner feelings at that moment.

Revision quiz: plot summary

Q

Use the words and phrases listed in the panel to fill in the blanks in this summary of Act 3:

banishes
Benvolio
Capulet
Capulets
disown
duel
forget
Friar Laurence
Juliet
kills
Lady Capulet
Mantua
marry
Mercutio
Montagues
Nurse
Paris
Prince Escalus
refuses
Romeo
secret
Thursday
Tybalt
Verona

The young men of _____ are out and about on the streets. Tybalt is looking for _____. When he finds him, he challenges him to a _____. Romeo refuses to fight Tybalt. The reason for this is that Romeo has married _____ and is now related to the _____, but he cannot reveal this because the marriage is a _____.

_____, who feels he has to defend Romeo's honour, steps in to fight Tybalt. When Romeo tries to stop the fight, _____ wounds Mercutio and runs from the scene. Before he dies, Mercutio curses both the _____ and the Capulets. When Tybalt returns, Romeo _____ him. Benvolio persuades Romeo to hide before _____ _____ arrives.

_____ explains what has happened and the Prince _____ Romeo from Verona. Juliet is distraught when she finds out what has happened. The _____ promises to bring Romeo to her before he leaves Verona. Romeo also feels despair and the Nurse has to stop him from killing himself. _____ _____ persuades Romeo that there is still a chance that the situation can be sorted out in time. Romeo and Juliet spend the night together before he must leave for _____.

Meanwhile Capulet has decided to agree to _____ marrying his daughter on the coming _____. Believing that Juliet's recent distress has been caused by Tybalt's death, _____ thinks this news will cheer her up. Juliet _____, but Capulet says he will _____ her if she does not marry Paris. Juliet appeals to _____ for help, but she abandons her. The Nurse advises Juliet to _____ Romeo and to _____ Paris, who is a much better catch. Juliet decides that she will turn to Friar Laurence for help.

ACT 4 † Scene 1

Plot summary

Friar Laurence and Paris are discussing the marriage arrangements for Paris and Juliet when Juliet enters in a distressed state. Paris and Juliet take part in an awkward conversation, which is cut short when Juliet asks Friar Laurence to hear her confession. After Paris has left, Juliet discusses her situation with Friar Laurence, who has a plan to reunite her with Romeo. Juliet is to pretend to agree to marry Paris. On the night before her proposed marriage she is to take a potion that will make it appear that she is dead, but from which she will awake after forty-two hours. By this time she will have been laid to rest in the Capulets' tomb. Friar Laurence will write to Romeo to let him know what is happening and to tell him to come back to meet Juliet at the tomb and bring her with him into exile.

Poor soul, thy face is much abused with tears.

PARIS, Act 4, Scene 1, 29

Verona. Friar Laurence's cell.

Enter FRIAR LAURENCE and COUNTY PARIS.

FRIAR

On Thursday, sir? The time is very short.

PARIS

My father Capulet will have it so,

And I am nothing slow to slack his haste.

FRIAR

You say you do not know the lady's mind.

Uneven is the course. I like it not.   5

PARIS

Immoderately she weeps for Tybalt's death,

And therefore have I little talked of love;

For Venus smiles not in a house of tears.

Now, sir, her father counts it dangerous

That she do give her sorrow so much sway,   10

And in his wisdom hastes our marriage

To stop the inundation of her tears,

Which, too much minded by herself alone,

May be put from her by society.

Now do you know the reason of this haste.   15

FRIAR [*aside*]

I would I knew not why it should be slowed.

[*to PARIS*] Look, sir, here comes the lady toward my cell.

Enter JULIET.

PARIS

Happily met, my lady and my wife!

JULIET

That may be, sir, when I may be a wife.

PARIS

That 'may be' must be, love, on Thursday next.   20

JULIET

What must be shall be.

FRIAR

                    That's a certain text.

---

2 *father:* future father-in-law

3 *nothing ... haste:* not at all anxious to make him go any slower in arranging my marriage to Juliet

4 *the lady's mind:* what Juliet thinks of this

5 *Uneven ... course:* this is an irregular business

6 *Immoderately ... death:* her sorrow at Tybalt's death is out of control

8 *Venus:* goddess of love

9 *counts:* considers

10 *That ... sway:* that she allows her sorrow to control her too much

11 *hastes:* hurries, brings forward the day of

12 *inundation:* flooding

13 *too ... alone:* she is thinking about too much when she is alone

14 *May ... society:* some company may make her forget her grief

15 *Now ... know:* now you know

16 *I would ... slowed:* I wish I didn't know why the marriage of Juliet and Paris has to be delayed

18 *Happily met:* I am glad to bump into you

21 *a certain text:* a true proverb; for sure

PARIS

Come you to make confession to this father?

JULIET

To answer that, I should confess to you.

PARIS

Do not deny to him that you love me.

JULIET

25   I will confess to you that I love him.

PARIS

So will ye, I am sure, that you love me.

JULIET

If I do so, it will be of more price,

Being spoke behind your back, than to your face.

PARIS

Poor soul, thy face is much abused with tears.

JULIET

30   The tears have got small victory by that,

For it was bad enough before their spite.

PARIS

Thou wrongest it more than tears with that report.

JULIET

That is no slander, sir, which is a truth.

And what I spake, I spake it to my face.

PARIS

35   Thy face is mine, and thou hast slandered it.

JULIET

It may be so, for it is not mine own.

[*to FRIAR*] Are you at leisure, holy father, now,

Or shall I come to you at evening mass?

FRIAR

My leisure serves me, pensive daughter, now.

40   My lord, we must entreat the time alone.

PARIS

God shield I should disturb devotion!

Juliet, on Thursday early will I rouse ye.

Till then, adieu, and keep this holy kiss.

Exit PARIS.

---

26 *that:* tell him that

27–8 *If . . . face:* if I say that I love you behind your back, it will mean more than if I had said it to your face

29 *much abused:* wronged, spoiled

30–1 *The . . . spite:* my tears have not ruined my face; it was bad enough already

32 *Thou . . . report:* your criticism of your face wrongs it more than your tears do

33 *slander:* lie, false accusation

34 *spake:* said
to my face: openly, and also about her face

36 *not mine own:* Juliet's hidden meaning is that her face is not her own since it belongs to Romeo
37 *at leisure:* free

39 *My . . . now:* sorrowful girl, I'm now free to see you
40 *we . . . alone:* we must ask you to let us have time to ourselves

41 *God . . . devotion!* God forbid that I should disturb a religious purpose
42 *rouse ye:* wake you
43 *holy:* virtuous, innocent

JULIET

O shut the door, and when thou hast done so,

Come weep with me. Past hope, past cure, past help!   45

FRIAR

O, Juliet, I already know thy grief.

It strains me past the compass of my wits.

I hear thou must, and nothing may prorogue it,

On Thursday next be married to this County.

JULIET

Tell me not, Friar, that thou hearest of this,   50

Unless thou tell me how I may prevent it.

If in thy wisdom thou canst give no help,

Do thou but call my resolution wise

And with this knife I'll help it presently.

God joined my heart and Romeo's, thou our hands;   55

And ere this hand, by thee to Romeo's sealed,

Shall be the label to another deed,

Or my true heart with treacherous revolt

Turn to another, this shall slay them both.

Therefore, out of thy long-experienced time,   60

Give me some present counsel; or, behold,

'Twixt my extremes and me this bloody knife

Shall play the umpire, arbitrating that

Which the commission of thy years and art

Could to no issue of true honour bring.   65

Be not so long to speak. I long to die

If what thou speakest speak not of remedy.

FRIAR

Hold, daughter. I do spy a kind of hope,

Which craves as desperate an execution

As that is desperate which we would prevent.   70

If, rather than to marry County Paris,

Thou hast the strength of will to slay thyself,

Then is it likely thou wilt undertake

A thing like death to chide away this shame,

That copest with death himself to 'scape from it.   75

And, if thou darest, I'll give thee remedy.

JULIET

O bid me leap, rather than marry Paris,

From off the battlements of any tower,

47 *It ... wits:* your situation is an unbearable strain on my mind

48 *may prorogue:* can postpone

49 *this County:* Count Paris

53–4 *Do ... presently:* agree that I should take my own life and I'll stab myself immediately

56 *ere:* before
sealed: bound by law

57 *Shall ... deed:* will sign another marriage contract

59 *this:* the knife she is carrying
both: her hand and her heart

60–1 *out ... counsel:* give me the benefit of your experience and wisdom

61–5 *behold ... bring:* this knife will make the decision for me that no legal authority could honourably make

66–7 *I ... remedy:* the time has come for me to die, unless you can solve my problem

69–70 *Which ... prevent:* we must take desperate measures to prevent a desperate situation

73–4 *thou ... shame:* you are prepared to try something near to death to get rid of this disgrace

75 *That ... it:* you must confront death to escape the shame of marrying Paris

78 *battlements:* low wall along the top of a castle, with spaces through which people could defend the castle from attack

79	*in thievish ways:* in places where thieves are found
81	*charnel house:* dungeon containing the bones of the dead
83	*reeky . . . skulls:* foul-smelling shinbones and yellow skulls without lower jaws
88	*unstained:* faithful, pure
91	*look:* see to it
93	*vial:* beaker
94	*distilling liquor:* liquid that will penetrate the body
95	*presently:* at once, instantly
96	*humour:* fluid
97	*native progress:* natural rhythm *surcease:* cease to operate
98	*testify thou livest:* give evidence that you are alive
100	*wanny:* pale *eyes' windows:* eyelids
102	*Each . . . government:* each part of the body will be unable to move
104	*borrowed . . . death:* disguise as a corpse
110	*In . . . bier:* dressed in your best clothes with your face uncovered as you are laid out
111	*vault:* tomb
112	*kindred:* relatives
113	*against . . . awake:* in expectation of your re-awakening
114	*our drift:* what we are up to
115	*hither:* here
117	*bear thee hence:* take you away

Or walk in thievish ways, or bid me lurk

80 Where serpents are. Chain me with roaring bears,

Or hide me nightly in a charnel house,

O'ercovered quite with dead men's rattling bones,

With reeky shanks and yellow chapless skulls.

Or bid me go into a new-made grave

85 And hide me with a dead man in his tomb —

Things that, to hear them told, have made me tremble —

And I will do it without fear or doubt,

To live an unstained wife to my sweet love.

FRIAR

Hold, then. Go home, be merry, give consent

90 To marry Paris. Wednesday is tomorrow.

Tomorrow night look that thou lie alone.

Let not the Nurse lie with thee in thy chamber.

Take thou this vial, being then in bed,

And this distilling liquor drink thou off;

95 When presently through all thy veins shall run

A cold and drowsy humour. For no pulse

Shall keep his native progress, but surcease.

No warmth, no breath, shall testify thou livest.

The roses in thy lips and cheeks shall fade

100 To wanny ashes, thy eyes' windows fall

Like death when he shuts up the day of life.

Each part, deprived of supple government,

Shall, stiff and stark and cold, appear like death.

And in this borrowed likeness of shrunk death

105 Thou shalt continue two-and-forty hours,

And then awake as from a pleasant sleep.

Now, when the bridegroom in the morning comes

To rouse thee from thy bed, there art thou dead.

Then, as the manner of our country is,

110 In thy best robes uncovered on the bier

Thou shalt be borne to that same ancient vault

Where all the kindred of the Capulets lie.

In the meantime, against thou shalt awake,

Shall Romeo by my letters know our drift.

115 And hither shall he come. And he and I

Will watch thy waking, and that very night

Shall Romeo bear thee hence to Mantua.

And this shall free thee from this present shame,
If no inconstant toy nor womanish fear
Abate thy valour in the acting it.   120

JULIET

Give me, give me! O, tell not me of fear!

FRIAR

Hold. Get you gone. Be strong and prosperous
In this resolve. I'll send a friar with speed
To Mantua, with my letters to thy lord.

JULIET

Love give me strength, and strength shall help afford.   125
Farewell, dear father.

Exeunt.

119–20 *If . . . it:* if no change of mind or the fear a woman might feel at doing something like this affects your determination to do what I suggest

122 *prosperous:* successful

123 *resolve:* agreed decision, plan

124 *thy lord:* your husband (Romeo)

125 *afford:* carry this out

Key points

This scene features an embarrassing interview between Juliet and Paris, Juliet's suicidal thoughts, and details of the Friar's plan to save her from having to marry Paris.

Timeline

Sunday	Monday	Tuesday	Wednesday	Thursday

- In Act 3, Scene 3, the Nurse and Friar Laurence had to restrain Romeo from suicide. Now, when Juliet visits the Friar, she too feels suicidal. The reason is the same in both cases: they have to endure separation because of Romeo's banishment and they short-sightedly believe that this makes life not worth living.

- The key feature of this scene is Friar Laurence's desperate but ingenious scheme to reunite Romeo and Juliet so that they may go into exile together. This plan, as we are to discover, carries its own risks, and is destined to go disastrously wrong. Nevertheless, Juliet is prepared to do anything to avoid marrying Paris and to remain faithful to her husband.

- Romeo and Juliet is a fast-moving play. A lot has happened in the two days since the events of the opening scene. Notice the number of references in this scene to Thursday as the date chosen for the marriage of Juliet and Paris. This tactic creates a sense of urgency that will be increased in the next scene.

- The conversation between Juliet and Paris at the start of this scene is uncomfortable. Juliet is quite cold and formal and gives Paris no encouragement. However, Paris remains determined to marry her, even though he is not convinced that she loves him.

Useful quotes

> And therefore have I little talked of love;
> For Venus smiles not in a house of tears.
>
> (Paris, lines 7–8)

> O bid me leap, rather than marry Paris,
> From off the battlements of any tower
>
> (Juliet, lines 77–8)

> God shield I should disturb devotion!
> Juliet, on Thursday early will I rouse ye.
> Till then, adieu, and keep this holy kiss.
>
> (Paris, lines 41–3)

> And this shall free thee from this present shame,
> If no inconstant toy nor womanish fear
> Abate thy valour in the acting it.
>
> (Friar Laurence, lines 118–20)

? Questions

1 Write out the text of what you imagine Friar Laurence and Paris might have been saying to each other before this scene begins.

2 When Friar Laurence says 'I like it not' (line 5), what does Paris think is the reason for the Friar's concerns?

3 What is the real reason for the Friar's concerns?

4 Describe the behaviour of Paris towards Juliet in this scene.

5 Describe the behaviour of Juliet towards Paris in this scene.

6 Friar Laurence shows skill and tact in dealing with Paris. Agree or disagree with this statement and give reasons for your answer.

7 What is Friar Laurence's plan?

8 What is your opinion of Friar Laurence's plan? What does Juliet think of it?

9 Is the Friar's behaviour what you would expect of a holy man? Give reasons for your answer.

10 Can you think of a better plan than that proposed by Friar Laurence? Explain your thinking.

Talking point

Romeo and Juliet are both very quick to consider suicide in response to Romeo's banishment. What does this tell us about them? Does it mean they are unable to face up to their situation? Is it because they are young and have not developed the skills to deal with life's knocks? Does it suggest that they live in a violent society? Is it likely that a modern play would feature so many references to suicide?

Plot summary

Juliet carries through the first stage of the Friar's plan. She finds her father making preparations for her wedding to Paris and pretends that, having spoken to Friar Laurence, she wants to apologise and ask him to forgive her disobedience. Capulet is so pleased at Juliet's change of heart that he gives orders for the marriage to take place a day earlier. He will oversee the wedding preparations himself, and hurries off to tell Paris the good news.

> *I have learnt me to repent the sin*
> *Of disobedient opposition*
> *To you and your behests, and am enjoined*
> *By holy Laurence to fall prostrate here*
> *And beg your pardon.*
>
> JULIET, Act 4, Scene 2, 16–20

Verona. The Capulets' house.

Enter CAPULET, LADY CAPULET, NURSE, and two or three SERVINGMEN.

CAPULET
So many guests invite as here are writ.

Exit a SERVINGMAN.

Sirrah, go hire me twenty cunning cooks.

SERVINGMAN
You shall have none ill, sir. For I'll try if they can lick their fingers.

CAPULET
5   How canst thou try them so?

SERVINGMAN
Marry, sir, 'tis an ill cook that cannot lick his own fingers. Therefore he that cannot lick his fingers goes not with me.

CAPULET
Go, be gone.

Exit SERVINGMAN.

We shall be much unfurnished for this time.

10   What, is my daughter gone to Friar Laurence?

NURSE
Ay, forsooth.

CAPULET
Well, he may chance to do some good on her.
A peevish self-willed harlotry it is.

Enter JULIET.

NURSE
See where she comes from shrift with merry look.

CAPULET
15   How now, my headstrong! Where have you been gadding?

JULIET
Where I have learnt me to repent the sin
Of disobedient opposition
To you and your behests, and am enjoined
By holy Laurence to fall prostrate here
20   And beg your pardon. Pardon, I beseech you!
Henceforward I am ever ruled by you.

---

1 *writ:* written down (on Capulet's guest list)

2 *Sirrah:* a form of address used by a master to a servant
  cunning: skilled

3 *none ill:* no bad ones
  try: test to see

6 *'tis . . . fingers:* this is a proverb for those who have no faith in their own abilities
7 *goes:* comes

9 *We . . . time:* we will not be ready for the wedding

11 *forsooth:* indeed

13 *A . . . is:* Juliet is a disagreeable, headstrong hussy

14 *shrift:* confession

15 *gadding:* roaming around

18 *behests:* commands
  enjoined: given orders
19 *prostrate:* flat on the ground
20 *beseech:* ask, beg

21 *Henceforward . . . you:* from now on I will always do what you tell me to

CAPULET

Send for the County. Go tell him of this.

I'll have this knot knit up tomorrow morning.

JULIET

I met the youthful lord at Laurence' cell

And gave him what becomèd love I might,   25

Not stepping o'er the bounds of modesty.

CAPULET

Why, I am glad on't. This is well. Stand up.

This is as't should be. Let me see the County.

Ay, marry, go, I say, and fetch him hither.

Now, afore God, this reverend holy Friar,   30

All our whole city is much bound to him.

JULIET

Nurse, will you go with me into my closet

To help me sort such needful ornaments

As you think fit to furnish me tomorrow?

LADY CAPULET

No, not till Thursday. There is time enough.   35

CAPULET

Go, Nurse, go with her. We'll to church tomorrow.

Exeunt JULIET and NURSE.

LADY CAPULET

We shall be short in our provision.

'Tis now near night.

CAPULET

                  Tush, I will stir about,

And all things shall be well, I warrant thee, wife.

Go thou to Juliet, help to deck up her.   40

I'll not to bed tonight. Let me alone.

I'll play the housewife for this once. What, ho!

They are all forth. Well, I will walk myself

To County Paris, to prepare him

Against tomorrow. My heart is wondrous light,   45

Since this same wayward girl is so reclaimed.

Exeunt.

22 *County:* Paris

23 *this … up:* you married

25 *becomèd:* appropriate, proper

26 *o'er the bounds:* outside the boundaries

27 *on't:* to hear it

31 *bound to him:* in his debt

32 *closet:* private apartment

33 *sort:* pick out
needful ornaments: necessary accessories
34 *furnish:* adorn, decorate

37 *provision:* catering, food and drink

38 *stir about:* stay up

39 *warrant:* guarantee

40 *deck up her:* get her dressed

41 *Let me alone:* leave it to me

43 *They … forth:* all the servants are out

45 *Against:* for
wondrous: amazingly
46 *reclaimed:* returned to obedience

Key points

In this scene Juliet begins to put Friar Laurence's plan in action, but immediately events take an unexpected turn when Capulet declares that the wedding will take place tomorrow, Wednesday.

Timeline

Sunday	Monday	Tuesday	Wednesday	Thursday

- At the start of this scene we see a busy Capulet making arrangements for the wedding, even though Juliet has told him that she will not marry Paris. It is clear that he expects her to do what he has told her rather than what she wants in the end. It also seems that he is planning a larger and more lavish event than he described in Act 3, Scene 4.

- Juliet misleads her father into thinking that she is sorry for her disobedience and is now willing to marry Paris. This is exactly what Capulet wanted to hear.

- Capulet is so pleased with Juliet's news that he changes the date of the marriage from Thursday to Wednesday. This change will have deadly consequences. It shortens by a day the time the Friar has to send his message about Juliet to Romeo in Mantua. The change of date also means that Juliet must now take her potion twenty-four hours earlier than she had been instructed.

- Friar Laurence's careful plan for Romeo and Juliet to meet at the tomb when Juliet awakes, and then to go into exile together, is now in danger.

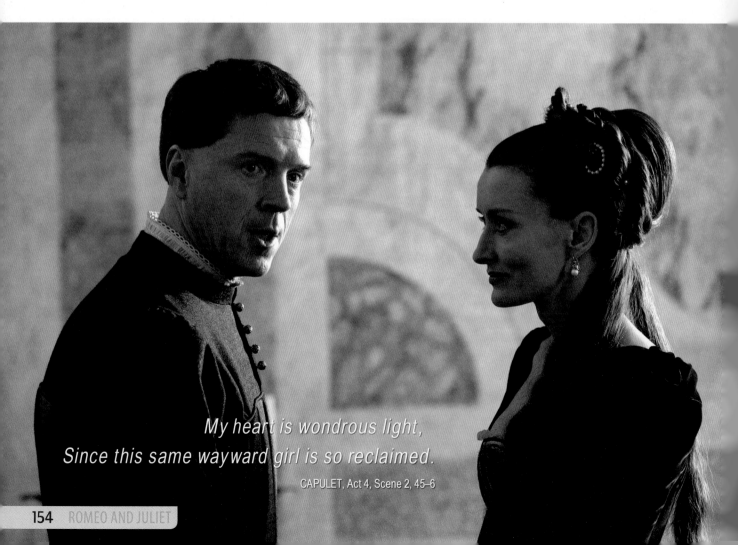

My heart is wondrous light,
Since this same wayward girl is so reclaimed.

CAPULET, Act 4, Scene 2, 45–6

Useful quotes

> *Pardon, I beseech you!*
> *Henceforward I am ever ruled by you.*
>
> (Juliet, lines 20–1)

> *Send for the County. Go tell him of this.*
> *I'll have this knot knit up tomorrow morning.*
>
> (Capulet, lines 22–3)

Questions ?

1 Why is Capulet giving his servant a list of guests at the start of this scene?

2 Does this suggest that Capulet believes Juliet has no choice but to marry Paris?

3 What effect does Capulet hope Juliet's visit to Friar Laurence will have on her?

4 Do you think Juliet gives her father a convincing explanation of her visit to the Friar's cell?

5 When Juliet hears that her father proposes to have her married 'tomorrow morning' (Wednesday) rather than on Thursday, why does she not object?

6 Dramatic irony occurs when a character does not recognise the full significance of what he or she is saying. Find an example of dramatic irony in this scene. Write out the relevant line(s) and explain why the quotation is an example of dramatic irony.

Talking point

The Capulets are a wealthy family and appear to have a large staff of servants. What would it be like to have servants? Do you think you would be comfortable with people serving you and your family? Would you mind sharing your home with them? Would it make you feel better about yourself?

ACT 4 ✝ Scene 3

Plot summary

Alone in her bedroom, Juliet is afraid of taking Friar Laurence's potion and being enclosed in the tomb. She is tempted to call back her mother and the Nurse to comfort her, but accepts that she must act alone if she is to play her part in the Friar's grim plan. She fears that the potion may not work, and that she will be forced to marry Paris. She wonders if the potion is really a poison prepared by the Friar to kill her, to save himself from dishonour if her marriage to Romeo becomes public knowledge. She fears that she may wake before Romeo arrives to rescue her from the tomb, and be stuck there among evil spirits. She nevertheless takes the potion and falls on her bed in a trance.

Romeo, Romeo, Romeo. Here's drink.
I drink to thee.

JULIET, Act 4, Scene 3, 58–9

Verona. Juliet's apartment in the Capulets' house.

Enter JULIET and NURSE.

JULIET

Ay, those attires are best. But, gentle Nurse,

I pray thee leave me to myself tonight.

For I have need of many orisons

To move the heavens to smile upon my state,

Which, well thou knowest, is cross, and full of sin.   5

Enter LADY CAPULET.

LADY CAPULET

What, are you busy, ho? Need you my help?

JULIET

No, madam. We have culled such necessaries

As are behoveful for our state tomorrow.

So please you, let me now be left alone,

And let the Nurse this night sit up with you.   10

For I am sure you have your hands full all

In this so sudden business.

LADY CAPULET

               Good night.

Get thee to bed, and rest. For thou hast need.

Exeunt LADY CAPULET and NURSE.

JULIET

Farewell! God knows when we shall meet again.

I have a faint cold fear thrills through my veins   15

That almost freezes up the heat of life.

I'll call them back again to comfort me.

Nurse! — What should she do here?

My dismal scene I needs must act alone.

Come, vial.   20

What if this mixture do not work at all?

Shall I be married then tomorrow morning?

No, no! This shall forbid it. Lie thou there.

She lays down a knife.

What if it be a poison which the Friar

Subtly hath ministered to have me dead,   25

Lest in this marriage he should be dishonoured,

Margin glosses:

1 *attires:* clothes

3 *orisons:* prayers

4 *state:* condition, life

5 *cross:* perverse

7–8 *We . . . tomorrow:* we have picked out everything we need for tomorrow's ceremony

8 *behoveful:* necessary

15 *faint . . . veins:* my fear makes me shiver and feel cold and faint

17 *them:* Lady Capulet and the Nurse

19 *dismal scene:* dreadful performance

20 *vial:* container of poison

21 *do:* does

25 *ministered:* doctored, tampered with

Handwritten annotations: foreshadowing/fate — Soliloquy

29 *he . . . man:* he has always shown himself to be a holy man

32 *redeem:* save, rescue

33 *stifled:* smothered
vault: tomb

34 *healthsome:* healthy, fresh

35 *strangled ere:* suffocated before

36 *like:* likely

37 *conceit:* fantasy, image

39 *receptacle:* storehouse

42 *green in earth:* newly buried

43 *festering . . . shroud:* rotting in his grave-clothes

44 *spirits resort:* ghosts hang out

45 *Alack:* an expression of regret or sorrow

46 *loathsome:* disgusting, revolting

47 *mandrakes:* plants that were supposed to shriek when uprooted, and cause madness to whoever uprooted them

49 *distraught:* deeply upset or disturbed

50 *Environèd:* surrounded

53 *rage:* madness

56 *spit:* stab through, pierce

Because he married me before to Romeo?
I fear it is. And yet methinks it should not,
For he hath still been tried a holy man.
30 How if, when I am laid into the tomb,
I wake before the time that Romeo
Come to redeem me? There's a fearful point!
Shall I not then be stifled in the vault,
To whose foul mouth no healthsome air breathes in,
35 And there die strangled ere my Romeo comes?
Or, if I live, is it not very like
The horrible conceit of death and night,
Together with the terror of the place —
As in a vault, an ancient receptacle
40 Where for this many hundred years the bones
Of all my buried ancestors are packed;
Where bloody Tybalt, yet but green in earth,
Lies festering in his shroud; where, as they say,
At some hours in the night spirits resort —
45 Alack, alack, is it not like that I,
So early waking — what with loathsome smells,
And shrieks like mandrakes torn out of the earth,
That living mortals, hearing them, run mad —
O, if I wake, shall I not be distraught,
50 Environèd with all these hideous fears,
And madly play with my forefathers' joints,
And pluck the mangled Tybalt from his shroud,
And, in this rage, with some great kinsman's bone,
As with a club dash out my desperate brains?
55 O, look! Methinks I see my cousin's ghost
Seeking out Romeo, that did spit his body
Upon a rapier's point. Stay, Tybalt, stay!
Romeo, Romeo, Romeo. Here's drink.
[*drinks*] I drink to thee.

She falls upon her bed within the curtains.

Key points

This is the scene in which Juliet, full of fear, takes the sleeping potion that will make it appear as though she has died.

Timeline

Sunday	Monday	Tuesday	Wednesday	Thursday

- Juliet expresses her fears as to what may happen when she takes the sleeping drug: it may poison her, she may wake before Romeo arrives to rescue her, she may die from breathing the foul air in the tomb, or be so desperate that she will seize the bone of some ancestor and dash her brain out. Her imagination is running riot.

- This scene reminds us of how young and vulnerable Juliet is, and that she is facing a desperate situation on her own. She does not want to drink the potion, but she also knows that she cannot marry Paris in the morning. She is still in a state of terror as she takes the drug and falls asleep.

- There is also a real sense of sadness early in the scene when Juliet says good night to her mother and the Nurse. Her line, 'Farewell! God knows when we shall meet again' (line 14), is uttered once they are out of earshot. Although we may hope that something will happen to save Juliet, we know, thanks to the Prologue, that Juliet will die soon and therefore probably will never see them again.

Useful quotes

> *Farewell! God knows when we shall meet again.*
> *I have a faint cold fear thrills through my veins*
> *That almost freezes up the beat of life.*
>
> (Juliet, lines 14–16)

> *How if, when I am laid into the tomb,*
> *I wake before the time that Romeo*
> *Come to redeem me?*
>
> (Juliet, lines 30–2)

> *What if it be a poison which the Friar*
> *Subtly hath ministered to have me dead,*
> *Lest in this marriage he should be dishonoured,*
> *Because he married me before to Romeo?*
>
> (Juliet, lines 24–7)

> *O, if I wake, shall I not be distraught,*
> *Environèd with all these hideous fears,*
> *And madly play with my forefathers' joints*
> *And pluck the mangled Tybalt from his shroud*
>
> (Juliet, lines 49–52)

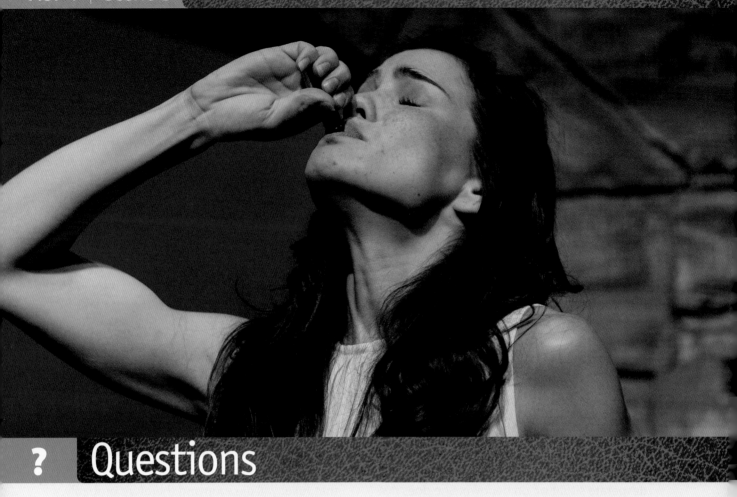

? Questions

1. How does Juliet manage to persuade everyone to leave her alone in her bedroom?

2. Imagine you are the Nurse. Write a short piece setting out your thoughts at this point in the play and your hopes for Juliet's future. Try to capture her tone of voice, her coarse language and her rambling style.

3. Why is Juliet afraid to take the potion? What does she imagine might happen?

4. What does Juliet think will happen if she does not take the potion?

5. How do you feel about Juliet's dilemma? Does she deserve our pity and/or our admiration?

6. What does this scene tell us about Juliet's character?

7. Imagine Juliet could write a short note to Romeo before she takes the potion. What would she write?

8. This scene requires a bed to be on the stage. If you were directing the play, what type of bed would you choose to use? You may like to illustrate your description with a drawing or photo.

Talking point

Juliet places a great deal of trust in Friar Laurence's plan and in his skills with plants and potions. What makes us trust another person? Does trust have to be earned? Do we tend to assume that we can trust people who are 'experts' in something that we do not know much about, such as doctors or lawyers? What would the world be like if you couldn't trust other people?

ACT 4 † Scene 4

Plot summary

This scene is taken up with preparations for Juliet's wedding feast. At three o'clock in the morning, Capulet is overseeing last-minute preparations for the day ahead. As Paris approaches with musicians, Capulet orders the Nurse to waken Juliet.

Come, stir, stir, stir! The second cock hath crowed.
The curfew-bell hath rung. 'Tis three o'clock.

CAPULET, Act 4, Scene 4, 3–5

Verona. The Capulets' house.

Enter LADY CAPULET and NURSE, with herbs.

LADY CAPULET
Hold, take these keys and fetch more spices, Nurse.

NURSE
They call for dates and quinces in the pastry.

Enter CAPULET.

CAPULET
Come, stir, stir, stir! The second cock hath crowed.
The curfew-bell hath rung. 'Tis three o'clock.
5   Look to the baked meats, good Angelica.
Spare not for the cost.

NURSE
                              Go, you cot-quean, go.
Get you to bed! Faith, you'll be sick tomorrow
For this night's watching.

CAPULET
No, not a whit. What, I have watched ere now
10   All night for lesser cause, and ne'er been sick.

LADY CAPULET
Ay, you have been a mouse-hunt in your time.
But I will watch you from such watching now.

Exeunt LADY CAPULET and NURSE.

CAPULET
A jealous hood, a jealous hood!

Enter three or four Servingmen with spits and logs and baskets.
Now, fellow, what is there?

FIRST SERVINGMAN
15   Things for the cook, sir; but I know not what.

CAPULET
Make haste, make haste.

Exit FIRST SERVINGMAN.
                              Sirrah, fetch drier logs.
Call Peter. He will show thee where they are.

---

1   *spices:* spices were very expensive and kept in a locked chest

2   *quinces:* pear-shaped fruits
pastry: kitchen

3   *the second cock:* the cockerel crows for the second time at 3 a.m. or later
4   *The ... rung:* the bell has rung for the end of curfew. Dawn has come
5   *baked meats:* meat pies
Angelica: the Nurse's name

6   *cot-quean:* interfering man

8   *watching:* staying awake

9   *whit:* bit
ere: before

11   *mouse-hunt:* man who pursued women

12   *will ... now:* keep an eye on you now to prevent you from eyeing up other women

13   *hood:* woman

spits: devices for roasting meat over a fire

16   *Sirrah:* a form of address used by a master to a servant

SECOND SERVINGMAN

I have a head, sir, that will find out logs

And never trouble Peter for the matter.

CAPULET

Mass, and well said! A merry whoreson, ha!   20

Thou shalt be loggerhead.

Exit SECOND SERVINGMAN.

                Good faith, 'tis day!

The County will be here with music straight,

For so he said he would.

Music plays.

             I hear him near.

Nurse! Wife! What, ho! What, Nurse, I say!

Enter NURSE.

Go waken Juliet. Go and trim her up.   25

I'll go and chat with Paris. Hie, make haste,

Make haste! The bridegroom he is come already.

Make haste, I say.

Exit CAPULET.

18 *I . . . logs:* my wooden head makes me an expert at finding logs

20 *Mass!* by the Mass (an oath)
    whoreson: bastard (not intended as an insult)
21 *loggerhead:* blockhead (he's still joking about wooden logs)

22 *County:* Paris
    straight: immediately

25 *trim her up:* get her dressed
26 *Hie, make haste:* go, quickly

Key points

This scene is necessary to fill in the time between Juliet taking the sleeping potion and the discovery early next morning of her supposed death.

Timeline

Sunday	Monday	Tuesday	Wednesday	Thursday

- This scene has the function of building up suspense. We know that it is only a matter of time before the Capulets discover Juliet's body. In many stage productions, Juliet's bed remains visible to the audience while the action in this scene takes place.

- In contrast to Juliet's still body, there is a busy and celebratory atmosphere in this scene as the household prepares for the wedding banquet. There is plenty of joking and banter between the Capulets and their staff. Everybody is looking forward to a happy occasion. We know that their hopes are about to be dashed.

- We see a friendly conversation take place between Capulet and the Nurse that contrasts strongly with their previous exchange in Act 3, Scene 5. Now that Juliet has agreed to the marriage, the Nurse and Capulet are in better form and back on the same side.

? Questions

1 Describe the atmosphere in this scene.

2 There is a strong emphasis in this scene on the need to hurry. How is this suggested?

3 Look again at the exchange between Capulet and the Nurse in lines 5–10. What does it tell us about their relationship?

4 What does Lady Capulet reveal about her husband?

5 At the end of this scene, Capulet goes off to greet Paris. Both men are looking forward to the day ahead and, as we have seen, Capulet is in very good form. Write a short script of what the two men say to each other.

6 If you were watching this scene in the theatre and Juliet's bed remained visible on stage, what impact would that have on your response to the other events on stage?

Talking point

There are some good examples of banter and gentle teasing in this scene. What makes for good banter? Do you need to make it clear that you are being playful in case you offend someone? Is your body language important? Are there some situations where banter would be inappropriate?

Plot summary

The Nurse, in jolly form, tries to wake Juliet, but the potion has worked and Juliet looks as if she is dead. The Capulets and the Nurse are convinced that she is. Her parents' harshness towards her in the past gives way to expressions of sorrow and loss. Paris and Friar Laurence arrive to find Juliet's parents grieving. Paris is distraught at his loss. Friar Laurence, knowing the truth, encourages the Capulets and Paris not to grieve, trying to comfort them with the thought that Juliet is in heaven. The Capulets must now attend Juliet's funeral rather than her wedding.

As the mourners leave, Peter, the Nurse's servant, asks the musicians to play a popular song to comfort him. He jokes with the musicians as they wait for the mourners to return from the funeral for dinner.

Alas, alas! Help, help! My lady's dead!
O weraday that ever I was born!
NURSE, Act 4, Scene 5, 14–15

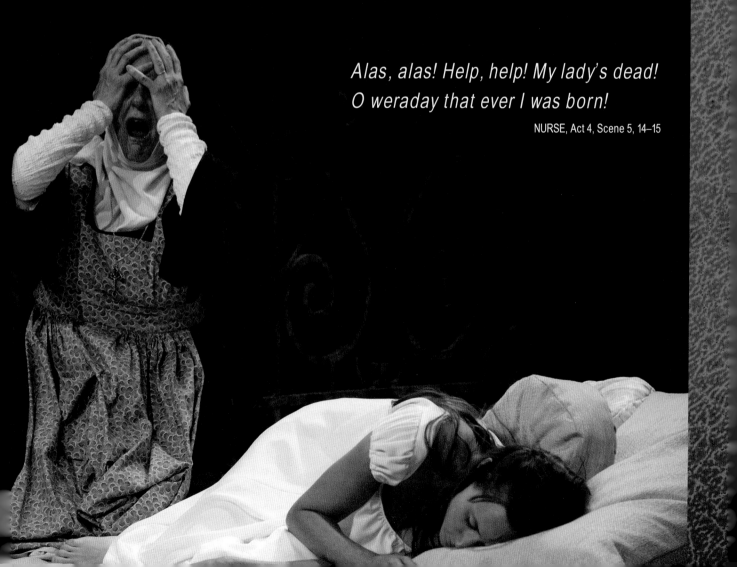

Verona. Juliet's apartment in the Capulets' house.

NURSE goes to curtains.

NURSE
Mistress! What, mistress! Juliet! Fast, I warrant her, she.
Why, lamb! Why, lady! Fie, you slug-a-bed!
Why, love, I say! Madam! Sweetheart! Why, bride!
What, not a word? You take your pennyworths now.
5   Sleep for a week. For the next night, I warrant,
The County Paris hath set up his rest
That you shall rest but little. God forgive me!
Marry, and amen! How sound is she asleep!
I needs must wake her. Madam, madam, madam!
10 Ay, let the County take you in your bed.
He'll fright you up, i' faith. Will it not be?
What, dressed, and in your clothes, and down again?
I must needs wake you. Lady! Lady! Lady!
Alas, alas! Help, help! My lady's dead!
15 O weraday that ever I was born!
Some aqua vitae, ho! My lord! My lady!

Enter LADY CAPULET.

LADY CAPULET
What noise is here?

NURSE
                                        O lamentable day!

LADY CAPULET
What is the matter?

NURSE
                                        Look, look! O heavy day!

LADY CAPULET
O me, O me! My child, my only life!
20 Revive, look up, or I will die with thee!
Help, help! Call help!

Enter CAPULET.

CAPULET
For shame, bring Juliet forth. Her lord is come.

NURSE
She's dead, deceased. She's dead, alack the day!

Glossary (left margin):

curtains: around Juliet's bed

1 *Fast:* fast asleep

2 *slug-a-bed:* lazybones

4 *pennyworths:* brief sleep, nap

6 *set . . . rest:* decided

8 *sound:* soundly

11 *fright you up:* scare you awake

12 *down again:* laid down again

15 *O weraday:* oh no, how unfortunate

16 *aqua vitae:* a strong drink (to revive her)

17 *lamentable:* deplorable, miserable

18 *heavy:* sad, mournful

23 *alack:* an expression of regret or sorrow

LADY CAPULET

Alack the day, she's dead, she's dead, she's dead!

CAPULET

Ha! Let me see her. Out, alas! She's cold,   25

Her blood is settled, and her joints are stiff.

Life and these lips have long been separated.

Death lies on her like an untimely frost

Upon the sweetest flower of all the field.

NURSE

O lamentable day!

LADY CAPULET

            O woeful time!   30

CAPULET

Death, that hath ta'en her hence to make me wail,

Ties up my tongue and will not let me speak.

Enter FRIAR LAURENCE and the COUNTY PARIS.

FRIAR

Come, is the bride ready to go to church?

CAPULET

Ready to go, but never to return.

O son, the night before thy wedding day   35

Hath death lain with thy wife. There she lies,

Flower as she was, deflowerèd by him.

Death is my son-in-law. Death is my heir.

My daughter he hath wedded. I will die

And leave him all. Life, living, all is death's.   40

PARIS

Have I thought long to see this morning's face,

And doth it give me such a sight as this?

LADY CAPULET

Accursed, unhappy, wretched, hateful day!

Most miserable hour that e'er time saw

In lasting labour of his pilgrimage!   45

But one, poor one, one poor and loving child,

But one thing to rejoice and solace in,

And cruel death hath catched it from my sight.

NURSE

O woe! O woeful, woeful, woeful day!

Most lamentable day, most woeful day   50

26 *settled:* still, no longer circulating

28 *untimely:* out of season

31 *ta'en her hence:* taken her away
wail: lament

35 *son:* Paris, whom Capulet hoped would be his son-in-law

37 *deflowerèd by him:* losing her virginity to death

40 *living:* possessions, property

41 *Have ... face:* have I longed for this day to come

43 *Accursed:* cursed, ill-fated

44 *e'er:* ever

45 *In ... pilgrimage:* in the endless work of time's movements

47 *solace:* take comfort

48 *catched:* snatched

51 *behold:* see, observe

53 *black:* dark, diabolical

55 *Beguiled:* cheated, deceived

60 *Uncomfortable:* without comfort

61 *To ... solemnity:* to ruin our celebration

65–6 *Confusion's ... confusions:* your violent behaviour will not cure the effects of this terrible blow

67 *part:* a share

69 *Your part in her:* her body

70 *his part:* her soul
eternal: endless, everlasting
71 *promotion:* marriage
72 *For ... advanced:* because it was your idea of happiness to see her do well

75 *ill:* badly

76 *well:* happy in heaven

77–8 *She's ... young:* it is better to die as a young bride than to live to be an old married woman
79 *rosemary:* a plant symbolising remembrance

81 *array:* clothes
bear: carry
82 *fond:* foolish
lament: grieve, be sad
83 *nature's ... merriment:* if we use reason and common sense we will see how laughable our tears are, since Juliet is happy
84–5 *All ... funeral:* all the items that were to be used for Juliet's wedding are now to be used for her funeral

That ever, ever I did yet behold!
O day, O day, O day! O hateful day!
Never was seen so black a day as this.
O woeful day! O woeful day!

PARIS

55 Beguiled, divorcèd, wrongèd, spited, slain!
Most detestable death, by thee beguiled,
By cruel, cruel thee quite overthrown.
O love! O life! — Not life, but love in death!

CAPULET

Despised, distressèd, hated, martyred, killed!
60 Uncomfortable time, why camest thou now
To murder, murder our solemnity?
O child! O child! My soul, and not my child!
Dead art thou — alack, my child is dead,
And with my child my joys are burièd.

FRIAR

65 Peace, ho, for shame! Confusion's cure lives not
In these confusions. Heaven and yourself
Had part in this fair maid. Now heaven hath all,
And all the better is it for the maid.
Your part in her you could not keep from death,
70 But heaven keeps his part in eternal life.
The most you sought was her promotion,
For 'twas your heaven she should be advanced.
And weep ye now, seeing she is advanced
Above the clouds, as high as heaven itself?
75 O, in this love, you love your child so ill
That you run mad, seeing that she is well.
She's not well married that lives married long,
But she's best married that dies married young.
Dry up your tears and stick your rosemary
80 On this fair corpse, and, as the custom is,
In all her best array bear her to church.
For though fond nature bids us all lament,
Yet nature's tears are reason's merriment.

CAPULET

All things that we ordainèd festival
85 Turn from their office to black funeral.

[handwritten note:] Paris also really loved Juliet

Our instruments to melancholy bells;

Our wedding cheer to a sad burial feast;

Our solemn hymns to sullen dirges change;

Our bridal flowers serve for a buried corpse;

And all things change them to the contrary.   90

FRIAR ·

Sir, go you in; and, madam, go with him;

And go, Sir Paris. Every one prepare

To follow this fair corpse unto her grave.

The heavens do lour upon you for some ill.

Move them no more by crossing their high will.   95

Exeunt all except the NURSE, casting rosemary on her and shutting the curtains.

Enter MUSICIANS.

FIRST MUSICIAN

Faith, we may put up our pipes and be gone.

NURSE

Honest good fellows, ah, put up, put up!

For well you know this is a pitiful case.

FIRST MUSICIAN

Ay, by my troth, the case may be amended.

Exit NURSE.

Enter PETER.

PETER

Musicians, O musicians, 'Heart's ease', 'Heart's ease'!   100

O, an you will have me live, play 'Heart's ease'.

FIRST MUSICIAN

Why 'Heart's ease'?

PETER

O musicians, because my heart itself plays 'My heart is full of woe!' O play me some merry dump to comfort me.

FIRST MUSICIAN

Not a dump we! 'Tis no time to play now.   105

PETER

You will not then?

FIRST MUSICIAN

No.

---

86 *Our ... bells:* our music will be the dismal death-knell
87 *cheer:* food and drink
88 *sullen dirges:* gloomy funeral songs
89 *serve:* will do
90 *all ... contrary:* everything is now to be used for the other purpose

94 *lour ... ill:* frown in anger because of some sin you have committed
95 *Move ... will:* do not upset them further by opposing their heavenly decision

96 *put up:* pack up

99 *the case ... amended:* the fiddler is making a pun on the Nurse's 'pitiful case' in line 98. She was referring to Juliet. He is referring to his broken instrument case, which can be fixed ('amended')
    Exit Nurse: this is the last we see of the Nurse

100 *'Heart's ease':* a popular song
101 *an:* if

103–4 *'My ... woe':* another popular song
104 *dump:* sad piece of music, mournful tune

108 *soundly:* logically

110 *gleek:* jeer, mockery
give you: nickname you
111 *minstrel:* mocking word for musician

112 *serving-creature:* mocking term for a servant

114 *pate:* head
carry no crotchets: not put up with your moods
re ... fa: musical notes

117 *put ... wit:* put away your dagger and show your intelligence

118 *dry-beat:* defeat you without drawing blood

120 *griping:* painful

121 *doleful dumps:* sad songs

124 *Catling:* a lute-string

126 *Rebeck:* fiddle

127 *sound for silver:* play music for money

128 *Soundpost:* part of a bass viol

PETER
I will then give it you soundly.

FIRST MUSICIAN
What will you give us?

PETER
110   No money, on my faith, but the gleek. I will give you the minstrel.

FIRST MUSICIAN
Then I will give you the serving-creature.

PETER
Then will I lay the serving-creature's dagger on your pate. I will carry no crotchets. I'll re you, I'll fa you. Do
115   you note me?

FIRST MUSICIAN
An you re us and fa us, you note us.

SECOND MUSICIAN
Pray you put up your dagger, and put out your wit.

PETER
Then have at you with my wit! I will dry-beat you with an iron wit, and put up my iron dagger. Answer me like men.
120   'When griping griefs the heart doth wound,
      And doleful dumps the mind oppress,
      Then music with her silver sound' —
Why 'silver sound'? Why 'music with her silver sound'?
What say you, Simon Catling?

FIRST MUSICIAN
125   Marry, sir, because silver hath a sweet sound.

PETER
Pretty! What say you, Hugh Rebeck?

SECOND MUSICIAN
I say 'silver sound' because musicians sound for silver.

PETER
Pretty too! What say you, James Soundpost?

THIRD MUSICIAN
Faith, I know not what to say.

PETER

O, I cry you mercy! You are the singer. I will say for you.   130
It is 'music with her silver sound' because musicians have
no gold for sounding.

> 'Then music with her silver sound
> With speedy help doth lend redress.'

Exit PETER.

FIRST MUSICIAN

What a pestilent knave is this same!   135

SECOND MUSICIAN

Hang him, Jack! Come, we'll in here, tarry for the
mourners, and stay dinner.

Exeunt.

130	*cry you mercy:* beg your pardon
132	*for sounding:* as a reward for their music, and for jingling in their pockets
134	*redress:* comfort, help
135	*pestilent knave:* very annoying fellow
136	*Jack:* name for a person of bad reputation and behaviour
	tarry: delay
137	*stay:* wait for

Key points

If the last scene lacked drama, this one certainly makes up for it. The Capulets and Paris, thinking Juliet is dead, witness the unintended results of their attempts to force Juliet into a marriage she did not want.

Timeline

Sunday	Monday	Tuesday	Wednesday	Thursday

- The supposed death of Juliet brings out the true feelings of her parents for her. Lady Capulet is ready to die with Juliet if she does not revive; she mourns the loss of her 'loving child', the only comfort of her life (lines 46–7). Capulet, who not long ago had called Juliet offensive names and declared himself and his wife cursed in having her, now calls her 'the sweetest flower of all the field' (line 29). He laments that death has married his only heir, and that when he dies he will leave everything he has to death. He loves Juliet so much that he says, 'with my child my joys are burièd' (line 64).

- Paris also blames 'detestable death' for having cheated and deceived him (line 56). He has looked forward to his marriage to Juliet, but it has been snatched away from him at the last moment.

- Friar Laurence, the only person present who knows that Juliet is alive, rebukes her parents for not thinking that their daughter is now happy in heaven, and suggests that it is better to die as a young bride than to live as an old married woman (lines 77–8). This response to their pain and grief seems rather harsh in the circumstances: parents are entitled to be upset over the loss of a child; and, as we and the Friar know, Juliet is not in heaven.

- The stage direction 'Exit Nurse' marks the final appearance of the Nurse in the play.

- This scene ends with some comic exchanges between the musicians who were hired for the wedding celebrations. This short episode suggests that life must go on, despite a tragic death.

Useful quotes

> Death lies on her like an untimely frost
> Upon the sweetest flower of all the field.
>
> (Capulet, lines 28–9)

> Heaven and yourself
> Had part in this fair maid. Now heaven hath all,
> And all the better is it for the maid.
>
> (Friar Laurence, lines 66–8)

> Beguiled, divorcèd, wrongèd, spited, slain!
> Most detestable death, by thee beguiled
>
> (Paris, lines 55–6)

> She's not well married that lives married long,
> But she's best married that dies married young.
>
> (Friar Laurence, lines 77–8)

? Questions

1 What do we learn about the Nurse from her reaction to Juliet's body?

2 How do Capulet and Lady Capulet respond to their loss?

3 Some commentators find the responses of the Nurse and the Capulets to Juliet's 'death' ridiculous and childish. Would you agree? Give reasons for your answer.

4 Do you feel sorry for the Nurse and the Capulets? Explain your answer.

5 How does Paris react to Juliet's supposed death? Is this an appropriate response? Do you have sympathy for him? Explain your answers.

6 Write out your own version of the speech of consolation (lines 65–83) delivered by Friar Laurence.

7 Do you think the Capulets and Paris would have found the Friar's speech helpful? Explain your answer.

8 How do Peter and the musicians respond to the death of Juliet?

9 Of all the responses in this scene, whose do you find the more convincing? Give reasons for your answer.

10 Imagine you are Lady Capulet. Write a letter to your parents telling them about the death of their granddaughter, Juliet.

Talking point

Death is never easy to deal with but it is particularly shocking when it involves a young and healthy person. What traditions do we have as a society to help and support bereaved families? Is it important to talk about the person who has passed away? What other services are available to help people handle their loss and grief?

ACT 4 ⚔ Key moments

Scene 1
- Juliet meets Paris at Friar Laurence's cell, and does not encourage his affections.
- Friar Laurence devises a plan to relieve Juliet's desperate situation. He recommends that she take a sleeping drug that will make her appear dead. He promises to write to Romeo and arrange for him to collect Juliet when she wakes in the Capulets' tomb.

Scene 2
- Juliet apologises to her father and pretends to consent to marry Paris. Capulet is delighted and brings forward the wedding date by one day.

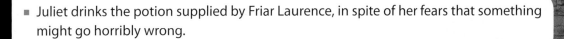

Scene 3
- Juliet drinks the potion supplied by Friar Laurence, in spite of her fears that something might go horribly wrong.

Scene 4
- The Capulet household is preparing for the wedding. Capulet orders that Juliet should be woken up.

Scene 5
- The Nurse finds Juliet apparently dead. Friar Laurence attempts to console the mourners as they prepare for Juliet's funeral.

ACT 4 ⚔ Speaking and listening

1 Select a student to play the part of Paris. He is questioned by members of the class on how he feels about his suitability as Capulet's choice of husband for Juliet, now that this prospect is at an end. Questions he might be asked include: whether he still loves Juliet, whether he blames anybody for what has happened, or whether he can think of any explanation for what has happened to him.

2 In pairs, imagine you are choosing actors to play the roles of Romeo and Juliet. Discuss the features you would want (age, build, etc.). Then look through the various photos in this book and decide which casting decisions, in your opinion, work best for Romeo and Juliet. Choose your favourite photo for each of these two characters and say what you like about it. Come together as a class and compare your selections.

Q Revision quiz: plot summary

Use the words and phrases listed in the panel to fill in the blanks in this summary of Act 4:

Capulet
confession
deathlike
die
fears
forgiveness
Friar Laurence
funeral
heaven
Juliet
kill
life
marriage
marry
musicians
Nurse
Paris
plan
potion
Romeo
sleeping
time
tomb
wedding
Wednesday

Paris and Friar Laurence are discussing the ▭ plans when Juliet arrives to seek the Friar's help. Paris tries to woo her, but Juliet remains distant. She asks the Friar to hear her ▭ and this means that ▭ must leave. Juliet would rather ▭ than marry Paris, but the Friar comes up with a plan to avoid the wedding and reunite her with ▭.

Following Friar Laurence's advice, Juliet returns home and begs her father's ▭ for her earlier disobedience. She tells him that she will ▭ Paris. ▭ is delighted with this news and decides he can't wait any longer than necessary: he changes the day of the wedding to ▭. This unexpected change will threaten the Friar's ▭ as it will give him less ▭ to get a message to Romeo.

▭ convinces the Nurse and Lady Capulet to leave her alone to pray and get some rest ahead of her wedding day. She is in a terrible situation. If she does not take the ▭ drug, she must marry Paris. If she does take it, she worries that it will ▭ her or perhaps she will wake up inside the Capulets' ▭ and suffocate in the stale air or be attacked by evil spirits. Despite her ▭, she takes the ▭ and falls into a ▭ sleep.

The wedding preparations are in full swing. When Capulet hears Paris and the ▭ approaching, he sends the Nurse to wake Juliet. The ▭ discovers Juliet's cold and stiff body and calls the others. Juliet's parents are grief-stricken. They cannot believe that they have lost their only child. Paris feels that he has been cheated out of his future happiness. ▭ ▭ tries to console them with the idea that Juliet is in ▭. Their thoughts turn from planning a ▭ to planning a ▭. When they leave, the musicians and servants illustrate that ordinary ▭ must go on.

ACT 5 ✝ Scene 1

Romeo has had a happy dream and is feeling optimistic. Then his servant Balthasar brings him news that Juliet is dead, and that her body lies in the Capulets' tomb. Romeo has been expecting a letter from Friar Laurence, but Balthasar tells him he has brought no such letter. Romeo is determined to be with Juliet that night. He calls on an Apothecary (expert in medicines) who is poor and starving. Romeo knows that this Apothecary is in need of money and persuades him to break the law by selling Romeo a deadly poison. Romeo sets out for the Capulets' tomb in Verona.

> *Green earthen pots, bladders, and musty seeds,*
> *Remnants of packthread and old cakes of roses*
> *Were thinly scattered, to make up a show.*
>
> ROMEO, Act 5, Scene 1, 46–8

Mantua. A street.

Enter ROMEO.

ROMEO
If I may trust the flattering truth of sleep,
My dreams presage some joyful news at hand.
My bosom's lord sits lightly in his throne,
And all this day an unaccustomed spirit
5 Lifts me above the ground with cheerful thoughts.
I dreamt my lady came and found me dead —
Strange dream that gives a dead man leave to think! —
And breathed such life with kisses in my lips
That I revived and was an emperor.
10 Ah me! How sweet is love itself possessed,
When but love's shadows are so rich in joy!

Enter BALTHASAR, Romeo's man, booted.
News from Verona! How now, Balthasar?
Dost thou not bring me letters from the Friar?
How doth my lady? Is my father well?
15 How fares my lady Juliet? That I ask again,
For nothing can be ill if she be well.

BALTHASAR
Then she is well, and nothing can be ill.
Her body sleeps in Capel's monument,
And her immortal part with angels lives.
20 I saw her laid low in her kindred's vault
And presently took post to tell it you.
O, pardon me for bringing these ill news,
Since you did leave it for my office, sir.

ROMEO
Is it e'en so? Then I defy you, stars!
25 Thou knowest my lodging. Get me ink and paper,
And hire posthorses. I will hence tonight.

BALTHASAR
I do beseech you, sir, have patience.
Your looks are pale and wild and do import
Some misadventure.

[handwritten margin note: Dramatic irony / Foreshadowing]

[handwritten margin note: very quick decision]

---

1 *If . . . sleep:* Romeo has had a good dream. He believes that this means good luck for him
2 *presage:* forecast
3 *My bosom's lord:* Cupid, the god of love, is in my heart
4 *unaccustomed spirit:* lightness that I'm not used to

10–11 *How . . . joy!* when dreams of love are so joyful, love itself is much more so

booted: wearing boots (meaning he has ridden there on a horse)

16 *ill:* bad

18 *Capel's monument:* the tomb of the Capulets
19 *immortal part:* soul
20 *her kindred's vault:* the tomb of her relatives
21 *And . . . post:* and set off immediately to ride here

23 *did . . . office:* made it my duty

24 *Is . . . so?* Is it true?
I defy you, stars! Romeo is standing up in defiance of his bad luck
25 *my lodging:* where I live
26 *posthorses:* horses kept at inns for the speedy delivery of messages
hence: leave here
27 *beseech:* ask, beg
28–9 *do . . . misadventure:* mean that some awful event is about to happen

Mantua: another city in northern Italy; about 35 km from Verona

ROMEO

Tush, thou art deceived. *No more*

Leave me and do the thing I bid thee do. *romantic* 30

Hast thou no letters to me from the Friar? *language*

BALTHASAR

No, my good lord.

ROMEO

No matter. Get thee gone

And hire those horses. I'll be with thee straight.

Exit BALTHASAR.

Well, Juliet, I will lie with thee tonight.

Let's see for means. O mischief, thou art swift 35

To enter in the thoughts of desperate men.

I do remember an apothecary,

And hereabouts 'a dwells, which late I noted

In tattered weeds, with overwhelming brows,

Culling of simples. Meagre were his looks. 40

Sharp misery had worn him to the bones.

And in his needy shop a tortoise hung,

An alligator stuffed, and other skins

Of ill-shaped fishes; and about his shelves

A beggarly account of empty boxes, 45

Green earthen pots, bladders, and musty seeds,

Remnants of packthread and old cakes of roses

Were thinly scattered, to make up a show.

Noting this penury, to myself I said,

'An if a man did need a poison now 50

Whose sale is present death in Mantua,

Here lives a caitiff wretch would sell it him.'

O, this same thought did but forerun my need,

And this same needy man must sell it me.

As I remember, this should be the house. 55

Being holiday, the beggar's shop is shut.

What, ho! Apothecary!

Enter APOTHECARY.

APOTHECARY

Who calls so loud?

33	*straight:* immediately
35	*for means:* how this can be done
	swift: quick, speedy
37–8	*apothecary ... dwells:* expert in medicine who lives around here
38	*which ... noted:* whom I noticed lately
39	*weeds:* clothes
	overwhelming brows: bushy and overhanging eyebrows
40	*Culling of simples:* picking out herbs from which to make medicines
	Meagre: thin, gaunt
42	*needy:* almost empty
45	*beggarly account:* miserable collection
46	*Green earthen:* unfired clay (i.e. fragile and cheap)
	bladders: animal bladders used for storing liquid
47	*Remnants ... roses:* bits of cord and pressed rose petals for perfume
48	*show:* display
49	*penury:* extreme poverty
50–2	*'An ... him':* if a man needed poison, the sale of which is punishable by immediate death in Mantua, here is a desperate creature who would sell it to him
53	*forerun my need:* predict what I would need

ROMEO

Come hither, man. I see that thou art poor.

Hold, there is forty ducats. Let me have

60 A dram of poison, such soon-speeding gear

As will disperse itself through all the veins,

That the life-weary taker may fall dead

And that the trunk may be discharged of breath

As violently as hasty powder fired

65 Doth hurry from the fatal cannon's womb.

APOTHECARY

Such mortal drugs I have. But Mantua's law

Is death to any he that utters them.

ROMEO

Art thou so bare and full of wretchedness

And fearest to die? Famine is in thy cheeks.

70 Need and oppression starveth in thine eyes.

Contempt and beggary hangs upon thy back.

The world is not thy friend, nor the world's law,

The world affords no law to make thee rich.

Then be not poor, but break it and take this.

APOTHECARY

75 My poverty but not my will consents.

ROMEO

I pay thy poverty and not thy will.

APOTHECARY

Put this in any liquid thing you will

And drink it off, and if you had the strength

Of twenty men, it would dispatch you straight.

ROMEO

80 There is thy gold — worse poison to men's souls,

Doing more murder in this loathsome world,

Than these poor compounds that thou mayst not sell.

I sell thee poison. Thou hast sold me none.

Farewell. Buy food and get thyself in flesh.

85 Come, cordial and not poison, go with me

To Juliet's grave. For there must I use thee.

Exeunt.

---

58 *hither:* here

59 *there . . . ducats:* here are forty gold coins (a large sum)

60 *dram:* small measure
soon-speeding gear: fast-acting stuff

61 *disperse:* spread

63 *trunk . . . breath:* the body may be deprived of oxygen

66 *mortal:* fatal, deadly

67 *utters:* dispenses, gives out

68–9 *Art . . . die?* Do you fear death, even though your life is so miserable?

70 *starveth:* produce the signs of starvation

71 *Contempt . . . back:* you're weighed down by the way people treat you

72–4 *The world . . . this:* as the world hasn't treated you kindly and the law doesn't look after you or make you rich, you should break the law and take my money

75 *My . . . consents:* I don't want to do it, but I am so poor that I have to

78 *if:* even if

79 *dispatch you straight:* end your life immediately

80–2 *There . . . sell:* here is your payment – although money does more harm and causes more deaths in this horrible world than poison does

82 *compounds:* mixtures

84 *in flesh:* nourished, fattened up

85 *cordial:* medicine

Key points

This scene shows fate working to frustrate Friar Laurence's plan. Romeo receives incorrect information and is going to return to Verona to die.

Timeline

Sunday	Monday	Tuesday	Wednesday	Thursday

- This scene opens with a disturbing irony as Romeo has had a good dream and is feeling positive about the future. He is happy and looking forward to receiving news from Verona. This optimistic mood is immediately destroyed when Balthasar, Romeo's loyal servant, arrives with news of Juliet's death (which he does not know is false).

- Balthasar provides the necessary link between Capulet's decision to bring forward the day of the wedding, and Romeo's suicide. Balthasar's success in reaching Romeo with the false news that Juliet is dead results in Romeo's immediate decision to return to Verona and poison himself alongside Juliet's body.

- Romeo purchases the poison from a poverty-stricken Apothecary. It is only because he is desperate for money that he is prepared to risk selling such a deadly poison. Potions and poisons were commonly used in Shakespeare's day and feature in several of his plays.

- In Act 2, Scene 3, Friar Laurence spoke of the power of plants to cure and to kill. He used plants to make Juliet's sleeping potion, hoping that it would help her out of a desperate situation. The Apothecary's poison has no purpose other than death. However, in his final comments, Romeo calls it a 'cordial' (a tonic or healing drink): 'Come, cordial and not poison, go with me to Juliet's grave. For there must I use thee' (lines 85–6). Unfortunately, Romeo now sees death as the only way to cure his unhappiness and be reunited with Juliet; whereas the opposite is true: if he chooses life, he'll find out about the Friar's plan and really be reunited with Juliet.

Useful quotes

If I may trust the flattering truth of sleep,
My dreams presage some joyful news at hand.
(Romeo, lines 1–2)

Put this in any liquid thing you will
And drink it off, and if you had the strength
Of twenty men, it would dispatch you straight.
(Apothecary, lines 77–9)

Her body sleeps in Capel's monument,
And her immortal part with angels lives.
(Balthasar, lines 18–19)

Come, cordial and not poison, go with me
To Juliet's grave. For there must I use thee.
(Romeo, lines 85–6)

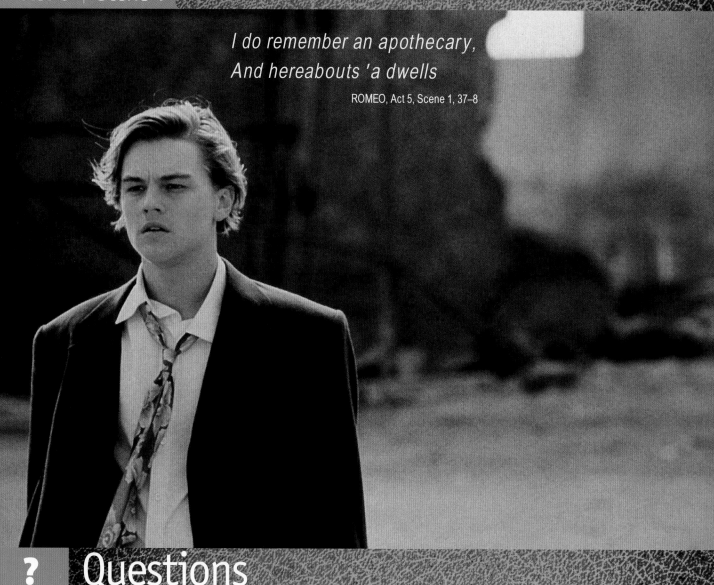

I do remember an apothecary,
And hereabouts 'a dwells

ROMEO, Act 5, Scene 1, 37–8

? Questions

1 Describe Romeo's mood at the start of this scene.

2 What effect does Balthasar's news have on Romeo?

3 In what way does Romeo see himself as a victim of fate?

4 How does Romeo plan to respond to Juliet's death?

5 How does Romeo persuade the Apothecary to sell him the poison?

6 Describe Romeo's mood at the end of this scene.

7 Compare the Romeo we see in this scene with the miserable, lovesick Romeo of Act 1 (just a few days earlier).

8 Imagine you are the Apothecary. Write a note about the man who gave you forty ducats (a handsome sum) for some deadly poison, and how you felt about making this sale.

Talking point

Romeo is able to get the deadly but illegal poison because he has money, which the Apothecary needs. Can money solve most problems? Does money make people do the wrong thing? Does money make life easier? Is it bad to have too much money?

Friar John tells Friar Laurence that he was unable to deliver the letter to Romeo about Juliet's real condition. Instead, he was delayed in Verona because an outbreak of plague prevented him from leaving an infected house. Realising that his plan has gone wrong, and that Romeo will not be in the tomb when Juliet awakes, Friar Laurence intends to go to the Capulets' tomb himself and bring Juliet back to his cell until Romeo arrives. He sends Friar John to get a crowbar, so that he can open the tomb.

> *Friar John, go hence.*
> *Get me an iron crow, and bring it straight*
> *Unto my cell.*
>
> FRIAR LAURENCE, Act 5, Scene 2, 20–2

Verona. Friar Laurence's cell.

Enter FRIAR JOHN.

FRIAR JOHN
Holy Franciscan friar, brother, ho!

Enter FRIAR LAURENCE.

FRIAR LAURENCE
This same should be the voice of Friar John.

Welcome from Mantua. What says Romeo?

Or, if his mind be writ, give me his letter.

FRIAR JOHN

5   Going to find a bare-foot brother out,

One of our order, to associate me

Here in this city visiting the sick,

And finding him, the searchers of the town,

Suspecting that we both were in a house

10   Where the infectious pestilence did reign,

Sealed up the doors, and would not let us forth,

So that my speed to Mantua there was stayed.

FRIAR LAURENCE
Who bare my letter, then, to Romeo?

FRIAR JOHN
I could not send it — here it is again —

15   Nor get a messenger to bring it thee,

So fearful were they of infection.

FRIAR LAURENCE
Unhappy fortune! By my brotherhood,

The letter was not nice, but full of charge

Of dear import; and the neglecting it

20   May do much danger. Friar John, go hence.

Get me an iron crow, and bring it straight

Unto my cell.

FRIAR JOHN
           Brother, I'll go and bring it thee.

Exit FRIAR JOHN.

---

4   *if . . . writ:* if he has written down his thoughts in a letter

5   *Going . . . out:* going to seek out another Franciscan friar
6   *associate me:* go with me

8   *searchers:* health officers, whose job was to report on dead bodies

10   *pestilence:* plague (a deadly and highly infectious disease)
     did reign: had taken over
11   *forth:* go out
12   *speed:* quick journey
     stayed: prevented

13   *bare:* carried, delivered

18   *nice:* unimportant, trivial
     charge: serious business
19   *dear import:* urgent importance

21   *crow:* crowbar
     straight: immediately

FRIAR LAURENCE

Now must I to the monument alone.

Within three hours will fair Juliet wake.

She will beshrew me much that Romeo   25

Hath had no notice of these accidents.

But I will write again to Mantua,

And keep her at my cell till Romeo come.

Poor living corpse, closed in a dead man's tomb!

Exit.

23 *must I:* I must go
    monument: Capulets' tomb

25 *beshrew:* rebuke, criticise

26 *notice:* warning
    accidents: events

Key points

This scene provides further confirmation of the cruelty of fate. This time fate has intervened to prevent Friar Laurence's letter from leaving Verona, which means that Romeo is unaware of the truth about Juliet.

Timeline

Sunday	Monday	Tuesday	Wednesday	Thursday

- Friar Laurence does not know that Balthasar has given Romeo news that Juliet is dead. However, he does know that he must reach Juliet in the tomb before she awakes. He plans to take her to his cell and keep her hidden there until Romeo comes.

- Although Shakespeare gives a very clear indication of the time frame within which the events of the play take place, there is a problem concerning Juliet and the sleeping potion. Friar Laurence told her that his potion would keep her in a deathlike state for 'two-and-forty hours' (Act 4, Scene 1, line 105). As Juliet took the potion on Tuesday evening, this means that she is not due to wake up until Thursday afternoon. However, she does wake up much earlier than that. This difference could indicate the unreliability of potions or perhaps Shakespeare wasn't great at maths – we'll never know.

- Friar Laurence's final speech (lines 23–9) is another example of a soliloquy. There are no other characters on stage, so his words are for the audience only. In this speech he is telling the audience what he is thinking and what he is planning to do.

Useful quotes

> Unhappy fortune! By my brotherhood,
> The letter was not nice, but full of charge
> Of dear import; and the neglecting it
> May do much danger.
>
> (Friar Laurence, lines 17–20)

> Now must I to the monument alone.
> Within three hours will fair Juliet wake.
>
> (Friar Laurence, lines 23–4)

> Poor living corpse, closed in a dead man's tomb!
>
> (Friar Laurence, line 29)

? Questions

1 Who was to deliver Friar Laurence's letter to Romeo?

2 Why did the letter not leave Verona?

3 What does this mean for Romeo and Juliet?

4 Up to now, Friar Laurence has had a logical solution to each problem. Has he one now?

5 What important piece of information do we, the audience, know that Friar Laurence does not know?

6 This scene shows that accident and chance can have major consequences. Develop this idea. Mention other examples in the play.

7 Friar Laurence intends to write another letter to Romeo in Mantua (line 27). Write the letter for him.

8 Imagine you are directing a stage or film version of the play and consider how you would cast the part of Friar Laurence. What sort of actor would you look for (think about age, height, build, voice, etc.)? You may like to include photos or drawings as part of your answer.

Talking point

There is only one scene left in the play and we know (thanks to the Prologue) that it will feature the deaths of Romeo and Juliet. Does this knowledge make the play less interesting for you? Or are you still interested to find out exactly how it all happens? Can you think of any other plays or of novels or films that reveal the ending first?

ACT 5 † Scene 3

Paris arrives at the churchyard in the dark of night to adorn Juliet's grave with flowers and perfumes. He sees Romeo opening the Capulets' tomb and thinks he has come back to abuse and dishonour the bodies inside. Paris challenges Romeo, who tries to persuade him to walk away. Paris refuses and Romeo kills him, laying his body in the tomb near Juliet. Romeo cannot believe how beautiful and alive Juliet appears. He poisons himself. Friar Laurence arrives too late to save the lives of Paris and Romeo. Juliet wakes up. The Friar tries to persuade her to leave with him, saying he will take her to a convent of nuns. Juliet refuses to leave. Friar Laurence panics and runs away. Juliet kills herself with Romeo's dagger. Paris's page leads the night watchmen to the tomb. On discovering the bodies, they send messengers to the Prince, Capulet and Montague and search the graveyard. Friar Laurence is arrested, along with Romeo's servant, Balthasar.

When Prince Escalus and the others have arrived, Friar Laurence makes a long speech telling them what has happened. Balthasar explains about his visit to Mantua and returning with Romeo. Romeo has left a letter for his father, which backs up the other stories. The heads of the feuding families, Montague and Capulet, now make peace and promise to honour their dead children.

Death, that hath sucked the honey of thy breath,
Hath had no power yet upon thy beauty.

ROMEO, Act 5, Scene 3, 92–3

Verona. A churchyard.

Enter PARIS and his PAGE, with flowers and sweet water.

PARIS

Give me thy torch, boy. Hence, and stand aloof.

Yet put it out, for I would not be seen.

Under yond yew trees lay thee all along,

Holding thy ear close to the hollow ground.

5 So shall no foot upon the churchyard tread,

Being loose, unfirm, with digging up of graves,

But thou shalt hear it. Whistle then to me,

As signal that thou hearest something approach.

Give me those flowers. Do as I bid thee, go.

PAGE [*aside*]

10 I am almost afraid to stand alone

Here in the churchyard. Yet I will adventure.

PAGE retires.

PARIS

Sweet flower, with flowers thy bridal bed I strew —

O woe! Thy canopy is dust and stones —

Which with sweet water nightly I will dew;

15 Or, wanting that, with tears distilled by moans.

The obsequies that I for thee will keep

Nightly shall be to strew thy grave and weep.

PAGE whistles.

The boy gives warning something doth approach.

What cursèd foot wanders this way tonight

20 To cross my obsequies and true love's rite?

What, with a torch! Muffle me, night, awhile.

PARIS retires.

Enter ROMEO and BALTHASAR, with a torch, a mattock and a crow of iron.

ROMEO

Give me that mattock and the wrenching iron.

Hold, take this letter. Early in the morning

See thou deliver it to my lord and father.

25 Give me the light. Upon thy life I charge thee,

Whate'er thou hearest or seest, stand all aloof

Page: a young attendant
sweet: perfumed

1 *Hence ... aloof:* go and stand a distance from here

2 *it:* the flame of the torch

3 *lay ... along:* lie flat, straight out

4–7 *Holding ... it:* if you hold your ear close to the ground, you'll hear the footsteps of anyone coming here, since the soil is loose and the ground is hollow

10 *stand:* remain

11 *adventure:* take my chances

retires: moves to the side or back of the stage

12 *strew:* scatter

13 *canopy:* curtains above bed

14 *dew:* wet, wash

15 *wanting:* lacking
distilled: squeezed out

16 *obsequies:* funeral ceremonies, rituals of remembrance
keep: observe, continue to perform

20 *cross:* interfere with, spoil
rite: rituals, traditions

21 *What ... awhile:* Paris, seeing that the others have a torch, wants the darkness of night to hide him from view

mattock: a kind of pick-axe
crow of iron: iron crowbar

22 *wrenching iron:* crowbar

25 *charge:* instruct, command

26 *Whate'er ... aloof:* no matter what you hear or see, remain at a distance

And do not interrupt me in my course.

Why I descend into this bed of death

Is partly to behold my lady's face,

But chiefly to take thence from her dead finger 30

A precious ring, a ring that I must use

In dear employment. Therefore hence, be gone.

But if thou, jealous, dost return to pry

In what I farther shall intend to do,

By heaven, I will tear thee joint by joint 35

And strew this hungry churchyard with thy limbs.

The time and my intents are savage-wild,

More fierce and more inexorable far

Than empty tigers or the roaring sea.

BALTHASAR

I will be gone, sir, and not trouble ye. 40

ROMEO

So shalt thou show me friendship. Take thou that.

Live, and be prosperous; and farewell, good fellow.

BALTHASAR [*aside*]

For all this same, I'll hide me hereabout.

His looks I fear, and his intents I doubt.

BALTHASAR retires.

ROMEO

Thou detestable maw, thou womb of death, 45

Gorged with the dearest morsel of the earth,

Thus I enforce thy rotten jaws to open,

And in despite I'll cram thee with more food.

ROMEO begins to open the tomb.

PARIS [*aside*]

This is that banished haughty Montague

That murdered my love's cousin — with which grief 50

It is supposèd the fair creature died —

And here is come to do some villainous shame

To the dead bodies. I will apprehend him.

[*to ROMEO*] Stop thy unhallowed toil, vile Montague!

Can vengeance be pursued further than death? 55

Condemnèd villain, I do apprehend thee.

Obey, and go with me. For thou must die.

---

27 *course:* plan of action

28–32 *Why . . . employment:* I'm going into the tomb to see Juliet again and to get back her wedding ring, which is important to me. Romeo is deceiving Balthasar about his real purpose, which is to kill himself

33 *jealous:* suspicious, curious

34 *what I farther:* whatever else I

36 *hungry churchyard:* the graveyard is waiting to be filled with dead bodies

37 *intents:* intentions

38 *inexorable:* unalterable, cannot be stopped

41 *that:* presumably Romeo is handing him money/his purse

44 *doubt:* am suspicious about (what Romeo intends to do)

45–8 *Thou . . . food:* Romeo sees death as a creature with a huge appetite – it has swallowed Juliet and now Romeo will force it to swallow him

48 *despite:* hatred

49 *haughty:* scornful, arrogant

50 *my love's cousin:* Tybalt

51 *fair creature:* Juliet

52 *shame:* disgraceful act (e.g. steal body parts for the purposes of witchcraft)

53 *apprehend:* arrest

54 *unhallowed toil:* unholy work

55 *Can . . . death?* Are you about to take revenge on the dead bodies of Tybalt and Juliet?

ROMEO

I must indeed; and therefore came I hither.

Good gentle youth, tempt not a desperate man.

60 Fly hence and leave me. Think upon these gone.

Let them affright thee. I beseech thee, youth,

Put not another sin upon my head

By urging me to fury. O, be gone!

By heaven, I love thee better than myself,

65 For I come hither armed against myself,

Stay not, be gone. Live, and hereafter say

A madman's mercy bid thee run away.

PARIS

I do defy thy conjuration

And apprehend thee for a felon here.

ROMEO

70 Wilt thou provoke me? Then have at thee, boy!

They fight.

PAGE

O Lord, they fight! I will go call the Watch.

Exit PAGE.

PARIS falls.

PARIS

O, I am slain! If thou be merciful,

Open the tomb, lay me with Juliet.

PARIS dies.

ROMEO

In faith, I will. Let me peruse this face.

75 Mercutio's kinsman, noble County Paris!

What said my man when my betossèd soul

Did not attend him as we rode? I think

He told me Paris should have married Juliet.

Said he not so? Or did I dream it so?

80 Or am I mad, hearing him talk of Juliet,

To think it was so? O, give me thy hand,

One writ with me in sour misfortune's book.

I'll bury thee in a triumphant grave.

A grave? O, no, a lantern, slaughtered youth,

59 *gentle youth:* Romeo does not yet recognise Paris

60 *Fly hence:* get away from here quickly
gone: dead

61 *affright thee:* make you afraid
beseech: beg

62–3 *Put ... fury:* don't make me so angry that I commit another sin by killing you

68 *conjuration:* a request and a warning

69 *felon:* criminal

71 *Watch:* officers of the law

74 *peruse:* examine

76 *betossèd:* troubled
77 *attend:* pay attention to
rode: travelled from Mantua to Verona

82 *One ... book:* both our names are written in the book of bitter bad luck
83 *triumphant:* splendid
84 *lantern:* structure on the top of the tomb to let in light

He opens the tomb.

For here lies Juliet, and her beauty makes   85

This vault a feasting presence full of light.

Death, lie thou there, by a dead man interred.

He lays him in the tomb.

How oft when men are at the point of death

Have they been merry, which their keepers call

A lightning before death! O how may I   90

Call this a lightning? O my love, my wife!

Death, that hath sucked the honey of thy breath,

Hath had no power yet upon thy beauty.

Thou art not conquered. Beauty's ensign yet

Is crimson in thy lips and in thy cheeks,   95

And death's pale flag is not advancèd there.

Tybalt, liest thou there in thy bloody sheet?

O, what more favour can I do to thee

Than with that hand that cut thy youth in twain

To sunder his that was thine enemy?   100

Forgive me, cousin! Ah, dear Juliet,

Why art thou yet so fair? Shall I believe

That unsubstantial death is amorous,

And that the lean abhorrèd monster keeps

Thee here in dark to be his paramour?   105

For fear of that I still will stay with thee

And never from this palace of dim night

Depart again. Here, here will I remain

With worms that are thy chambermaids. O here

Will I set up my everlasting rest   110

And shake the yoke of inauspicious stars

From this world-wearied flesh. Eyes, look your last!

Arms, take your last embrace! And, lips, O you

The doors of breath, seal with a righteous kiss

A dateless bargain to engrossing death!   115

Come, bitter conduct, come, unsavoury guide!

Thou desperate pilot, now at once run on

The dashing rocks thy seasick weary bark!

Here's to my love! [*drinks*] O true Apothecary,

Thy drugs are quick! Thus with a kiss I die.   120

He falls.

---

86 *a feasting presence:* like a hall fit for a feast

87 *interred:* buried

89 *keepers:* jailers

94 *ensign:* banner

99 *in twain:* in two

100 *To … enemy:* to take my own life

101 *cousin:* Tybalt

103 *unsubstantial:* bodiless, invisible
     amorous: loving

105 *paramour:* lover

106 *still will stay:* will stay forever

109 *chambermaids:* room mates

111–12 *And … flesh:* and free my weary body from the burden of my unfortunate destiny

114 *righteous:* pure, honourable

115 *A … death:* an unending agreement with death, which takes over everything

116 *Come … guide!* this poison will take and guide me to the next world

117–18 *Thou … bark!* I am like a sailor whose ship is about to be wrecked on rocks

119 *true:* reliable, truthful

Enter FRIAR LAURENCE, with lantern, crow, and spade.

FRIAR

Saint Francis be my speed! How oft tonight

Have my old feet stumbled at graves! Who's there?

BALTHASAR

Here's one, a friend, and one that knows you well.

FRIAR

Bliss be upon you! Tell me, good my friend,

125   What torch is yond that vainly lends his light

To grubs and eyeless skulls? As I discern,

It burneth in the Capels' monument.

BALTHASAR

It doth so, holy sir; and there's my master,

One that you love.

FRIAR

                Who is it?

BALTHASAR

                     Romeo.

FRIAR

How long hath he been there?

BALTHASAR

130   Full half an hour.

FRIAR

Go with me to the vault.

BALTHASAR

                  I dare not, sir.

My master knows not but I am gone hence,

And fearfully did menace me with death

If I did stay to look on his intents.

FRIAR

135   Stay then; I'll go alone. Fear comes upon me.

O much I fear some ill unthrifty thing.

BALTHASAR

As I did sleep under this yew tree here,

I dreamt my master and another fought,

And that my master slew him.

---

121   *speed:* protector
      oft: often

126   *discern:* see, observe

132   *knows ... hence:* doesn't know that I'm still here

133   *menace:* threaten

134   *his intents:* what he wanted to do

136   *ill:* bad
      unthrifty: unfortunate

139   *slew:* killed

FRIAR

Romeo!

He stoops and looks on the blood and weapons.

Alack, alack, what blood is this which stains   140

The stony entrance of this sepulchre?

What mean these masterless and gory swords

To lie discoloured by this place of peace?

He enters the tomb.

Romeo! O, pale! Who else? What, Paris too?

And steeped in blood? Ah, what an unkind hour   145

Is guilty of this lamentable chance!

The lady stirs.

JULIET rises.

JULIET

O comfortable Friar! Where is my lord?

I do remember well where I should be,

And there I am. Where is my Romeo?   150

FRIAR

I hear some noise. Lady, come from that nest

Of death, contagion, and unnatural sleep.

A greater power than we can contradict

Hath thwarted our intents. Come, come away.

Thy husband in thy bosom there lies dead;   155

And Paris too. Come, I'll dispose of thee

Among a sisterhood of holy nuns.

Stay not to question, for the Watch is coming.

Come, go, good Juliet. I dare no longer stay.

JULIET

Go, get thee hence, for I will not away.   160

Exit FRIAR.

What's here? A cup, closed in my true love's hand?

Poison, I see, hath been his timeless end.

O churl! Drunk all, and left no friendly drop

To help me after? I will kiss thy lips.

Haply some poison yet doth hang on them   165

To make me die with a restorative.

[*kisses him*] Thy lips are warm!

Glossary

140 *Alack:* an expression of regret or sorrow
141 *sepulchre:* tomb
142 *masterless:* abandoned by their owners
   gory: bloody
143 *discoloured:* stained with blood
145 *unkind:* unnatural
146 *lamentable chance:* grim turn of fortune
148 *comfortable:* comfort-bringing
   lord: husband (Romeo)
154 *thwarted our intents:* spoiled our plans
156 *dispose of:* make arrangements for
162 *timeless:* eternal, everlasting
163 *churl:* a term of abuse
164 *after:* follow you (in death)
165 *Haply:* perhaps
166 *restorative:* the kiss she gives Romeo

WATCHMAN [*within*]
Lead, boy. Which way?

JULIET
Yea, noise? Then I'll be brief. O happy dagger!

She snatches Romeo's dagger.

170   This is thy sheath; there rust, and let me die.

She stabs herself and falls.

Enter Paris's PAGE and the WATCH.

PAGE
This is the place. There, where the torch doth burn.

FIRST WATCHMAN
The ground is bloody. Search about the churchyard.
Go, some of you. Whoe'er you find attach.

Exeunt some of the WATCH.
Pitiful sight! Here lies the County slain!

175   And Juliet bleeding, warm, and newly dead,
Who here hath lain these two days burièd.
Go, tell the Prince. Run to the Capulets.
Raise up the Montagues. Some others search.

Exeunt others of the WATCH.
We see the ground whereon these woes do lie,

180   But the true ground of all these piteous woes
We cannot without circumstance descry.

Enter some of the WATCH, with BALTHASAR.

SECOND WATCHMAN
Here's Romeo's man. We found him in the churchyard.

FIRST WATCHMAN
Hold him in safety till the Prince come hither.

Enter FRIAR LAURENCE and another of the WATCH.

THIRD WATCHMAN
Here is a Friar that trembles, sighs, and weeps.

185   We took this mattock and this spade from him
As he was coming from this churchyard's side.

FIRST WATCHMAN
A great suspicion! Stay the Friar too.

---

within: from off stage

169   *brief:* quick
      happy: fortunately convenient

170   *This ... sheath:* my body will be your holder

173   *Whoe'er ... attach:* arrest everyone you find

174   *County:* Paris
      slain: murdered

178   *Raise:* waken

179   *woes:* miserable creatures (Romeo, Juliet and Paris)
180–1   *But ... descry:* however, we won't know the reasons for these pitiful deaths until we examine in detail what happened

183   *in safety:* securely

187   *Stay:* detain

Enter the PRINCE and ATTENDANTS.

PRINCE

What misadventure is so early up,

That calls our person from our morning's rest?

Enter CAPULET, LADY CAPULET and OTHERS.

CAPULET

What should it be, that is so shrieked abroad?   190

LADY CAPULET

O the people in the street cry 'Romeo',

Some 'Juliet', and some 'Paris'; and all run

With open outcry toward our monument.

PRINCE

What fear is this which startles in your ears?

FIRST WATCHMAN

Sovereign, here lies the County Paris slain;   195

And Romeo dead; and Juliet, dead before,

Warm and new killed.

PRINCE

Search, seek, and know, how this foul murder comes.

FIRST WATCHMAN

Here is a Friar, and slaughtered Romeo's man,

With instruments upon them fit to open   200

These dead men's tombs.

CAPULET

O heavens! O wife, look how our daughter bleeds!

This dagger hath mista'en, for, lo, his house

Is empty on the back of Montague,

And it mis-sheathèd in my daughter's bosom!   205

LADY CAPULET

O me! This sight of death is as a bell

That warns my old age to a sepulchre.

Enter MONTAGUE and OTHERS.

PRINCE

Come, Montague. For thou art early up

To see thy son and heir now early down.

188 *misadventure … up:* accident has occurred at such an early hour

189 *our person:* me

190 *What … abroad?* What can have happened that everybody is shouting on the streets?

193 *open:* public
monument: tomb

195 *Sovereign:* your excellence

199 *man:* Balthasar

200 *instruments:* tools

203–5 *This … bosom!* this dagger has gone astray since its sheath is empty on Romeo's back and it has been wrongly placed in Juliet's chest

207 *warns … sepulchre:* calls my older body to its grave

209 *early down:* die young

MONTAGUE

210   Alas, my liege, my wife is dead tonight!

Grief of my son's exile hath stopped her breath.

What further woe conspires against mine age?

PRINCE

Look, and thou shalt see.

MONTAGUE

O thou untaught! What manners is in this,

215   To press before thy father to a grave?

PRINCE

Seal up the mouth of outrage for awhile,

Till we can clear these ambiguities

And know their spring, their head, their true descent.

And then will I be general of your woes

220   And lead you, even to death. Meantime forbear,

And let mischance be slave to patience.

Bring forth the parties of suspicion.

FRIAR

I am the greatest, able to do least,

Yet most suspected, as the time and place

225   Doth make against me, of this direful murder.

And here I stand, both to impeach and purge

Myself condemnèd and myself excused.

PRINCE

Then say at once what thou dost know in this.

FRIAR

I will be brief, for my short date of breath

230   Is not so long as is a tedious tale.

Romeo, there dead, was husband to that Juliet;

And she, there dead, that Romeo's faithful wife.

I married them; and their stolen marriage day

Was Tybalt's doomsday, whose untimely death

235   Banished the new-made bridegroom from the city;

For whom, and not for Tybalt, Juliet pined.

You, to remove that siege of grief from her,

Betrothed and would have married her perforce

To County Paris. Then comes she to me

240   And with wild looks bid me devise some mean

To rid her from this second marriage,

Glossary (left margin)

210   *liege:* lord

210–11   *my wife . . . breath:* Lady Montague died tonight from a broken heart caused by Romeo's banishment

214   *untaught:* ignorant, rude (referring to Romeo)

214–15   *What . . . grave?* Montague pitifully rebukes his dead son for dying before him

216   *mouth of outrage:* expressions of grief; also the entrance to the tomb

217   *ambiguities:* doubts, confusions

218   *And . . . descent:* and find out how they started and what course they took

219   *general . . . woes:* the leader of your mourning

220   *to death:* if sorrow were to kill me
      forbear: refrain, take a step back

221   *let . . . patience:* let our sense of our misfortune give way to patience

222   *Bring . . . suspicion:* bring the suspects forward

223   *greatest:* most involved

225   *make against me:* throw suspicion on me

226   *both . . . purge:* to accuse myself and also to declare my innocence

229–30   *my short . . . tale:* I won't live long enough to tell a painstakingly detailed story

233   *stolen:* secret

234   *doomsday:* day of death

237   *You . . . her:* you, the Capulets, to take away her powerful sorrow

238   *Betrothed:* promised her in marriage
      perforce: against her will

240   *mean:* method

241   *rid her from:* help her prevent

And here I stand, both to impeach and purge
Myself condemnèd and myself excused.

FRIAR LAURENCE, Act 5, Scene 3, 226–7

Or in my cell there would she kill herself.

Then gave I her — so tutored by my art —

A sleeping potion; which so took effect

As I intended, for it wrought on her   245

The form of death. Meantime I writ to Romeo

243 *so … art:* guided by my skills (with plants)

245 *wrought:* produced

246 *form:* look and features of

That he should hither come as this dire night

To help to take her from her borrowed grave,

Being the time the potion's force should cease.

250 But he which bore my letter, Friar John,

Was stayed by accident and yesternight

Returned my letter back. Then all alone

At the prefixèd hour of her waking

Came I to take her from her kindred's vault;

255 Meaning to keep her closely at my cell

Till I conveniently could send to Romeo.

But when I came, some minute ere the time

Of her awakening, here untimely lay

The noble Paris and true Romeo dead.

260 She wakes; and I entreated her come forth

And bear this work of heaven with patience.

But then a noise did scare me from the tomb,

And she, too desperate, would not go with me,

But, as it seems, did violence on herself.

265 All this I know; and to the marriage

Her Nurse is privy; and if aught in this

Miscarried by my fault, let my old life

Be sacrificed, some hour before his time,

Unto the rigour of severest law.

PRINCE

270 We still have known thee for a holy man.

Where's Romeo's man? What can he say to this?

BALTHASAR

I brought my master news of Juliet's death;

And then in post he came from Mantua

To this same place, to this same monument.

275 This letter he early bid me give his father,

And threatened me with death, going in the vault,

If I departed not and left him there.

PRINCE

Give me the letter. I will look on it.

Where is the County's page that raised the Watch?

280 Sirrah, what made your master in this place?

PAGE

He came with flowers to strew his lady's grave,

And bid me stand aloof, and so I did.

Anon comes one with light to ope the tomb,

And by and by my master drew on him.

And then I ran away to call the Watch.   285

PRINCE

This letter doth make good the Friar's words,

Their course of love, the tidings of her death.

And here he writes that he did buy a poison

Of a poor 'pothecary, and therewithal

Came to this vault to die, and lie with Juliet.   290

Where be these enemies? Capulet, Montague,

See what a scourge is laid upon your hate,

That heaven finds means to kill your joys with love.

And I, for winking at your discords too,

Have lost a brace of kinsmen. All are punished.   295

CAPULET

O brother Montague, give me thy hand.

This is my daughter's jointure, for no more

Can I demand.

feud is being resolved

MONTAGUE

        But I can give thee more.

For I will raise her statue in pure gold,

That whiles Verona by that name is known,   300

There shall no figure at such rate be set

As that of true and faithful Juliet.

CAPULET

As rich shall Romeo's by his lady's lie,

Poor sacrifices of our enmity!

PRINCE

A glooming peace this morning with it brings.   305

The sun for sorrow will not show his head.

Go hence, to have more talk of these sad things.

Some shall be pardoned, and some punishèd.

For never was a story of more woe

Than this of Juliet and her Romeo.   310

Exeunt.

---

282 *aloof:* aside

283 *Anon . . . ope:* soon someone carrying a light came to open
284 *by and by:* immediately

287 *tidings:* news

289 *therewithal:* with the poison

292 *scourge:* punishment

293 *joys:* children

294 *winking at:* ignoring
      discords: feud
295 *brace of kinsmen:* two relatives (Mercutio and Paris)

297 *my daughter's jointure:* the handshake of Montague is now the only marriage settlement Capulet can get from his former enemy

299 *raise her statue:* see that a statue of her is made

300 *whiles:* as long as

301 *at . . . set:* be valued so highly

303 *As . . . lie:* a splendid image of Romeo will be placed alongside the equally rich image of Juliet
304 *enmity:* hostility, feud

305 *glooming:* sad, dull

Key points

This scene features the final working-out of what the Prologue told us at the beginning of the play, i.e. that Romeo and Juliet are doomed to take their own lives, and that this is necessary before their families' feud can end.

Timeline

Sunday	Monday	Tuesday	Wednesday	Thursday

- Since we know that both Romeo and Juliet will die at the close of the play, our real interest is in how Shakespeare will bring their deaths about.

- Friar Laurence is unaware that Balthasar has told Romeo that Juliet is dead. Thus, he thinks all he has to do is reach Juliet in the Capulets' tomb before she awakes, and then keep her at his cell until Romeo arrives there.

- It is important to realise that Shakespeare makes Balthasar's success in arriving in Mantua with false news to Romeo, rather than Friar John's failure to arrive with the truth that Juliet is alive, the catalyst for (event that brings about) Romeo's suicide, and as a result of that, Juliet's.

- What would have happened if Shakespeare had used Balthasar (as he does) to tell his false news to Romeo, but had not used Friar John at all? The answer is certain: Romeo's suicide and then Juliet's. What if Shakespeare had not used Balthasar at all, but had left the Friar John incident as it is? The answer is clear: Friar Laurence would still have found time to reach the tomb so that he would be beside Juliet when she woke. Romeo, not having had news of Juliet's supposed death, would not have taken poison or rushed to the tomb, but found his way to Friar Laurence's cell to be reunited with Juliet. Therefore, it is Balthasar's action, performed in ignorance of the facts, that brings about the tragic end of the play.

- The Capulets' tomb (or vault) is not the type of coffin-sized grave that we are used to seeing. It is a large monument, partly above and partly below ground level, that is sealed by a heavy door. It is possible to walk around inside it

and it can hold many bodies. It contains the remains of many of Juliet's ancestors and, by the end of the play, the dead bodies of Tybalt, Paris, Romeo and Juliet.

- Romeo has a clear plan of what he wants to do. He has the tools he needs to open the tomb, and the poison to take his life. He has written a letter for his father, which he gives to Balthasar along with some money. He has not told Balthasar that he intends to poison himself, but Balthasar is worried about Romeo's safety.

- The meeting of Romeo and Paris is most unfortunate. Unaware of Romeo's love for Juliet, Paris assumes that his motives for opening the tomb are malicious. Paris feels he must stop him, but Romeo will not let anyone stop him. Romeo pleads with Paris to walk away; he does not want to kill another person. When Paris refuses, Romeo kills him. It is another wasted life.

- It is also unfortunate that Friar Laurence arrives moments too late to save Romeo. He is in time to save Juliet, but the approach of the watchmen scares him and provides an opportunity for Juliet to stab herself.

- Friar Laurence's final speech (lines 229–69) informs the other characters of what has happened (and allows the audience to understand and remember the story of the play).

- There is one hopeful result of all the tragic events: the feud is over. This will prevent further deaths, but it is too late for the six characters who have already died, most of them young: Mercutio, Tybalt, Paris, Romeo, Juliet and Lady Montague.

Useful quotes

The obsequies that I for thee will keep
Nightly shall be to strew thy grave and weep.

(Paris, lines 16–17)

Stay not, be gone. Live, and hereafter say
A madman's mercy bid thee run away.

(Romeo, lines 66–7)

O true Apothecary,
Thy drugs are quick! Thus with a kiss I die.

(Romeo, lines 119–20)

A greater power than we can contradict
Hath thwarted our intents.

(Friar Laurence, lines 153–4)

Capulet, Montague,
See what a scourge is laid upon your hate,
That heaven finds means to kill your joys with love.
And I, for winking at your discords too,
Have lost a brace of kinsmen. All are punished.

(Prince Escalus, lines 291–5)

Poor sacrifices of our enmity!

(Capulet, line 304)

Questions ?

1 Why is Paris visiting Juliet's grave?

2 Why does Romeo lie to Balthasar (lines 28–32)?

3 Romeo describes Paris as 'one writ with me in sour misfortune's book' (line 82). Is this an accurate account of the lives of Romeo and Paris?

4 What is Paris's dying wish? In your opinion, why did Romeo carry it out?

5 How does Romeo feel as he prepares to die? Is he happy, sad or both? Is he relieved, afraid or both? Explain your answers with reference to the text.

6 Is Friar Laurence justified in running away from the tomb?

7 What is your opinion of the behaviour of Friar Laurence in this scene as a whole?

8 Juliet quickly decides that suicide is her only option. Suggest why she thinks this.

9 In your opinion, who is most to blame for this sequence of tragic events?

10 Is there any reason for hope at the end of the play?

11 Imagine that you are a newspaper journalist. Write an article on what has happened overnight in Verona's graveyard. Remember to give it an eye-catching headline.

12 Write a review of *Romeo and Juliet* for the school magazine or website. Say why you would or would not recommend the play to other students.

Talking point

Why do we read sad stories and watch sad plays and films? Do they seem more real than works that have a happy ending? Do they make you feel better or worse? Do they help you cope with situations in your own life or make your life seem less difficult in comparison?

ACT 5 ✝ Key moments

Scene 1

- In Mantua, Romeo's servant, Balthasar, tells him that Juliet is dead.
- Romeo buys a deadly poison from the Apothecary, which he intends to use when he gets to Juliet's grave.

Scene 2

- Friar Laurence learns that Friar John has not been able to deliver the letter he sent to Romeo. He hurries to the tomb before Juliet awakes.

Scene 3

- At the tomb, Romeo is challenged by Paris, who has come to pay his respects to Juliet. Romeo and Paris fight, and Paris is killed. As he is dying, he asks Romeo to place his body with Juliet's.
- Romeo takes the poison, and dies.
- When Juliet wakes, Friar Laurence tries to explain to her what has happened. He offers to enrol her in a convent. She refuses to leave with him.
- Juliet seizes Romeo's dagger and stabs herself to death.
- Friar Laurence tells Prince Escalus of his part in the events that have led to the tragic deaths of Romeo, Juliet and Paris.
- Capulet and Montague make peace.

ACT 5 ✝ Speaking and listening

1 Select one student to play Friar Laurence. The rest of the class is then divided into five groups, each representing a surviving character: the Prince, Capulet, Lady Capulet, Montague and Benvolio. Each group should agree a list of questions that they think their character would like to ask Friar Laurence about his part in the lives and deaths of Romeo and Juliet. The group should then select a spokesperson to interrogate the Friar. At the end, each group must decide whether their character thinks Friar Laurence should be punished for his actions.

2 In small groups, select any passage that you consider to be important from the three scenes in Act 5. Then discuss how it might be performed on stage. Where should the characters involved be positioned on stage? Which character should be closest to the audience? How would the characters stand, sit, move? What gestures might they make, if any? Should they have any props? How do they speak? Should there be any pauses in the dialogue? What would their facial expressions be? Finally, try acting out the passage to see whether your ideas work in practice.

Revision quiz: plot summary Q

Use the words and phrases listed in the panel to fill in the blanks in this summary of Act 5:

Apothecary

Balthasar

Capulet

Capulets

convent

corpse

Friar John

Friar Laurence

hide

Juliet

kills

Mantua

Montague

open

Page

Paris

plague

poison

Prince

Romeo

sleeping

stabs

statues

tomb

Verona

Exiled in _____, Romeo is beginning to feel positive about the future. His hopes are dashed when his servant _____ arrives with the news that _____ is dead. Romeo decides to buy a deadly poison from a poor _____ and travel to _____ to die alongside Juliet's body.

_____ _____ explains to Friar Laurence that he was detained in Verona because of an outbreak of _____ and could not deliver the letter to _____. Friar Laurence realises that he needs to be inside the Capulets' _____ when the _____ drug wears off and Juliet awakes. He will then _____ Juliet until Romeo arrives.

Late at night, Paris visits the _____ 'tomb to pay homage to Juliet. When he sees Romeo trying to _____ the tomb he assumes that Romeo (a Montague) has come to damage the tomb of the Capulets. _____ tries to arrest Romeo. They fight and Romeo _____ Paris. Paris asks Romeo to place his _____ beside Juliet's, which Romeo does. Romeo then takes the _____ and dies in Juliet's arms.

_____ _____ arrives just before Juliet wakes up. He tries to persuade her to leave with him so he can arrange for her to live in a _____. She refuses to go. As the watchmen arrive, the Friar runs off, leaving Juliet alone. She takes Romeo's dagger and _____ herself. The watchmen find the bodies in the tomb and arrest Balthasar and Friar Laurence in the graveyard.

When Prince Escalus, Capulet, Lady Capulet, Montague and others arrive, Friar Laurence tells them all he knows about what happened to Romeo and Juliet. Balthasar and Paris's _____ fill in the gaps in his story. Romeo's letter to _____ gives further confirmation. The _____ blames the feud for the deaths. Montague and _____ shake hands and decide to build _____ to their dead children.

Romeo and Juliet ✝ Crossword

Across

3 Who tries to stop the fight between the servants in the opening scene?

5 Who is Romeo's father?

6 Who is Romeo in love with at the start of the play?

9 Who is killed by Tybalt?

11 Who bans fighting on the streets of Verona?

13 Who do Juliet's parents want her to marry?

14 Who does Juliet ask about Romeo's identity at the Capulets' feast?

Down

1 What is the name of the friar who is meant to take the letter to Romeo in Mantua?

2 Who kills Paris?

4 Who is Juliet's mother?

7 Who is Tybalt's cousin?

8 Who wants to attack Romeo at the Capulets' feast?

10 Who narrates the Prologue?

12 _ _ _ _ _ Laurence. What is the missing title?

Characters

In terms of the number of lines spoken, the main roles in *Romeo and Juliet* are: Romeo (speaks 20 per cent of the lines), Juliet (18 per cent), Friar Laurence (11 per cent), the Nurse (9 per cent), Capulet (9 per cent) and Mercutio (8 per cent).

Other characters make significant contributions. For example, Benvolio, Lady Capulet, Prince Escalus and Paris have influential roles. Tybalt speaks only 36 lines, but his importance in the development of the plot is out of all proportion to the number of his appearances on the stage.

Changing times

Remember that our responses to some of the characters and events in *Romeo and Juliet* are quite different from those of Shakespeare's first audiences.

Take Juliet and her parents, Capulet and Lady Capulet, as an example. In the play, Capulet is very interested in Juliet's welfare. He thinks that she will have a happy and prosperous future if she marries Count Paris. Paris, a rich and admirable young man, wants to marry Juliet and has sought the approval of her parents. Capulet eventually arranges a marriage between Paris and Juliet, without consulting Juliet. Meanwhile Juliet has secretly married Romeo, without consulting her parents.

Most members of Shakespeare's first audiences would have had sympathy with Capulet here, rather than with Juliet. They would have believed that parents have absolute authority over their children. Juliet's actions would have been seen as disrespectful and disobedient.

Modern audiences, on the other hand, have greater sympathy for Juliet. They tend to think that Romeo and Juliet should be free to marry for love, and to make their own choices, with or without consulting their parents. It is Capulet's actions that may be seen as disrespectful and authoritarian.

Casting decisions have changed too. In Shakespeare's day women and girls were not allowed to act. This means that the part of the Nurse was played by a man, and the other female parts, including Juliet's, were played by specially trained boy actors, dressed as females.

In modern productions of the play, Juliet is usually played by an actress. However, by the time an actress is able to play this part well, she is usually too old to look like a girl of not quite fourteen years. The part is straightforward, but the language is often quite complex and can take years of experience to master.

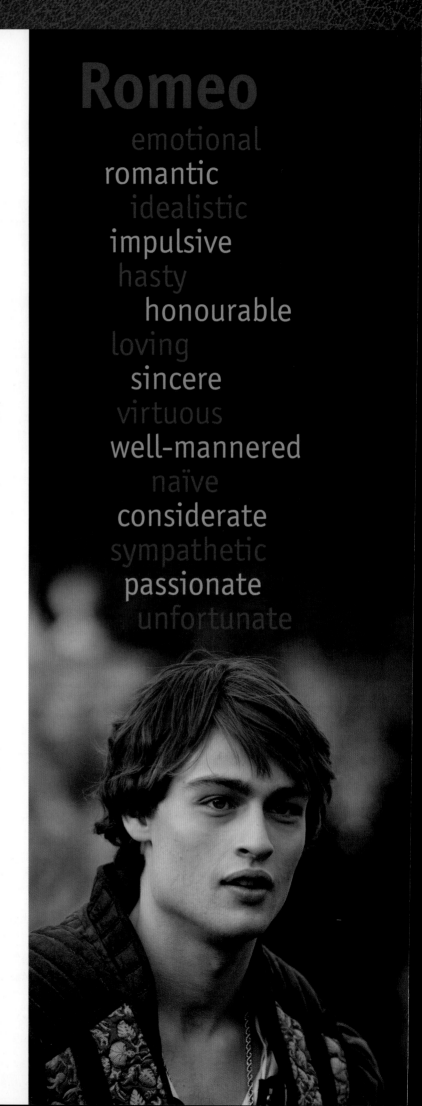

Romeo

emotional
romantic
idealistic
impulsive
hasty
honourable
loving
sincere
virtuous
well-mannered
naïve
considerate
sympathetic
passionate
unfortunate

Although Romeo is the hero of the play, he is not an entirely attractive character.

At the beginning, he is a source of amusement to his friends, as he pines for Rosaline, whom he loves, or thinks he loves, although she does not return his love. He is moody, withdrawn and inclined to exaggerate his feelings for Rosaline. The shallowness of those feelings is shown in the speed with which he forgets her as soon as he sees Juliet. Friar Laurence makes this point well:

> *Is Rosaline, that thou didst love so dear,*
>
> *So soon forsaken? Young men's love then lies*
>
> *Not truly in their hearts, but in their eyes.*
>
> (Act 2, Scene 3, lines 62–4)

The astonished Friar makes this remark after Romeo has told him that he has forgotten Rosaline's name and all the misery she brought him, because he is now in love with Juliet, whom he has just met but wants to marry immediately. The Friar gives Romeo a piece of useful advice: 'Wisely and slow. They stumble that run fast' (Act 2, Scene 3, line 90).

Unfortunately this is not Romeo's style. His motto is: 'I stand on sudden haste' (Act 2, Scene 3, line 89). He insists on acting on the spur of the moment, a tendency that proves fatal to him and to his hopes for a happy future. Romeo's encounter with Tybalt in Act 3, Scene 1 shows this side of his character in action. He starts out being reasonable and sensible, but then Mercutio's death causes him to lose self-control and he is drawn into a duel with Tybalt.

At first Romeo refuses to duel with Tybalt and does all he can to make peace with him. When the fiery Mercutio, disgusted by Romeo's peaceful response to an insult, feels he has to step in and fight Tybalt, Romeo tries to stop them. In the confusion, Tybalt kills Mercutio. It is only when Tybalt returns to cause further trouble that Romeo loses his patience, challenges him to a duel and kills him. Romeo is banished from Verona as a result.

In defence of Romeo's killing of Tybalt, it should be remembered that (a) Tybalt came with the intention of killing Romeo and (b) Romeo is bound by the code of honour in drama to avenge the murder of his friend (Mercutio). Tybalt is the only truly unlikeable character in the play, and it can be said that Romeo

behaves with great patience in the face of this bully, who insults and provokes him in the presence of his friends.

It is a tribute to Romeo's character that everybody in the play likes him except the hate-filled Tybalt. Romeo's friends and parents are devoted to him. Friar Laurence, his confessor and advisor, does everything he can to help him. Even Capulet, head of the rival family, speaks highly of him, pointing out to Tybalt that Romeo carries himself like a well-mannered gentleman:

> *And, to say truth, Verona brags of him*
>
> *To be a virtuous and well-governed youth.*
>
> (Act 1, Scene 5, lines 65–6)

Romeo's big weakness is his frequent loss of self-control. When things go against him, he displays childish rage and grief. He cannot control his feelings when he gets news of his banishment. He claims this is worse than a death sentence (because it means living without Juliet) and the Nurse has to restrain him from killing himself. The Friar then helps him to see reason and respond more sensibly and maturely to his situation.

Left to himself, Romeo is likely to make foolish decisions. It is no great surprise that later in the play, when he hears that Juliet is dead, he again determines to take his own life. He decides this without making the slightest effort to check the truth or otherwise of what he has heard.

Romeo's two vital decisions in the play, concerning his marriage and his death, are made with ridiculous speed and lack of thought. However, he is not quite as impetuous and rash as Tybalt (in pursuit of trouble) or Mercutio (in pursuit of honour).

As Romeo's death approaches, there are signs that he has grown in maturity. He is less changeable in his moods and less inclined to panic. He has learned to recognise and accept realities and to form balanced judgements. In other words, adversity has made a man of him.

He has developed a new concern for others. For example, he shows sympathy for the Apothecary as a victim of poverty and starvation. He sees that a cruel world treats him unfairly and he gives him gold in exchange for the illegal poison:

> *Famine is in thy cheeks.*
> *Need and oppression starveth in thine eyes.*
> *Contempt and beggary hangs upon thy back.*
> *The world is not thy friend, nor the world's law,*
> *The world affords no law to make thee rich.*
>
> (Act 5, Scene 1, lines 69–73)

Before he poisons himself, Romeo writes a letter to his father and tells his servant Balthasar to see that it is safely delivered. He thinks of Balthasar's future welfare, giving him money and perhaps his purse, and advising him to 'Live, and be prosperous' (Act 5, Scene 3, line 42).

When Paris challenges him at the entrance to Juliet's tomb, mistakenly believing that he is about to abuse the corpses of Juliet and Tybalt, Romeo begs him to go away:

> *By heaven, I love thee better than myself,*
> *For I come hither armed against myself,*
> *Stay not, be gone. Live, and hereafter say*
> *A madman's mercy bid thee run away.*
>
> (Act 5, Scene 3, lines 64–7)

It is only after Paris refuses to leave and instead tries to arrest Romeo that Romeo fights and kills him, not yet knowing his identity. When he realises that the man he has killed is Paris, Romeo grieves over what he has done and places Paris's body next to Juliet's in the tomb, as a fellow victim of fate.

Romeo's progress towards emotional maturity comes in three stages:

1. His education begins after the Friar and the Nurse prevent him from killing himself. The Friar takes charge at this point. In a lengthy speech (Act 3, Scene 3, lines 109–55) he teaches Romeo that it is useless to criticise fortune. He also shows him that he is more fortunate than he thinks. After all, Juliet is still alive, he has survived Tybalt's attempt to kill him, and the Prince, who had a legal right to sentence him to death for killing Tybalt, has merely sentenced him to exile. When Romeo stops his weeping and complaining and goes to console Juliet, he has taken his first step towards maturity.

2. As he begins his descent from Juliet's window to head for exile in Mantua, Juliet asks: 'O, thinkst thou we shall ever meet again?' and Romeo replies: 'I doubt it not; and all these woes shall serve for sweet discourses in our time to come' (Act 3, Scene 5, lines 51–3). Romeo is growing in maturity: he has thrown off despair and is facing the future with some degree of hope.

3. When Romeo re-appears at the beginning of Act 5 in Mantua, his first words indicate that he is a stronger and more optimistic man. He has had a happy dream, which makes him look forward to a better future: 'My dreams presage some joyful news at hand' (Act 5, Scene 1, line 2). It is then that he receives the most terrible news that Juliet is dead and buried. The earlier Romeo would almost certainly have reacted to this news with an hysterical outburst, as he did when he heard of his banishment. Now he responds with calm simplicity: 'Is it e'en so? Then I defy you, stars!' (line 24). By denying the power of fortune, Romeo is declaring that he will no longer be its plaything, he is no longer under its control. Nevertheless, his solution is still to take his own life – a response that we consider wrong.

The Prologue to the play, however, suggests that all that happens in the play, and all that happens to the characters, is controlled by fate, fortune or the stars. In other words, no matter how Romeo and Juliet behave, their deaths are inevitable. Fate has decided that the feud between their families can be ended only by their deaths. The decision of both to die can thus be seen as a terrible sacrifice undertaken to achieve a noble aim: the end of generations of murderous strife between the two households.

Notice that when Paris tells Romeo in the graveyard that he is going to kill him, 'for thou must die', Romeo replies: 'I must indeed; and therefore came I hither' (Act 5, Scene 3, lines 57–8). This reply indicates that he has come willingly to embrace the inevitable end of his life's journey. As the Prologue puts it, Romeo is one of 'a pair of star-crossed lovers' who 'doth with their death bury their parents' strife' (lines 6 and 8).

Juliet

inexperienced
loving
spontaneous
generous
frank
faithful

unfortunate
strong
practical
straightforward
tactful
courageous
clever
capable
strong-willed

One of the most important aspects of Juliet is her youth. The entire action of the play, which is spread over just five days, takes place as Juliet approaches her fourteenth birthday. She is not yet familiar with all of society's rules and conventions, and is very open and honest about her feelings.

Juliet's simplicity and frankness are among her most attractive qualities. She tends to say what she means and to mean what she says. She falls in love with Romeo at the very first sight of him, as he does with her. After the briefest of conversations, before she even knows his name, she decides that she is in love with him and that she will never love any other man: 'If he be marrièd, my grave is like to be my wedding bed' (Act 1, Scene 5, lines 132–3).

When the Nurse tells her that he is a Montague, she is appalled that the one man she loves, and the only one she will love, is a member of a family that hates her own: 'My only love, sprung from my only hate!' (Act 1, Scene 5, line 136). Despite her age, Juliet is sufficiently mature to realise that she is facing a serious situation. She has met Romeo and fallen in love with him, without realising who and what he is, but it is too late to change what has already happened.

Juliet displays a degree of cunning in finding out who Romeo is. She does not want the Nurse to know of her interest in Romeo at this early stage, so she cannot ask her directly to identify him. Instead, she first asks her to name some other young men, and then, almost casually, as if she had no particular interest in him, asks her to identify Romeo: 'What's he that follows here, that would not dance?' (Act 1, Scene 5, line 130).

When it comes to her love for Romeo, Juliet is strong, practical and honest. In this regard, Romeo has a big advantage over her. Hiding in the orchard, he hears words from Juliet that she would not have spoken had she known he was listening:

> *O Romeo, Romeo, wherefore [why] art thou Romeo?*
> *Deny thy father and refuse thy name.*
> *Or, if thou wilt not, be but sworn my love,*
> *And I'll no longer be a Capulet.*
>
> (Act 2, Scene 2, lines 33–6)

He also hears her say that people's names do not matter, that Romeo would keep his 'dear perfection' (line 46) no matter what he was called, and that she wishes Romeo might take her in exchange for his name: 'Take all myself' (line 49).

The first real dialogue between Juliet and Romeo reveals a significant contrast between them. Juliet takes the lead in their conversation. She is not afraid to tell Romeo of the extent of her love for him. Her questions and comments to Romeo are all direct, straightforward and, above all, practical. Romeo's answers, however, are vague and full of romantic exaggeration.

Juliet's questions seek to find out the truth about Romeo:

> *Art thou not Romeo, and a Montague?*
> *How camest thou hither, tell me, and wherefore?*
> *By whose direction foundest thou out this place?*
> *What satisfaction canst thou have tonight?*
>
> (Act 2, Scene 2, lines 60, 62, 79, 126)

Romeo's answers consist mainly of poetic flights of fancy. To her question about whether he is Romeo and a Montague, he answers: 'Neither, fair maid, if either thee dislike' (line 61). Her next question, about how he came to her orchard, is answered: 'With love's light wings did I o'er-perch these walls' (line 66). When she enquires as to how he found her place, he tells her 'By love, that first did prompt me to inquire' (line 80).

Juliet's comments are also to the point. She advises him that if her relatives see him, they will murder him. In the lengthy speech in which she confesses her love for Romeo, her language is tactful, direct and clear. Her biggest fear is that because she has been so explicit about her love for him, Romeo will think she is 'too quickly won' (line 95). It is also Juliet who proposes marriage:

> *If that thy bent of love be honourable,*
> *Thy purpose marriage, send me word tomorrow, ...*
> *Where and what time thou wilt perform the rite,*
> *And all my fortunes at thy foot I'll lay*
>
> (Act 2, Scene 2, lines 143–7)

When Juliet is in serious trouble, separated from Romeo and threatened by her father with dismissal from the family home if she does not agree to marry Paris, she shows remarkable courage. She goes to Friar Laurence's cell to seek advice on avoiding a forced marriage to Paris, and he comes up with a plan. When she returns home, she is to drink a sleeping potion he gave her, which will make her seem as if she is dead, and from which she will not awake for forty-two hours. By the time she awakes, she will have been buried in the family tomb, and Romeo will be waiting for her.

When it comes to swallowing the sleeping potion, Juliet recognises how desperate the Friar's plan is. She fears that he may have given her a deadly poison rather than a sleeping potion. Then she worries that if she wakes before Romeo's arrival at the tomb, she will be unable to breathe properly, or will have her brains dashed out by 'some great kinsman's bone' (Act 4, Scene 3, line 53). She displays extraordinary courage when she confronts and overcomes these fears, and swallows the sleeping potion.

Act 3, Scene 5 represents one of the lowest points in Juliet's life. But in dealing with appalling situations created for her by those closest to her, she shows considerable presence of mind, resourcefulness and quickness of wit.

Her parents, knowing nothing of her marriage to Romeo, have arranged for Paris to be her husband. When she refuses to marry Paris, her father subjects her to foul abuse and threatens to throw her out of her home as if she were an animal: 'Graze where you will, you shall not house with me' (Act 3, Scene 5, line 189). Juliet pleads for mother's support: 'O sweet my mother, cast me not away!' (line 199), but Lady Capulet coldly abandons her:

Talk not to me, for I'll not speak a word.

Do as thou wilt, for I have done with thee.

(Act 3, Scene 5, lines 203–4)

Dismissed by her parents, Juliet looks to her Nurse for help and support. The Nurse, who knows that Juliet has just married Romeo, offers neither. Instead, she makes the ridiculous suggestion that Juliet should simply forget that she is married to Romeo and go ahead and marry Paris, thus committing bigamy.

Juliet holds her nerve and shows remarkable composure, cleverly hiding her intentions. First she pretends to be pleased with the Nurse's advice to marry Paris: 'Well, thou hast comforted me marvellous much' (Act 3, Scene 5, line 231). She is being sarcastic here, but the Nurse does not recognise the sarcasm, thinking instead that Juliet is being grateful to her.

Juliet then pretends that she wants to make her confession to Friar Laurence, and seek forgiveness for having displeased her father. What she really wants to do is to get the Friar's help in avoiding a second marriage. The Nurse agrees to tell Juliet's mother what Juliet wants her to hear: that she regrets upsetting her father. She wants her parents to think that she is now ready to marry Paris, and manages to convince the Nurse to think the same.

Juliet continues with the pretence in Act 4, Scene 2. Following Friar Laurence's advice, she tells her father that she will obey him: 'Henceforward I am ever ruled by you' (line 21). Her father is totally convinced: 'My heart is wondrous light, since this same wayward girl is so reclaimed' (lines 45–6).

Juliet also exhibits sound judgement. This emerges in her comments on the Nurse, whom she despises for her lack of morals. She calls her, in her absence, 'Ancient damnation! O most wicked fiend!' (Act 3, Scene 5, line 236). In other words, the Nurse is a damned old woman and an extremely wicked devil. This description is justified for two reasons. The Nurse has tried to persuade Juliet to do something Juliet finds morally and emotionally repulsive, and has been a hypocrite in criticising Romeo whom she previously praised. Juliet's rejection of the Nurse, who has been her lifelong companion, is a sign of Juliet's integrity and the sincerity of her love for Romeo.

Juliet also shows herself an expert in the clever use of ambiguous, or double-meaning, speech. A good example follows her mother's idea of sending someone to Mantua to poison Romeo. Juliet pretends to go along with this idea: 'Madam, if you could find out but a man to bear a poison, I would temper it' (Act 3, Scene 5, lines 96–7). This comment carries two meanings: the meaning Juliet has in mind and the different meaning that she knows her mother will take from it. What she has in mind is to secure a promise from her mother that nobody but she (Juliet) shall be allowed to mix the poison. The meaning her mother takes from the comment is that Juliet has a strong personal interest in poisoning Romeo. Her mother finds it easy to believe this because of another ambiguous comment Juliet has just made:

Indeed I never shall be satisfied

With Romeo, till I behold him – dead –

Is my poor heart so far a kinsman vexed.

(Act 3, Scene 5, lines 93–5)

This is a splendid example of ambiguity, since 'dead' can refer either to Romeo or to Juliet's heart; the first meaning is intended for her mother, the second (and real) one for herself.

The question is sometimes asked: Why does Juliet allow Romeo to leave Verona without her in Act 3, Scene 5, when she could easily have gone with him disguised as a boy? We know that she has the courage to take such a risk. However, if Shakespeare had allowed Juliet to escape with Romeo, and the play had ended happily for both of them, it would be a comedy, and not the tragedy that the Prologue warns us it is to be.

Friar Laurence

risk-taking

well-intentioned

peace-making

wise

fatherly

benevolent

pious

honest

unfortunate

trustworthy

innocent

eager

imperfect

crafty

secretive

Shakespeare presents Friar Laurence as a well-meaning character who wants to put an end to the feud that is disturbing the peace of Verona.

This aim explains why Friar Laurence agrees to conduct the secret marriage of Romeo and Juliet. He makes this clear to Romeo when he tells him his one reason for helping them:

> *In one respect I'll thy assistant be.*
> *For this alliance may so happy prove*
> *To turn your households' rancour to*
> *pure love.*
>
> (Act 2, Scene 3, lines 86–8)

In the scheme of the play, the Friar represents reason and common sense. Above all, he tries to control Romeo's tendency to go to extremes – of happiness and delight on the one hand, and of misery and despair on the other. The Friar has no time for such excess. He believes in moderation and self-control.

When Romeo hears that he has been banished from Verona and tries to stab himself, Friar Laurence rebukes him for not using his intelligence ('wit') but instead allowing himself to be burned away: 'Like powder in a skilless soldier's flask' (Act 3, Scene 3, line 133). In other words, Romeo is like an incompetent soldier who blows himself up with his own gunpowder. The Friar thinks of the impetuous Romeo as having gunpowder in his veins, and of love as being the fire that ignites it.

Later Romeo confirms the accuracy of the Friar's words when he asks the Apothecary for poison to act on his body: 'As violently as hasty powder fired doth hurry from the fatal cannon's womb' (Act 5, Scene 1, lines 64–5).

Friar Laurence's main function in the play is to act as a father figure to Romeo, who confides in him rather than in his own father, Montague. He also acts as Juliet's confessor and advisor when nobody else can help her.

His main characteristic is natural goodness and there is little doubt that whatever he does, he does with the best intentions. This includes his risky plan to re-unite Romeo and Juliet in the Capulet tomb. When his plan goes wrong, through the innocent intervention of others, he is prepared to face the consequences. He gives a full and honest account to Prince Escalus of his role in the lives and deaths of Romeo and Juliet, and leaves it to the Prince to pass judgement on what he has done:

> … if aught in this
> Miscarried by my fault, let my old life
> Be sacrificed, some hour before his time,
> Unto the rigour of severest law.

> (Act 5, Scene 3, lines 266–9)

Here he is telling the Prince that if he is found guilty of doing anything wrong in his efforts on behalf of Romeo and Juliet, he wants to be punished according to the law, even if this means being sentenced to death.

The Prince, an honest and fair-minded magistrate, expresses confidence in Friar Laurence as 'a holy man' (Act 5, Scene 3, line 270). Then, when he reads Romeo's letter to Montague, he confirms that: 'This letter doth make good the Friar's words' (line 286). It seems to be the Prince's verdict that Friar Laurence is free from guilt.

The most sensible view of Friar Laurence is that he is a good-natured, trustworthy priest whom Romeo and Juliet seek out when they are in trouble; a kindly man, anxious to be helpful to people in distress. It is not his fault that Capulet changed the wedding day, that Friar John was unable to deliver his letter to Romeo, or that Balthasar travelled to Mantua with news of Juliet's supposed death, leading to the tragic ending of the play. His own explanation is that fate, or providence, intervened to defeat his plans: 'A greater power than we can contradict hath thwarted our intents' (Act 5, Scene 3, lines 153–4).

Friar Laurence has been criticised for his conduct after Juliet awakes in the tomb to find Romeo dead. He tries to persuade her to leave Romeo's body so that he may take her to a convent of nuns. However, he panics when he hears others approach, and leaves Juliet on her own when she refuses to go with him. Juliet then kills herself with Romeo's dagger, something the Friar might have prevented had he remained with her.

There are other possible criticisms of Friar Laurence. Although his slogan is 'wisely and slow' (Act 2, Scene 3, line 90), he acts hastily in marrying Romeo and Juliet in secret, without witnesses, thus breaking church law. He also hides Juliet's marriage from her parents and Paris and then devises another plan to deceive them into believing that she is dead.

It is sometimes said that he risks poisoning Juliet when he gives her a sleeping potion. This does not make sense, however, as the point of his soliloquy at the beginning of Act 2, Scene 3 is to reveal that he is an expert with plants and herbs.

Friar Laurence is one of two characters in the play who take steps to end the feud between the Montagues and the Capulets. The other is Prince Escalus. The Prince works openly, by lecturing the troublemakers and warning them, on pain of death, to avoid public quarrels in the future. His intervention during the brawl in Act 1, Scene 1 is a good example. Friar Laurence works secretly, conducting a secret marriage, sending secret messages, giving Juliet a drug to take in secret. The problem is that when a link in the chain of secrecy is broken, the entire plan collapses, and disaster becomes inevitable. In this sense, Friar Laurence is the main agent of the tragedy.

The worst that can be said of Friar Laurence is that he takes too many chances, and does not have full control of the schemes he devises.

Friar Laurence gives a good summary of his role in the play in Act 5, Scene 3, lines 229–69.

The Nurse

entertaining
humorous
lively
plain-spoken
mature
experienced
ill-educated
coarse
vulgar
long-winded
talkative
insensitive
protective
immoral
unprincipled

Shakespeare makes the Nurse a source of lively entertainment, particularly in the first half of the play. She is a mature woman, wise in the ways of the world, and one of Shakespeare's finest comic creations.

While almost all the other characters (apart from the servants) are cultured, educated and sophisticated, the Nurse is of peasant origin, with little education. She is plainly spoken, often coarse, and cannot resist making rude and vulgar comments.

Act 1, Scene 3 shows her at her best as a comic character. When Lady Capulet asks the Nurse to tell her Juliet's age, Shakespeare might easily have allowed her to answer in a single sentence, but a straight answer is not in the Nurse's nature. She likes to ramble on at great length before coming to the point. This is her first attempt at an answer:

> I'll lay fourteen of my teeth –
> And yet, to my teen be it spoken, I have but four –
> She's not fourteen. How long is it now
> To Lammastide?

(Act 1, Scene 3, lines 13–16)

After this absurd comment that she is prepared to wager fourteen of her teeth even though she has only four, she gets around to revealing that Juliet will be fourteen on the night of 31 July ('Lammas Eve at night'; line 18). This should be the end of the discussion, but the Nurse is only warming up. She goes on a trip down memory lane to Juliet's childhood, and that of her own daughter, Susan:

> Susan and she – God rest all Christian souls –
> Were of an age. Well, Susan is with God.
> She was too good for me …
> 'Tis since the earthquake now eleven years …
> Sitting in the sun under the dovehouse wall …
> And then my husband – God be with his soul!
> 'A was a merry man – took up the child.

(Act 1, Scene 3, lines 19–21, 24, 28, 40–1)

These ramblings are mixed with sexual innuendo and jokes about marriage. Lady Capulet, unable to take any more, tries to halt the Nurse: 'Enough of this. I pray thee hold thy peace' (line 50). The

At the feast, Capulet chats about his youth, welcomes his guests and is a warm host. He is admirable in his defence of Romeo, who has gate-crashed the celebrations. His response is tolerant and fair. He has no time for Tybalt's complaint that Romeo is an enemy who has come to make a mockery of the event. Capulet points out that Romeo has a good reputation, whereas Tybalt is rude ('a princox'; Act 1, Scene 5, line 84).

Capulet had earlier given a sign of his reasonable side in his comment to Paris on the long-standing feud between the Capulets and the Montagues: 'and 'tis not hard, I think, for men so old as we to keep the peace' (Act 1, Scene 2, lines 2–3).

Halfway through the play, a new Capulet seems to emerge. He appears more like a tyrant than a caring father who loves his daughter. Earlier, he spoke of Juliet's value to him, and of her right to have a say in whom she marries. When she tries to exercise this right by refusing to marry Paris, Capulet declares, in anger, that she should be grateful to her parents for finding her a worthy man prepared to marry her when she herself is so unworthy:

> Doth she not give us thanks?
> Is she not proud? Doth she not count her blest,
> Unworthy as she is, that we have wrought
> So worthy a gentleman to be her bride?
>
> (Act 3, Scene 5, lines 142–5)

Then comes the terrible threat. If she refuses to do what he says, and to accept the husband he has chosen for her, he will drag her to the church himself. If she still rejects his demands, he tells her he is prepared to let her beg in the streets, or starve, or die.

This is an utterly disturbing scene, painful in the extreme for Juliet, but there are a number of things that explain Capulet's behaviour here. When we are judging him, we should think of the situation in which he finds himself.

Shakespeare has already shown him as a devoted father, who would not knowingly act against his daughter's best interests. When he orders Juliet to marry Paris, who, from Capulet's point of view, would make an ideal husband for her, he is ignorant of an all-important truth. Juliet has already married Romeo. We know

this, but Capulet does not. He is speaking and acting in the innocent belief that Juliet is free to marry Paris.

There can be no doubt that the anger Capulet displays towards Juliet springs from his love for her and his concern for her welfare. He is frustrated that she cannot see what is good for her. He loses his temper because she seems to him to be denying herself the best way to future happiness. As he sees it, he is being cruel to be kind.

In Shakespeare's time, arranged marriages were common among noble families and often did not involve the consent of the bride. These practices should be kept in mind when we are judging Capulet's comments to Juliet in Act 3, Scene 5. Law and custom were on his side.

We should also take account of Capulet's motive for arranging a speedy marriage of his daughter to Paris. He is concerned for Juliet's well-being. He thinks she is depressed as a result of Tybalt's death, and that marriage to Paris will restore her to happiness. His motive is explained to Juliet by Lady Capulet:

> Well, well, thou hast a careful father, child:
> One who, to put thee from thy heaviness,
> Hath sorted out a sudden day of joy
>
> (Act 3, Scene 5, lines 107–9)

In other words, Capulet, with the best of intentions, wants to take care of his only child, and relieve her depression, by having her speedily married. It is not his fault, or his wife's, that they do not know that the marriage would be unlawful because Juliet is already married.

It is only at the end of the play, when Juliet's body lies before him and Friar Laurence has told all he knows of what has led to her death, that Capulet is able to act in a situation that he at least partly understands. Then he cries out: 'O brother Montague, give me thy hand' (Act 5, Scene 3, line 296). This handshake marks the end of the deadly feud.

On the evidence of the play, we may conclude that Capulet is a good man caught up in circumstances that make it impossible for him to know the truth. Unlike the audience, he does not know all the facts and it is important to take this into account when judging his words and actions.

Lady Capulet

cold-hearted
unreasonable
unsympathetic
mean
sarcastic
vindictive
vengeful
retaliatory
selfish

Lady Capulet appears to be a cold-hearted woman. She is seldom seen in a sympathetic relationship with either her husband or her daughter.

Lady Capulet's first words in the play are a sarcastic comment intended to stop her husband from joining the street-fighting: 'A crutch, a crutch! Why call you for a sword?' (Act 1, Scene 1, line 69). In other words: there's no point asking for a sword; an old man like you should be calling for a crutch to help you get around! Lady Capulet is probably still in her twenties, having been a very young bride, and a mother around the age of thirteen or fourteen, so this comment indicates that there is a significant age gap between her and her husband.

She does not seem to have had as strong a role in Juliet's upbringing as the Nurse has. Indeed,

her relationship with her daughter appears to be rather formal. When she has to raise the issue of marriage with Juliet, she asks the Nurse to be present for the discussion (Act 1, Scene 3, lines 9–11), perhaps in recognition that the Nurse will have more influence over her daughter, or be able to offer her better support, than she will.

Lady Capulet tells Juliet that it is time for her to consider marriage and encourages her to look favourably on Paris. Her glowing description of Paris mainly focuses on his handsome appearance. She suggests that Juliet would be lucky to have such a man as her husband.

When Capulet agrees to the marriage of Juliet and Paris and sets a date, it is Lady Capulet's job to deliver the 'joyful tidings' (Act 3, Scene 5, line 104) to Juliet. Like Capulet, she expects Juliet to be pleased with the news and perhaps grateful that they have found her such an eligible husband as Paris. She does not understand Juliet's refusal.

Like her husband, Lady Capulet does not know that Juliet is already married, and believes that marriage to Paris will ease Juliet's current sadness and secure her future. Nevertheless, it is a strange mother who could wish her only daughter dead for refusing a suitor: 'I would the fool were married to her grave!' (line 140).

When Juliet, in extreme misery, appeals to her mother for sympathy, Lady Capulet's response is chilling:

Talk not to me, for I'll not speak a word.

Do as thou wilt, for I have done with thee.

(Act 3, Scene 5, lines 203–4)

Lady Capulet can also be fiery. Her first reaction to the news of Tybalt's death, before she knows anything about the circumstances that led to it, is to demand the death of Romeo: 'For blood of ours shed blood of Montague' (Act 3, Scene 1, line 147). When Benvolio explains how Tybalt provoked Romeo, Lady Capulet alleges that Benvolio's friendship with Romeo is causing him to lie on Romeo's behalf. She persists in her vengeful attitude, ignoring the fact that Tybalt has killed Mercutio: 'Romeo slew Tybalt. Romeo must not live' (line 179). She later considers instructing a man to poison Romeo (Act 3, Scene 5, lines 88–91).

When Juliet is found (apparently) dead in her bed, Lady Capulet cries out in grief that her life is not worth living without her only child:

O me, O me! My child, my only life!

Revive, look up, or I will die with thee!

Help, help! Call help!

(Act 4, Scene 5, lines 19–21)

When she arrives at Juliet's tomb and discovers the truth about her daughter, her first thought is not for Juliet or Romeo, but still for herself:

O me! This sight of death is as a bell

That warns my old age to a sepulchre.

(Act 5, Scene 3, lines 206–7)

This reference to 'old age' should not be taken literally. It may be that she feels too old to continue living, or simply a statement that the older parent should be in the grave before the younger child.

Mercutio

sociable
unromantic
coarse
plain-speaking
lively

entertaining
creative
articulate
mocking
witty
intelligent
loyal
fiery

Mercutio is one of the two principal comic characters in the play, the other being the Nurse.

Mercutio is not involved in the feud. He is neither a Montague nor a Capulet, but a relative of Prince Escalus. He is invited to the feast given by the Capulets, but at the same time is a close friend of Romeo and Benvolio, who are both Montagues.

Mercutio provides an interesting contrast to Romeo. Mercutio is sociable and witty whereas Romeo is moody and withdrawn. Mercutio's intelligence is at the other extreme from Romeo's passion. Mercutio listens to his head and Romeo to his heart. Romeo is a romantic dreamer whereas Mercutio, like the Nurse, takes an unromantic view of love. Mercutio is the champion of plain speaking, and sometimes of coarse language. He has no time for Romeo's idealistic fantasies about Rosaline and is suspicious of the strength of Romeo's feelings.

Mercutio is the most lively and dazzling of the characters in the play. He is an entertainer, gifted at playing with language, making puns and speeches full of flights of fancy. These speeches reveal his highly creative and insightful imagination; for example, his famous Queen Mab speech (Act 1, Scene 4, lines 53–95). They also show that he is a realist; he is not subject to delusions.

We appreciate Mercutio best as he makes his exit from the play, having been fatally wounded by Tybalt. As he is dying, he gives a wonderful, mocking speech, which is both deeply felt and grimly comic:

> *Ask for me tomorrow, and you shall find me a grave man. I am peppered, I warrant, for this world. A plague a' both your houses! Zounds, a dog, a rat, a mouse, a cat, to scratch a man to death! A braggart, a rogue, a villain, that fights by the book of arithmetic!*

(Act 3, Scene 1, lines 95–100)

Mercutio's curse, 'A plague a' both your houses', is significant. In Shakespeare's time a dying man's curse was believed to bring bad luck to those at whom it was directed, in this case the Montagues and the Capulets. His is the first death in the play; others will follow as a consequence.

Mercutio's death is dramatically necessary. It is the key moment in the tragedy since it spurs Romeo to act wrongly and take revenge, which in turn leads to his banishment and from that to the complications leading to his and Juliet's deaths.

It is interesting to consider the circumstances leading to Mercutio's death and what these tell us about his character. Romeo has a valid reason for declining to fight Tybalt. Juliet, the woman he has just married, is Tybalt's cousin. However, the marriage has not been made public and so no one else present can understand his refusal.

Mercutio feels that he must defend Romeo's honour, since Romeo refuses to defend it himself. This is clear from his challenge to Tybalt:

> O calm, dishonourable, vile submission!
>
> **Alla stoccata** *carries it away.*
>
> *Tybalt, you ratcatcher, will you walk?*
>
> (Act 3, Scene 1, lines 69–71)

In the first of these lines Mercutio is expressing contempt for Romeo's refusal to fight Tybalt and so defend his own honour; in the second, he is deploring the fact that Romeo's refusal means that Tybalt, wielder of the sword ('*Alla stoccata*'), gets away with calling Romeo a villain; and in the third, he is asking Tybalt, the cat with nine lives, to fight a duel.

Tybalt's response suggests that he is not particularly keen to fight Mercutio: 'What wouldst thou have with me?' (line 72). It is only when Mercutio threatens to beat him around the ears with his sword if he refuses to fight that Tybalt feels he has no choice. Given that Tybalt is usually spoiling for a fight, but has also turned down the chance of a duel with Mercutio earlier in the same scene, preferring to fight Romeo instead, it is possible that Mercutio's swordsmanship is superior to Tybalt's.

In turn, this implies that had the duel gone ahead without interference from Romeo, Mercutio would probably have won. Tybalt makes the sneaky strike that kills Mercutio during the confusion caused by Romeo's and Benvolio's intervention.

What might have happened if Romeo had not intervened and Mercutio had killed Tybalt? Well, Mercutio would have survived and the Prince (his relative) might, or might not, have sentenced him to death or, more likely, to banishment. Romeo would have avoided banishment, Juliet would not have been sad and Capulet would have had no reason to change his mind about delaying her wedding until she was sixteen. The feud between the Montagues and Capulets might well have died with Tybalt, in the absence of anybody else to keep it going. Montague and Capulet would then have been reconciled at some point, and the marriage of Romeo and Juliet would have been accepted by both families. Mercutio was on the point of bringing all of this to pass when the well-meaning action of Romeo ('I thought all for the best'; Act 3, Scene 1, line 102) turned the play to tragedy.

Tybalt

menacing
quarrelsome
troublemaker
fighter
killer
hate-filled
vengeful
violent
provocative
uncontrollable
temperamental
negative
destructive
villainous
angry

Tybalt, who is Lady Capulet's nephew, is a menacing character, a constant threat to peace and order in Verona. He appears to have no useful thing to do but roam the city flexing his muscles and causing trouble.

Hatred of all Montagues is his principal motive for taking action. This is made clear as soon as he makes his first appearance. In Act 1, Scene 1 he interrupts the ridiculous quarrel of the servants as Benvolio (a Montague) is trying to make peace. Tybalt's first impulse is to challenge Benvolio to a duel, with the intention of killing him: 'Turn thee, Benvolio, look upon thy death' (Act 1, Scene 1, line 60). When Benvolio declines to fight, Tybalt shows his contempt for a Montague who desires peace:

What, drawn, and talk of peace? I hate the word
As I hate hell, all Montagues, and thee.
Have at thee, coward!

(Act 1, Scene 1, lines 63–5)

Tybalt's desire is to keep the traditional feud between the Capulets and the Montagues going, since if peace is declared, his career as a specialist in the art of killing will be at an end. This explains his attempt to provoke Benvolio.

On this occasion, the arrival of Prince Escalus prevents further violence. However, Tybalt soon finds another opportunity to cause trouble, his victim this time being Romeo. Romeo is present, in disguise, at the Capulets' feast. When Tybalt recognises him he calls for his rapier and declares, 'To strike him dead I hold it not a sin' (Act 1, Scene 5, line 57). Capulet defends Romeo but Tybalt persists until Capulet forces him to leave. As he goes, he trembles with anger and vows revenge on Romeo (lines 87–90).

Tybalt's violent nature, his uncontrollable urge to kill, is demonstrated in its most dramatic form in Act 3, Scene 1, the turning-point of the play. Tybalt is searching for Romeo. When Romeo makes an appearance, Tybalt has found his target: 'Here comes my man' (line 52). The standard way to provoke a duel was to call somebody a villain, so this is what Tybalt does. However, Romeo is eager to make peace with Tybalt, who is Juliet's cousin and now related to Romeo through his secret marriage.

Instead, Mercutio fights Tybalt. Tybalt engages in foul play by thrusting his sword under Romeo's arm and fatally wounding the unsuspecting Mercutio. He leaves the scene, but quickly returns in a furious rage, determined to kill Romeo. Romeo, angered by Mercutio's death, loses his self-control and fights and kills Tybalt. As a result of Tybalt's intervention in the lives of others, two people die within minutes of each other: Mercutio and Tybalt himself; and Romeo will be banished from Verona.

Tybalt's role in the play is entirely negative. Without him, the old feud between the Montagues and the Capulets would have had a better chance of fading away, since the heads of the two families and their wives show little interest in keeping it going, and the Prince wants to suppress it, as we see in Act 1, Scene 1. Tybalt not only wants to maintain the feud, but also to extend it. The result is that the play features the deaths of four young and admirable characters (Romeo, Juliet, Mercutio and Paris), as well as the deaths of Tybalt and Lady Montague.

Tybalt's opposite in the play is Benvolio, who tries as hard to avoid or settle quarrels as Tybalt does to start and multiply them.

The characters who have the greatest influence on what happens in *Romeo and Juliet* are Friar Laurence and Tybalt. In their totally different ways, and for totally different reasons, these two characters help to shape events and outcomes, especially tragic ones, to a major extent.

Tybalt is the only significant character of whom nothing good can be said. He is the villain of the play. He is very consistent: full of anger and aggression, hot-headed and quarrelsome, the kind of person who feels only rage, an enemy of peace, always spoiling for a fight, acting without any rational motive, a professional troublemaker, lacking a sense of responsibility, filled with hatred, specialising in insulting others and violent in the extreme.

Tybalt's fate is to live by the sword and to die by the sword.

Benvolio

friendly
peacemaker
honest
reliable
fair-minded
trusted
balanced
reasonable
loyal
positive
caring

Benvolio is Romeo's cousin and his friend. He is the only member of either feuding family who tries to restore peace when the fight between the servants of the Montagues and the Capulets breaks out on the street: 'Part, fools! Put up your swords. You know not what you do' (Act 1, Scene 1, lines 57–8).

In the fateful scene during which Mercutio is killed by Tybalt, it is Benvolio who tries to convince Mercutio to go home and avoid trouble (Act 3, Scene 1, lines 1–2). He reminds Mercutio and Tybalt that they must not fight in public, which the Prince has already forbidden on pain of death. He suggests three practical ways of avoiding this punishment: to continue their business elsewhere; to discuss their differences calmly; or to leave separately (lines 46–9). Unfortunately, both Mercutio and Tybalt refuse to follow Benvolio's advice.

It is Benvolio who is asked by the Prince to say who began the fight that led to the deaths of Mercutio and Tybalt. The Prince, himself a wise and fair judge, asks Benvolio because he knows he will hear the truth from him. Benvolio gives an honest and balanced account, as an impartial judge might.

Benvolio (whose name suggests goodwill) is a loyal friend who always has Romeo's welfare at heart. Romeo's parents turn to Benvolio when they need someone to help them understand their son's depression. He tries to find Romeo when he leaves the Capulets' feast alone, wanting to be sure that Romeo is all right, but gives up searching when he realises that Romeo does not want to be found (Act 2, Scene 1, lines 41–2).

Benvolio is sympathetic to the miserable Romeo, whose love for Rosaline is not returned, but also practical and urges him to focus his attentions elsewhere. He realises that Romeo's love for her is not real and that she will be easily replaced in his affections.

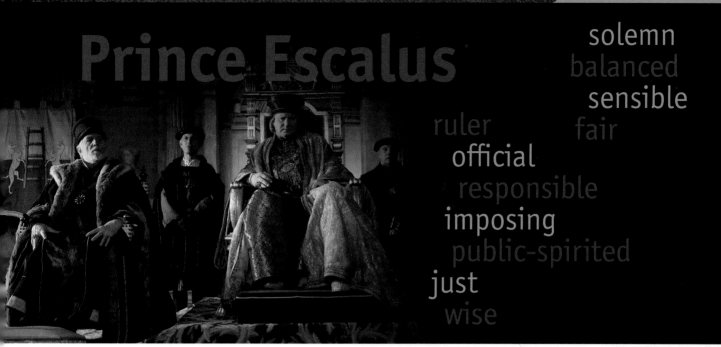

Prince Escalus

solemn
balanced
sensible
ruler   fair
official
responsible
imposing
public-spirited
just
wise

Prince Escalus of Verona, as well as being ruler of the city, is also its chief magistrate. He is responsible for enforcing the law and for keeping order in the city.

His biggest problem is the long-standing feud between two prominent families in the city, the Montagues and the Capulets. Rival supporters of these families engage in street riots that disturb the peace of Verona, as we see in Act 1, Scene 1 and Act 3, Scene 1.

The Prince's intervention in Act 1, Scene 1 shows his attitude to these riots. He refers to those taking part as: 'Rebellious subjects, enemies to peace' (line 74) and 'beasts, that quench the fire of your pernicious rage with purple fountains issuing from your veins' (lines 76–8). He threatens those who riot in the streets that in the future: 'Your lives shall pay the forfeit of the peace' (line 90). In other words, death will be the penalty for any more breaches of the peace.

The Prince is a just magistrate with an interest in the welfare of the city and an understanding of its needs. Above all, he recognises what will happen to everyone in Verona if the Montagues and the Capulets do not end their feud. He sees the feud as a wound in the body of the city, which must be healed. He knows from the beginning that keeping the peace is a matter of life and death.

The Prince's three appearances in the play are always at moments of crisis. His first is a solemn, official one (Act 1, Scene 1) when he acts decisively to stop a riot and then lays down the law (the death penalty) for future rioters.

On his second appearance (Act 3, Scene 1) he is accompanied by Montague and Capulet, their wives and followers. His purpose this time is to find out who began the brawl that led to the deaths of Mercutio (his own relative) and Tybalt (a Capulet). He shows wisdom in choosing Benvolio as his witness. His banishment of Romeo, rather than a sentence of death, is fair in the circumstances.

His third appearance is in the final scene of the play, when his task is to discover the cause of the tragic deaths of Romeo, Juliet and Paris (another member of his own family). Having heard the evidence supplied by Friar Laurence, Romeo's servant Balthasar and Paris's Page, the Prince turns his attention to Capulet and Montague, blaming them and their feud: 'See what a scourge is laid upon your hate' (Act 5, Scene 3, lines 292).

It is to the Prince's credit that he is prepared to take a share of the blame for not being active enough in dealing with the violence arising from the feud:

And I, for winking at your discords too,

Have lost a brace of kinsmen.

(Act 5, Scene 3, lines 294–5)

The two ('brace of') kinsmen the Prince is lamenting are Mercutio and Paris.

Paris

polite
civilised
respectful
tactful
unaware
sincere
eligible
devoted
honourable
noble
good
honest
straightforward
blameless
unfortunate

Paris is a handsome nobleman and a member of the Prince's family. Juliet's father, Capulet, decides that Juliet should marry Paris.

We first meet Paris in Act 1, Scene 2 and can see why Capulet might favour him as a future husband for his only daughter. Capulet confides in Paris, confessing that men as old as Montague and himself should be able to keep the peace. Paris is polite and respectful, paying tribute to Capulet's and Montague's honourable reputations. This provides him with a suitable opening to raise the subject of his wish to marry Juliet.

Capulet's reply shows how much he values Paris. Although he does not want Juliet to marry until she is sixteen, he encourages Paris to persist in making himself agreeable to Juliet: 'But woo her, gentle Paris, get her heart' (Act 1, Scene 2, line 16).

The problem for Paris is that despite the admiration of Capulet, Lady Capulet and the Nurse for his many fine qualities, Juliet is not particularly impressed. When Lady Capulet asks her whether she would be favourable to Paris as a suitor, her reply is less than enthusiastic (Act 1, Scene 3, lines 98–100). When she meets Romeo, however, and instantly decides that she can never marry anybody else, Paris can have no hope of winning her love.

Paris is a sorry victim of cruel circumstances. Capulet's comment on events in general applies particularly to Paris: 'Things have fallen out, sir, so unluckily' (Act 3, Scene 4, line 1). Paris does not know, nor does Capulet, that Juliet is already married, as he and Capulet plan his marriage to Juliet in a few days' time (lines 19–30). Paris anticipates the proposed wedding with enthusiasm: 'My lord, I would that Thursday were tomorrow' (line 29).

Paris goes through an awkward meeting with Juliet at Friar Laurence's cell. He is unaware of his true position in relation to Juliet. She gives him no hint that she is married; neither does Friar Laurence. Juliet brings their conversation to an end by turning to Friar Laurence for confession. The Friar dismisses him abruptly: 'My lord, we must entreat the time alone' (Act 4, Scene 1, line 40). Paris accepts this dismissal gracefully and tactfully:

> *God shield I should disturb devotion!*
>
> *Juliet, on Thursday early will I rouse ye.*
>
> *Till then, adieu, and keep this holy kiss.*
>
> (Act 4, Scene 1, lines 41–3)

The unfortunate Paris leaves, trying to convince himself that Juliet is willing to marry him. Meanwhile, Juliet is revealing her true feelings to Friar Laurence:

> *O bid me leap, rather than marry Paris,*
>
> *From off the battlements of any tower*
>
> (Act 4, Scene 1, lines 77–8)

Friar Laurence gives Juliet advice that can only add to the misery Paris must undergo. He suggests that she should consent to marry Paris, but take a sleeping drug that will make her appear dead, so that she may be laid to rest in the Capulets' tomb, where she will awaken to find Romeo waiting to take her to Mantua. In other words, she will give Paris hope for the future and then snatch it away.

Juliet's supposed death causes Paris to suffer intensely; as he himself puts it:

> *Beguiled, divorcèd, wrongèd, spited, slain!*
>
> *Most detestable death, by thee beguiled,*
>
> *By cruel, cruel thee quite overthrown.*
>
> (Act 4, Scene 5, lines 55–7)

The first word of this speech expresses a cruel irony. Paris thinks he has been cheated or deceived ('Beguiled') by death (that of Juliet), but Juliet is not dead at this point, merely sleeping. He has, however, been cheated and deceived, by being prevented from knowing that, almost from the beginning, his hope of marrying Juliet was a false one.

His visit to the graveyard with flowers to strew on Juliet's tomb shows Paris's dignity. He makes a moving promise to honour her death in a sincere and fitting way (Act 5, Scene 3, lines 12–17). This rhymed poem expresses sorrow for Juliet and his determination to make nightly visits to her grave to mourn her contrasts favourably with Romeo's despair and suicide when he thinks she is dead.

Paris is still unaware that Romeo is Juliet's husband. When he sees Romeo beginning to open the tomb, he assumes he is about 'to do some villainous shame to the dead bodies' (Act 5, Scene 3, lines 52–3). His insistence on trying to arrest Romeo as a criminal brings about his own death. Romeo tries to persuade Paris to walk away, but he refuses. Romeo is determined to enter the tomb and so he kills Paris.

Much can be said in favour of Paris. He is a model of correct behaviour in his dealings with Capulet and Juliet. He does the honourable thing (for the time) in asking Capulet's approval for his wooing of Juliet. His behaviour in this regard is in contrast to Romeo's secretive dealings. Paris always respects and honours Juliet. He is an innocent victim of circumstances created by others, and certainly does not deserve to die.

Shakespeare takes great care to show the nobility and goodness of Paris. He is remarkable for his honesty, his good manners and his tact. No blame can be attached to him for anything that goes wrong in the course of the action.

Paris's dying wish is that he be buried alongside Juliet. It seems that his love for her is true and sincere. Romeo recognises this and considers Paris a fellow loser in love: 'one writ with me in sour misfortune's book' (Act 5, Scene 3, line 82).

The following diagram illustrates the relationships and interactions between the characters in *Romeo and Juliet*.

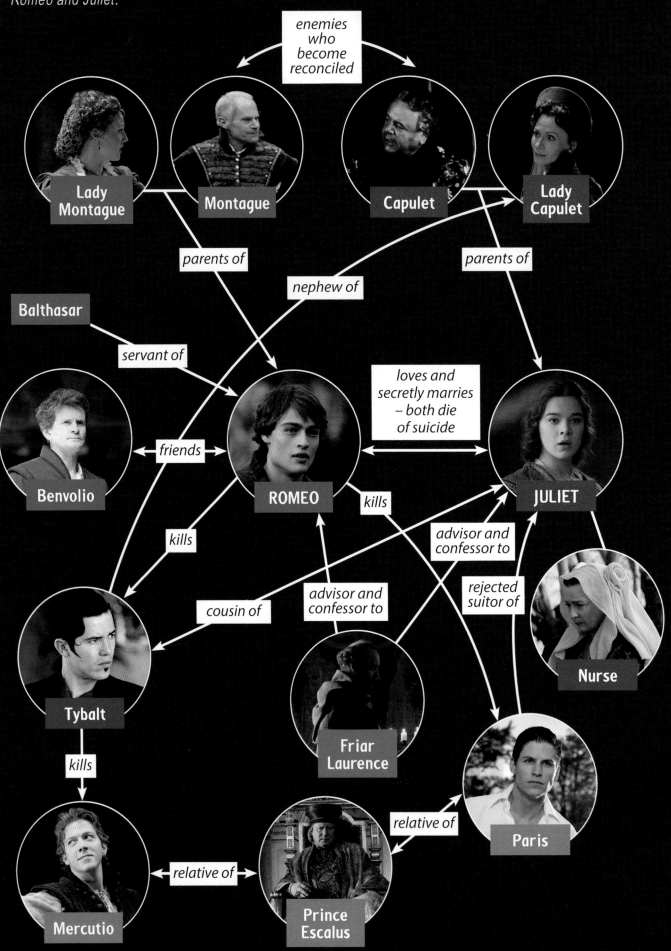

Love Hatred
Fate
Chance

Love

Love is a stronger force in the play than hatred, and is demonstrated in many more characters.

The 'star-crossed lovers'

The love of Romeo for Juliet and her love for him is the central theme of the play. On both sides, it is love at first sight and involves total commitment. They are entirely absorbed with each other: nothing or nobody else matters to them.

Their intense relationship and the secrecy with which it is surrounded leads to serious problems for both of them. Their secret and sudden marriage causes most of these problems.

Juliet commits herself to Romeo after the briefest of meetings, and before she knows his identity:

> *Go ask his name. If he be marrièd,*
> *My grave is like to be my wedding bed.*
>
> (Act 1, Scene 5, lines 132–3)

On their second meeting, she declares her unconditional love for him, even before he asks for this: 'I gave thee mine before thou didst request it' (Act 2, Scene 2, line 128).

The quality of Juliet's love for Romeo is frankly expressed to him in her most moving speech:

> *My bounty is as boundless as the sea,*
> *My love as deep. The more I give to thee,*
> *The more I have, for both are infinite.*
>
> (Act 2, Scene 2, lines 133–5)

Romeo's love for her is equally intense. He cannot bear the thought of separation from her. After his banishment from Verona, which to him means nothing other than banishment from Juliet, he says:

> *'Tis torture, and not mercy. Heaven is here,*
> *Where Juliet lives.*
>
> (Act 3, Scene 3, lines 29–30)

Have not saints lips,
and holy palmers too?

ROMEO, Act 1, Scene 5, 99

When Romeo thinks he may never see Juliet again, he prefers to die rather than live without her, and attempts to stab himself, only to be restrained by the Nurse. As for Juliet, when she is confronted with the threat of being married to Paris, and losing Romeo forever, she too prefers death: 'If all else fail, myself have power to die' (Act 3, Scene 5, line 243).

Finally, when Romeo thinks the sleeping Juliet is dead, he decides to join her by poisoning himself. Had he reacted less hastily, they would have been reunited when she awoke. When she wakes and finds him dead, she stabs herself to death with his dagger. Their love means so much to each of them that life without the other seems empty and meaningless. The world that surrounds them has no place for a love like theirs.

Their love is not the love of ordinary people who live in the real world. It is the love of two dramatic characters from the world of fiction.

Paris's love

Romeo and Juliet are not the only characters whose love is never in doubt. To achieve contrast, Shakespeare might have made Paris an unpleasant rival of Romeo's for Juliet's affections. Instead, he makes him thoroughly noble and honest and a suitable match for Juliet. Paris's love is as sincere as Romeo's, but is free from the extremes of emotion to which Romeo is prone. Romeo's love is passionate in the way it is expressed, whereas Paris is more restrained and gentle.

In the scene where Capulet offers him Juliet in marriage, Paris does not become wildly enthusiastic, as Romeo might in similar circumstances, but confines his expression of joy to a single sentence: 'My lord, I would that Thursday were tomorrow' (Act 3, Scene 4, line 29). Later, assuming that Juliet's distress must be due to Tybalt's death, he treats her with understanding and sympathy:

> *Immoderately she weeps for Tybalt's death,*
> *And therefore have I little talked of love*
>
> (Act 4, Scene 1, lines 6–7)

Paris has already shown the same consideration for her feelings in his conversation with Capulet. Anxious as he is to marry Juliet, he has sufficient tact and delicacy not to intrude on the family's grief. In the Friar's cell, the depth of his feeling for her is conveyed in his comment: 'Poor soul, thy face is much abused with tears' (Act 4, Scene 1, line 29).

The irony here is that Paris also deserves sympathy. His bright hopes are expressed in his greeting to her as she arrives at Friar Laurence's cell: 'Happily met, my lady and my wife!' (Act 4, Scene 1, line 18). As he speaks these words, he does not know that his hopes of sharing his love with Juliet can never be fulfilled.

The love Paris has for Juliet is lasting, even after her supposed death. He comes to the churchyard to do honour to her tomb, something he intends to do every night:

> The obsequies [ceremonies] that I for thee will keep
> Nightly shall be to strew thy grave and weep.
>
> (Act 5, Scene 3, lines 16–17)

Paris still regards Juliet as his 'true love' (Act 5, Scene 3, line 20). When he sees Romeo approach the tomb, he thinks of him as the enemy who killed Juliet's cousin Tybalt, thereby causing Juliet to die of grief. He imagines that Romeo has 'come to do some villainous shame' (line 52) to the dead bodies of Juliet and Tybalt, and tries to arrest him to prevent this. The best evidence of his love for Juliet comes with his dying words to Romeo:

> O, I am slain! If thou be merciful,
> Open the tomb, lay me with Juliet.
>
> (Act 5, Scene 3, lines 72–3)

Parental love

The love of parents for their children should also be considered. For example, the Montagues show great concern for Romeo's miserable mood at the start of the play and would love to be able to help him:

> Could we but learn from whence his sorrows grow,
> We would as willingly give cure as know.
>
> (Act 1, Scene 1, lines 147–8)

The main parent–child relationship in the play is the one between the Capulets and Juliet. Looking at his angry treatment of Juliet in Act 3, Scene 5, some audience members feel that Capulet is a tyrant. But the play as a whole shows him to be a father who loves his daughter and who is deeply concerned to ensure her future welfare.

For example, when Paris mentions the possibility of marriage to Juliet, Capulet's first thought is to protect her from the dangers of marriage at too young an age. He does not want his only child to marry before she is sixteen. His deep regard for her is clear: 'Earth hath swallowed all my hopes but she; she's the hopeful lady of my earth' (Act 1, Scene 2, lines 14–15).

Capulet's love for Juliet is best shown in his concern for her future happiness. This hope is frustrated when Juliet marries Romeo without his knowledge, never mind his permission. She continues to deceive her parents by keeping them in ignorance of this marriage. Knowing nothing about it, Capulet encourages Paris, a good and virtuous man, to regard Juliet as his future wife. Capulet does this in good faith, not because he wants to impose his will on Juliet, but because he wants the best for her.

Given the information that he has, Capulet cannot be faulted for promoting Paris as Juliet's future husband. He does not know that Juliet has married Romeo. He does not know that her grief is over the banishment of Romeo, and not, as everybody else thinks, over the death of Tybalt. He firmly believes that Paris is likely to make an ideal husband for Juliet, and is frustrated that Juliet appears not to realise what her best interests are. It is because he loves her that he becomes angry.

Both Capulet and Lady Capulet express genuine shock and sorrow when their daughter is found (apparently) dead in bed at the start of Act 4, Scene 5. The loss of their only child affects them deeply. Similarly, Montague reports that Lady Montague has died of a broken heart following Romeo's banishment. When they discover the truth about Romeo and Juliet, the love of these parents for their children proves stronger than their families' feud, and so their children's deaths bring about their reconciliation.

Hatred

Hatred is ever-present in the play in the form of the long-standing feud between the Montagues and the Capulets, which is best represented by Tybalt.

Montague–Capulet feud

When we say that the Montague and Capulet families are involved in a feud, we mean that the members of each family treat the members of the other family as their enemies. The Capulets have grown up to feel that they must hate all Montagues, and the Montagues have grown up to feel that they must hate all Capulets. The bad feeling is shared by the staff of the two households, who also hate each other.

When Capulets and Montagues meet in public places, fights and assaults easily occur, sometimes resulting in death. During the Capulets' feast, Tybalt recognises Romeo and immediately wants to kill him or drive him out simply because Romeo is a Montague and should not be at the Capulets' home (Act 1, Scene 5, lines 52–7). When Juliet falls in love with Romeo, she realises how unlucky she is that the only man she can ever love is the son of the one family she must hate: 'My only love, sprung from my only hate!' (Act 1, Scene 5, line 136).

What is the cause of this feud? How or when did it start? The play does not answer these questions. The Prologue informs us that the feud began long ago with some quarrel or grudge that nobody can remember, and that generations of both families have kept this quarrel alive. It also tells us that it will take the deaths of Romeo and Juliet to end the feud.

The action of *Romeo and Juliet* takes place inside five days: from a Sunday to the following Thursday. As far as the feud is concerned, Tybalt's death at the heart of the action is a major turning-point (Act 3, Scene 1, line 129). Before his death there were signs that the feud had almost run its course, and that several characters would like to see it end.

The heads of the feuding families, Capulet and Montague, do not appear to be fierce leaders at war with each other, or to want to inspire their followers to do the same. For example, when Capulet, wearing his fireside gown, shuffles to the scene of a minor disorder and calls for his sword, we cannot take him seriously as a feuding rioter. Lady Capulet tells him bluntly that it is not a sword, but a crutch that an old man like him should be looking for (Act 1, Scene 1, line 69).

Similarly, Montague speaks some fiery words, but he cannot follow these up with actions, because his wife plucks his arm and prevents him from joining in the riot: 'Thou shalt not stir one foot to seek a foe' (Act 1, Scene 1, line 73).

It is true that the Prince says:

> *Three civil brawls, bred of an airy word*
> *By thee, old Capulet, and Montague,*
> *Have thrice disturbed the quiet of our streets*
> (Act 1, Scene 1, lines 82–4)

However, the latest brawl, which the Prince has witnessed, seems to involve a lot of posturing, and is quickly brought to an end. Montague and Capulet are bound by the Prince to keep the peace. Later Capulet remarks that it is not hard for men as old as they are to cease feuding (Act 1, Scene 2, lines 2–3).

Other characters are in favour of bringing an end to the feud. Paris thinks it is a pity that the Montagues and Capulets have lived at odds for so long (Act 1, Scene 2, line 5). Benvolio, a Montague, is a constant peacemaker. He tries to suppress a brawl involving rival sets of servants, and invites Tybalt, a Capulet, to assist him in the effort (Act 1, Scene 1, lines 61–2). Later, Benvolio advises his friends to avoid trouble by keeping out of the way of the Capulets (Act 3, Scene 1, lines 1–4). When the excitable Mercutio invites Tybalt to fight, Benvolio tries to preserve the peace, asking them to go somewhere private to try to resolve their differences (lines 46–9).

It is worth noting that Capulet does not want the fiery Tybalt to renew the feud at the feast, saying of Romeo: 'I would not for the wealth of all the town here in my house do him disparagement' (Act 1, Scene 5, lines 67–8). He is willing to force his own relative, Tybalt, to leave rather than have him start a quarrel with Romeo. It seems that he thinks so little of the feud that he will not let it interrupt a party. This incident also shows that he admires Romeo, the son of his enemy Montague.

The feud survives mainly in a few high-spirited, hot-blooded young men, and among the servants of both households. Tybalt, by seeking out Romeo to challenge him, provides the excuse for a renewal of old hatreds. Once Tybalt dies, the ancient feud revives for a time. Lady Capulet, Tybalt's aunt, wants the Prince to have Romeo put to death, because 'Romeo slew Tybalt. Romeo must not live' (Act 3, Scene 1, line 179). Later, she comes up with a plan to have Romeo poisoned in Mantua (Act 3, Scene 5, lines 88–91).

As we were told in the Prologue, the feud ends with the deaths of Juliet, Capulet's daughter, and Romeo, Montague's son. The Prince observes that Capulet and Montague have been cruelly punished for whatever hatred they and their families have felt for each other: 'See what a scourge is laid upon your hate' (Act 5, Scene 3, line 292). Capulet and Montague then lay their hatred aside and shake hands. The feud can be seen as the means by which fate acts to bring about the tragic ending, and the tragic ending is the means by which the feud must end.

Tybalt's hatred

The one character who carries hate with him wherever he goes is Tybalt. He is not ashamed to acknowledge his hatred, which is mainly directed at members of the Montague family. He sums up his outlook when he tells the peacemaker Benvolio that he hates him, and all other Montagues, as much as he hates hell:

> *What, drawn, and talk of peace? I hate the word*
> *As I hate hell, all Montagues, and thee.*
> *Have at thee, coward!*
>
> (Act 1, Scene 1, line 63–5)

He expresses his hatred not only in words but also in action: whenever he appears, he provokes, or tries to provoke, anybody connected to the Montagues to a duel with the intention of killing them. While other characters are losing interest in the hateful feud, Tybalt works to keep it going.

Tybalt's death midway through the play revives dying hatreds for a while, especially in his aunt, Lady Capulet, who wants Romeo, who has killed him, put to death: 'Prince, as thou art true, for blood of ours shed blood of Montague' (Act 3, Scene 1, lines 146–8).

Fate

We are reminded of the power of fate throughout the play. Fate is the idea that some unseen power decides and governs everything that will happen to a person from birth to death. A person who believes that all events are decided in advance by fate is called a fatalist.

Before the play gets under way, we are warned that we are about to see how fate works:

> *From forth the fatal loins of these two foes*
> *A pair of star-crossed lovers take their life*
>
> (Prologue, lines 5–6)

The Prologue tells us that the two feuding families (the Capulets and the Montagues) are cursed by fate, and that a girl from one family and a boy from the other are doomed by the stars to become lovers and to take their own lives.

From the beginning, therefore, we are given the impression that a cruel fate is working against the happiness and lives of the two main characters. The term 'star-crossed lovers' means that they were born under unlucky stars, and doomed from birth to see their best hopes disappointed. No matter what they or others do, there is no chance that Romeo and Juliet will avoid the tragedy that fate has in store for them. Their destiny cannot be changed.

As the play progresses, Romeo and Juliet sense that fate is working against them, and express this idea quite often. Romeo, as he makes his way (in disguise) to the home of the Capulets, shudders at the thought that some unknown terror is lying in wait to destroy him. He fears that the feast he is going to will somehow lead to his early death:

> *For my mind misgives*
> *Some consequence, yet hanging in the stars,*
> *Shall bitterly begin his fearful date*
> *With this night's revels and expire the term*
> *Of a despisèd life, closed in my breast,*
> *By some vile forfeit of untimely death.*
>
> (Act 1, Scene 4, lines 106–11)

Juliet senses that the happiness she gets from her love for Romeo is too great to last, that it will leave her suddenly and without warning. She feels it is 'too like the lightning, which doth cease to be ere one can say "It lightens"' (Act 2, Scene 2, lines 119–20).

Even though the main characters act for the best, fate has arranged things so that their actions, more often than not, turn out for the worst. There is a good example of this in Act 3, Scene 1, when Romeo's well-meaning attempt to halt the fight between Tybalt and Mercutio results in Mercutio's death. All that Romeo can say is: 'I thought all for the best' (line 102).

The unintended outcome of Romeo's best efforts teaches him that fate has arranged incidents such as Mercutio's death to bring about further tragedies. One piece of bad luck leads to another:

> *This day's black fate on more days doth depend.*
> *This but begins the woe others must end.*
>
> (Act 3, Scene 1, lines 117–18)

As Romeo leaves her to go to Mantua, Juliet wonders if they will ever meet again. In spite of Romeo's efforts to console her, she has a horrifying, and true, vision of the future:

> *O God, I have an ill-divining soul!*
> *Methinks I see thee, now thou art so low,*
> *As one dead in the bottom of a tomb.*
>
> (Act 3, Scene 5, lines 54–6)

Here she paints an accurate picture of what fate has in store for both of them. The next time she sees him, he will be lying dead beside her as she wakes in the tomb.

Act 5 contains some striking comments on the workings of fate, with Romeo and Juliet as its victims. One notable example is found at the beginning of Act 5, Scene 1, when Romeo says: 'I dreamt my lady came and found me dead' (line 6). The dream, however, ends happily and Romeo is feeling positive about the future. Almost immediately Romeo's hopes are shattered by the arrival of his servant Balthasar with news that Juliet is dead. Romeo blames the stars that were present at his birth, but intends to fight against his fate: 'Then I defy you, stars!' (line 24).

Romeo can think of only one way to avoid his fate, and that is to take his own life. Balthasar's news is incorrect, but when Romeo hears it, he, in despair, buys the poison that will kill him. In this way, fate will no longer be able to punish him. By dying in Juliet's tomb, he will deprive his unlucky stars of their power:

> *And shake the yoke of inauspicious stars*
> *From this world-wearied flesh.*
>
> (Act 5, Scene 3, lines 111–12)

Friar Laurence tries to take on the role of a 'kindly fate' in the play as he attempts to direct the lives of Romeo and Juliet. He makes clever and elaborate plans for their happiness but these go disastrously wrong. The cruel fate that is governing the lives of the two young lovers is more powerful than anything Friar Laurence can do to oppose it:

> *A greater power than we can contradict*
> *Hath thwarted our intents.*
>
> (Act 5, Scene 3, lines 153–4)

Shakespeare's treatment of fate in the play reflects the widely held views of his time. It was believed that human beings could never be out of the range of the blows of fate. The stars were thought to govern the course of everybody's life, from birth to death. Tragedies such as *Romeo and Juliet* are founded on the idea that life offers no escape from destiny.

Modern audiences may find it hard to believe that our lives are ruled by fate, or that the fortunes of human beings are written in the stars. However, if what happens to Romeo and Juliet is decided by fate, then we cannot argue that they are responsible for their own downfall. It was unavoidable. Can we blame other characters in the play? For example, is Friar Laurence responsible? Or the parents of the two lovers? Or the troublemaker Tybalt? Or the society in which Romeo and Juliet have grown up, and the feud between their families? Or is it a combination of all these factors that led to their deaths?

Unawareness

Fate does not use a human villain or a supernatural being to bring about the sad destiny of Romeo and Juliet. Instead it relies on human unawareness or ignorance of the facts.

Characters often act without knowing the truth about the situation in which they find themselves. They observe terrible events, which some of them have helped to cause by doing things in ignorance of where these events might lead. No character in the play has access to all the knowledge that the audience is given by Shakespeare.

One simple example of this involves the First Watchman in Act 5, Scene 3. He cannot understand how Juliet, who has been buried for two days, is still bleeding and warm (lines 175–6) or, as he puts it later, 'Juliet, dead before, warm and new killed' (lines 196–7). However, we know what he does not know: that Juliet has not been

dead for two days but had taken drugs to make it appear as though she was, and that she has not been killed but has killed herself.

Even Prince Escalus is not aware of major happenings in the city he rules, and has to ask: 'What misadventure is so early up, that calls our person from our morning's rest?' (Act 5, Scene 3, lines 188–9). Those who have watched the play from the beginning are reminded that they have full knowledge of events, about which the characters remain in the dark. The Prince silences those around him until the truth about the deaths of Romeo, Juliet and Paris can be established ('Till we can clear these ambiguities'; line 217).

If they do see thee, they will murder thee.

JULIET, Act 2, Scene 2, 70

Friar Laurence knows more than any other character about what has led to these tragic deaths. He has to tell the others that Romeo and Juliet were married; that Juliet was grieving for Romeo, not for Tybalt; that he, Friar Laurence, gave Juliet a sleeping drug; that his letter telling Romeo of this drug was accidentally delayed; that when he arrived at the tomb, Romeo and Paris were dead; and that Juliet killed herself when she found Romeo dead. The other characters were unaware of all these events.

However, even Friar Laurence is not aware of everything. He does not know how Romeo or Paris came to be in the tomb. Paris's Page fills in one gap when he tells the Prince that Paris had come 'with flowers to strew his lady's grave' (line 281), but he does not know that the lady in question was Romeo's wife. Balthasar provides details of travelling from Mantua with Romeo.

Having heard what everyone has to say, the Prince feels able to tell Capulet and Montague that their feud was the main cause of the tragic deaths of their children. He declares that the feud led fate, or heaven, to invent a way to end it by destroying their children: 'heaven finds means to kill your joys with love' (line 293).

No character knows enough about the means used by fate to kill the young lovers. Only the audience or reader can give a full account of the way in which fate worked, because audience and reader are in possession of all the necessary facts.

Unawareness is a problem almost from the beginning of the play. Both Romeo and Juliet are early victims of this. They fall in love before either knows the identity of the other. The awful consequences of this unawareness become clear to them as soon as they learn the truth. Juliet expresses this best:

> My only love, sprung from my only hate!
> Too early seen unknown, and known too late!
>
> (Act 1, Scene 5, lines 136–7)

Romeo's closest friends, Benvolio and Mercutio, as we learn at the beginning of Act 2, are unaware that Romeo has forgotten Rosaline.

When Romeo joins them in Act 2, Scene 4, he is in good spirits, but Mercutio is unaware of the real reason for this (that he has arranged to marry Juliet).

When, at the beginning of Act 3, Romeo and Mercutio encounter a quarrelsome Tybalt, both Mercutio and Tybalt are unaware that Romeo has just married Juliet, Tybalt's cousin. Had Mercutio and Tybalt known that Romeo had become a relation of the Capulets, they would have understood why he could not fight with Tybalt. Furthermore, there would have been no reason for a duel between Mercutio and Tybalt, or later between Romeo and Tybalt, and two deaths and the banishment of Romeo would have been avoided.

Thus, unawareness of an essential fact is the means used by fate to help seal Romeo's doom. Mercutio and Tybalt die without awareness of the truth of the situation in which they die.

Unawareness is also an essential factor in Capulet's decision to attempt to force Juliet to marry Paris. He does this because he believes it is in her best interests and he is unaware that she is already married. One of the consequences of this unawareness is Juliet's death.

Paris is also a victim of unawareness. In good faith, he relies on Capulet's support and advice in pursuing Juliet, and eventually in thinking she will be his bride. This leads to further complications. But for his pointless pursuit of Juliet (unaware that she is married), Friar Laurence would not be forced to take the drastic step of giving Juliet a sleeping drug, which eventually leads to disaster.

Paris is unaware of the false position he is in both before and after Juliet's death. He takes on the role of Juliet's chief mourner, unaware that this role belongs to her husband, Romeo. When Paris goes to pay tribute at her tomb, he encounters Romeo and meets his death.

Balthasar plays a vital part in contributing to the final disaster when he reaches Romeo at Mantua to tell him that Juliet is dead. He believes this to be true. Again, Balthasar's unawareness that he is giving Romeo false news has disastrous consequences for both Romeo and Juliet.

Chance

Observe how many chance events, accidents and remarkable coincidences are crowded into a few days in the lives of Romeo and Juliet. Observe also how many of these chances, accidents and coincidences are unlucky for them.

The unluckiest chance of all is that the young lovers should happen to be children of families engaged in a long and deadly feud. Juliet comments on this:

> *My only love, sprung from my only hate! …*
> *Prodigious [unlucky] birth of love it is to me*
> *That I must love a loathèd enemy.*
>
> (Act 1, Scene 5, lines 136, 138–9)

It is another unlucky chance that Paris is anxious to marry Juliet at the worst possible time.

Romeo is constantly unlucky, although he always means well. He draws attention to this following his interference in the duel between Mercutio and Tybalt. His attempt to stop this duel accidentally costs Mercutio his life. Romeo comments: 'I thought all for the best' (Act 3, Scene 1, line 102).

Tybalt kills Mercutio and Romeo kills Tybalt in revenge. Imagine what might have happened if Romeo had not intervened. Perhaps Mercutio would have killed Tybalt. Mercutio might then have escaped with a warning from the Prince. Romeo would not have been banished. The feud would have died with Tybalt. The Montagues and Capulets might have been reconciled without further deaths.

It is also down to chance that Friar Laurence's letter to Romeo is prevented from leaving Verona. Friar John is unable to take the letter to Mantua because, before setting out, he chances to enter a house where the plague has struck and he is detained there to prevent it from spreading.

The timing of Romeo's arrival at the tomb is cruelly unlucky. Had he come a little later, he would have found Juliet awake. Instead, Romeo takes the poison just before Juliet awakes and just before Friar Laurence arrives at the tomb.

Friar Laurence is involved in another case of bad timing. The watchmen come as he is trying to persuade Juliet to leave the tomb with him. She refuses, and the Friar, fearful for his own safety, leaves on his own. His absence gives Juliet an opportunity to kill herself with Romeo's dagger.

Paris is also the victim of chance and coincidence. For example, it is unfortunate that his arrival in the churchyard to pay tribute to the supposedly dead Juliet coincides with Romeo's attempt to open her tomb. Because it is night, Romeo does not recognise Paris. He orders him to leave, but Paris refuses, believing that Romeo intends to harm the grave. Afraid that Paris will prevent him from entering the tomb, Romeo kills him. As he takes the hand of the dead Paris, Romeo makes an appropriate comment on his victim as 'One writ with me in sour misfortune's book' (Act 5, Scene 3, line 82).

Timeline

Shakespeare gives a clear indication of the play's time frame. It opens on a Sunday morning and ends, just four days later, at dawn on Thursday. The following table sets out the key events in the play by time and theme.

	Scene	LOVE
Sunday	Act 1, Scene 1	Romeo is besotted with Rosaline, but she does not return his feelings
	Act 1, Scene 2	Paris asks Capulet for Juliet's hand in marriage; Capulet says he must win her love
	Act 1, Scene 3	Lady Capulet tells Juliet to consider marriage to Paris
	Act 1, Scene 4	
	Act 1, Scene 5	Romeo and Juliet fall in love at first sight
	Act 2, Scene 1	Romeo leaves the feast but cannot bear to be away from Juliet and turns back to look for her
	Act 2, Scene 2	Juliet and Romeo declare their love and agree to marry the next day
Monday	Act 2, Scene 3	Friar Laurence agrees to marry Romeo and Juliet in secret
	Act 2, Scene 4	Romeo tells the Nurse of the plans for the secret marriage
	Act 2, Scene 5	The Nurse tells Juliet of the plans for the secret marriage
	Act 2, Scene 6	Juliet and Romeo meet at Friar Laurence's cell to marry in secret
	Act 3, Scene 1	
	Act 3, Scene 2	Juliet is upset at Tybalt's death but decides to remain loyal to Romeo
	Act 3, Scene 3	Juliet's love for him raises Romeo's spirits and his desire to live
	Act 3, Scene 4	Capulet offers Juliet to Paris in marriage to take place on Thursday
Tuesday	Act 3, Scene 5	■ Romeo and Juliet have spent the night together ■ Juliet refuses to marry Paris and is alienated from her family
	Act 4, Scene 1	
	Act 4, Scene 2	
	Act 4, Scene 3	
Wednesday	Act 4, Scene 4	
	Act 4, Scene 5 Act 5, Scene 1 [Mantua]	
	Act 5, Scene 2	
	Act 5, Scene 3	■ Paris arrives in the graveyard at night to pay tribute at Juliet's tomb ■ Romeo arrives at Juliet's tomb to kill himself
Thursday	Act 5, Scene 3	The lovers are dead

HATE (FEUD)	FATE/CHANCE
Street disturbance between Capulets and Montagues	Prince states that any further street violence will be punishable by death
	Capulet's servant cannot read the guest list for the feast and asks Romeo for help. Romeo sees Rosaline's name and decides to go to the feast
	Romeo has a strong sense of foreboding about going to the feast
Tybalt recognises Romeo and wants to kill him; Capulet stops Tybalt and sends him away	■ Romeo and Juliet do not realise who they are falling in love with ■ Tybalt vows to get revenge on Romeo
Tybalt has sent a challenge to Romeo	
■ Tybalt insults Romeo ■ Mercutio challenges Tybalt ■ Tybalt kills Mercutio ■ Romeo kills Tybalt ■ Lady Capulet demands that Romeo be put to death but the Prince banishes him instead	■ Romeo cannot fight Tybalt because they are now related by marriage, but the others do not know this ■ It is Romeo's intervention to stop the fight that allows Tybalt to kill Mercutio ■ Mercutio's dying curse condemns the Montagues and the Capulets
Friar Laurence tells Romeo of his banishment	Romeo intends to kill himself but is stopped by the Nurse
Romeo must leave Verona; he goes to Mantua	Juliet cannot marry Paris because she is already married to Romeo, but her parents do not know this
	Friar Laurence and Juliet make a plan to fake her death to avoid the marriage to Paris
	■ Juliet apologises to her father and says she will marry Paris ■ Capulet is delighted and changes the day of the wedding to Wednesday
	Juliet must now take the sleeping potion a day earlier than the Friar planned
	The Capulets are busy preparing for the wedding, unaware that it cannot take place
	Juliet's 'dead' body is found and the wedding becomes a funeral instead ■ Balthasar tells Romeo that Juliet is dead ■ Romeo buys a deadly poison from the Apothecary
	Friar John tells Friar Laurence that he was unable to deliver the letter to Romeo explaining about Juliet's fake death
	■ Romeo kills Paris ■ Romeo drinks the poison ■ Friar Laurence arrives as Juliet awakes; she refuses to leave with him. He goes to avoid the watchmen ■ Juliet kills herself
The feud is over	■ The Prince and families discover what has happened ■ The families are reconciled

The tragic pattern

The Prologue tells us in advance that the play is a tragedy in which Romeo and Juliet are doomed to take their own lives. Shakespeare has organised the events in the play in such a way that they lead to the deaths of Romeo and Juliet. This is known as the tragic pattern. Romeo and Juliet, and no others, are the tragic characters.

The tragic pattern is as follows:

- Romeo Montague is persuaded to attend the Capulets' feast, knowing that Rosaline, whom he loves, will be there.

- Romeo sees Juliet Capulet and falls instantly in love with her, and she with him, before they realise that their families are sworn enemies.

- Tybalt is ready to kill Romeo as a Montague and an enemy. When Capulet stops him, Tybalt vows to take revenge on Romeo.

- Romeo and Juliet marry secretly.

- Tybalt challenges Romeo to a duel. As he is now married to Juliet and related to Tybalt, Romeo refuses. Mercutio takes up Tybalt's challenge and is fatally wounded. Romeo then kills Tybalt.

- Romeo is banished from Verona by Prince Escalus. He goes to Mantua.

- Capulet decides that Juliet should marry Paris.

- Feeling trapped and desperate, Juliet consults Friar Laurence, who comes up with a dangerous plan. Juliet is to agree to marry Paris but the night before the wedding she will take a sleeping potion that will make it seem that she is dead. She will wake up in the Capulets' tomb, where Romeo (having been told what is going on) will be waiting for her.

- When Juliet tells Capulet that she will marry Paris, he decides to bring the wedding date forward by a day. This puts pressure on the Friar's already risky plan.

- All might still have worked out well for Romeo and Juliet but for the arrival of Balthasar to tell Romeo that Juliet is dead. This event exposes a weakness in the Friar's plan.

- In despair, Romeo buys a deadly poison to take when he reaches Juliet's tomb.

- Friar Laurence discovers that the letter he wrote to Romeo has not left Verona. He plans to bring Juliet from the tomb to his cell, where Romeo can come to get her.

- Once again the Friar's plan is undone. Romeo arrives at the tomb first and, believing Juliet to be dead, poisons himself.

- Juliet refuses to leave with Friar Laurence and, when he hides from the watchmen, she stabs herself. Her death completes the tragic pattern.

Exam tips

Read all the questions carefully. Make sure you understand what is being asked in each question. Then choose the one that you are best prepared to answer.

Make sure you deal equally with all the elements in the question.

You must support your answer with suitable reference to the play. In order to do this you must be thoroughly familiar with the details of the plot, as well as with the characters and their actions.

Your answers will benefit from brief, relevant quotations from the play. There is no need for lengthy quotations. Short quotations can make a point just as well, and leave more space for making further points.

From the beginning to the end of your answer, it is important to stay with the exact terms of the question you are dealing with. Remember that

marks are awarded for making relevant points clearly and economically.

Know in advance how much time you will give to each question, and stick to this plan. Giving too much time to one question will mean that you have too little time for other questions.

In your study of the play, you will have formed opinions on the play's characters, plot and themes. Examiners would like to know *your* opinions on these topics. This is why you should *think* about them in advance.

Your opinions should be based on facts presented in the play. For example, when you are judging characters, observe what they do and what they say, and also what other characters think and say about them.

Revising

When revising you should aim to gain a good knowledge of:

- **Characters:** the characters in the play, and how they relate to each other.

- **Plot:** the events in the play, and scenes in which something interesting, exciting, important, strange, unpleasant or pleasant happens.

- **Themes:** significant themes or ideas in the play, for example love, hatred, fate, chance.

You should cover the following four kinds of exam questions.

1 Questions about the plot of the play or about single scenes

To answer these, you need to know what happens in the play in general and in each individual scene. When you are looking at an individual scene, ask yourself:

- Is it exciting? Does it involve conflict, or suspense?

- Is it sad or happy?

- Does it include strange or surprising elements?

- What impact has it had on you?

- What does it tell you about the characters who feature in it?

2 Questions about the characters

When you are examining the characters, ask yourself:

- Looking at each character in turn, do you like or dislike the character? Why?
- Choosing two contrasting characters, what are the differences between them?
- Choosing a character you dislike, what happens to him or her?
- Choosing a character you like, what happens to him or her?
- Choosing two connected characters, what is the nature of the relationship between them?
- Is there tension or conflict between any characters?
- Does any character rebel against another, or hate another? Why?
- Which character do you find most interesting? Why?
- Does any character experience good luck or bad luck? How?
- Which characters deserve the titles hero, heroine or villain? Why?
- Which character would you like to play in a stage or film version of the play? Why?

3 Questions about themes

Think about ideas or subjects that keep on turning up in the course of the play. In the case of *Romeo and Juliet*, you will be conscious of such themes as:

love	hatred	feuds	revenge
fate	unawareness	accident	coincidence
chance	marriage	family	exile	death

When studying a theme, ask yourself:

- How is this theme introduced?
- How is this theme developed?
- Is this theme associated with a particular place or group of characters?
- What interests you about this theme?
- Is this theme relevant to your own life and/or to the world around you?
- What impression of this theme does the play leave you with?

4 General questions

Other questions that you should think about include:

- What is the world depicted in the play like?
- What impact or effect did the play have on you?
- Did you like or dislike the play?
- Would you recommend the play to students of your own age? Why or why not?

Past papers

It is worth looking at past exam papers in order to familiarise yourself with the types of questions asked. The following are some examples.

Higher Level Paper 2, 2013

1 Choose a character from a play you have studied.

    (a) What was your first impression of your chosen character? Support your answer with reference to the play.

    (b) To what extent does your impression of your chosen character change as the play progresses? Explain your answer with reference to your chosen play.

        OR

2 Choose a scene from a play you have studied that has a strong mood or atmosphere.

    (a) Describe what takes place in your chosen scene and identify the mood or atmosphere created. Support your answer with reference to the play.

    (b) Imagine you are directing your chosen scene on stage. Explain some of the decisions that you would make in order to create the mood or atmosphere successfully. Support your answer with reference to the play.

Higher Level Paper 2, 2011

1 Identify a hero, heroine or villain from a play you have studied. Explain why, in your opinion, this character deserves the title hero, heroine or villain. Support your answer with reference to the play.

        OR

2 Often plays combine both serious and light-hearted elements.

    (a) Did you find the play that you studied to be mainly serious or mainly light-hearted? Explain your answer with reference to the play.

    (b) Which element of the play had the greater impact on you, the serious element or the light-hearted element? Clearly explain your choice with reference to the play you have studied.

Ordinary Level Paper, 2013

Name a play or film you have studied in which there is a friendship between two characters.

  (a) Name both of the characters.

  (b) Which of the two characters did you prefer? Give reasons for your answer.

  (c) Do you think it is a good friendship? Give reasons for your answer.

Ordinary Level Paper, 2011

Name a play or film you have studied in which there is a likeable character.

  (a) Describe the character.

  (b) Describe the ending of the play or film.

  (c) Would you change the ending? Why / Why not?

Let me have
A dram of poison, such soon-speeding gear
As will disperse itself through all the veins

ROMEO, Act 5, Scene 1, 59–61

Sample questions and answers

Suitable for Higher Level

> **1** Select a play you have studied and choose from it a scene where conflict occurs.
>
> (a) Outline what happens in this scene.
>
> (b) What are the underlying causes of the conflict in this scene? Support your answer by reference to the play as a whole.

The play I have studied is William Shakespeare's *Romeo and Juliet*. The scene I have chosen to discuss is the first scene of Act 3.

(a) Romeo, a member of the Montague family, and his friends Benvolio and Mercutio, accompanied by their attendants, are together in a public place in Verona. Benvolio is afraid that members of a rival family, the Capulets, will turn up and start a brawl. He suggests that it will be safer for himself, Romeo and Mercutio to leave in order to avoid trouble. Mercutio does not agree.

Soon Tybalt, a quarrelsome Capulet, and some of his friends arrive. Tybalt becomes aggressive with Mercutio for being friendly with Romeo. Just when it looks as though Tybalt and Mercutio may fight a duel, Romeo arrives. Tybalt loses interest in annoying Mercutio, and turns his attention to Romeo, who has just married Juliet, Tybalt's cousin, in secret. Tybalt, not knowing that Romeo has married his cousin, challenges him to a duel. Romeo refuses to fight, even though Tybalt has insulted him by calling him a villain.

Mercutio, who is also unaware that Romeo has just married, thinks Romeo has disgraced himself by not taking up Tybalt's challenge, and challenges Tybalt himself. As they fight, Romeo tries to stop them. In the confusion, Tybalt inflicts a fatal wound on Mercutio, and leaves the scene. Mercutio dies almost immediately of his wounds, but not before he curses both the Montagues and the Capulets. Tybalt returns to provoke Romeo to a duel. This time Romeo is so angry with Tybalt that he accepts his challenge. Romeo kills Tybalt.

The Prince, who is responsible for law and order, listens to a witness statement from Benvolio, before sentencing Romeo to banishment from Verona.

(b) There are a few causes underlying the conflict in this scene. The most important of these is the long-standing feud between the two noble families in Verona, the Montagues and the Capulets. When members of either of these families come in contact with members of the other family, conflict is likely to arise, sometimes leading to death. Some members of both families seem to be growing tired of this feud, but Tybalt is not one of them.

There is an underlying cause for Tybalt's involvement in the conflict dramatised in this scene. Earlier in the play, Tybalt discovered that Romeo was at the feast in the Capulets' home, and tried to have him expelled. Capulet defended Romeo's presence there, and sent Tybalt away instead. This enraged Tybalt, who from that moment was determined to fight and kill Romeo. When his chance comes in this scene, it is Tybalt, not Romeo, who is killed.

A further cause of conflict in the scene is that two of the three people involved, Tybalt and Mercutio, are unaware of one very important fact: that Romeo has just married Juliet. They are unaware of this because the marriage has been performed in secret by Friar Laurence. If Mercutio had known about the marriage, he would, as Romeo's loyal friend, have done all he could to keep him out of the conflict. Even Tybalt, whose whole career is one of conflict, would not have wanted to fight with Romeo on his wedding day. Also, Romeo's marriage to Juliet, Tybalt's cousin, has made Romeo one of Tybalt's relatives. If Tybalt had been aware of this new relationship, he would no longer have a motive to view Romeo as his enemy, and conflict would have been avoided. Thus, we might say that ignorance, or unawareness, on the part of two of the participants can partly be blamed for the conflict.

Finally, it is interesting that the Prince of Verona blames himself for allowing conflicts such as this one to develop. He later points out that if he had not largely ignored riotous behaviour in the past, he would not have lost his relative, Mercutio, in this brawl.

To sum up, the underlying causes of the conflict in this scene are the longstanding feud between the Capulets and the Montagues, the out-of-control Tybalt, unawareness on the part of Tybalt and Mercutio of Romeo's marriage, and the Prince's over-tolerance of street violence.

> **2** Choose your favourite character from a play you have studied.
>
> (a) Why do you find this character interesting? Support your answer by reference to the text.
>
> (b) Discuss the relationship between your chosen character and **ONE** other character in the play. Refer to the text in support of your answer.

Shakespeare's *Romeo and Juliet* is the play I have studied.

(a) My favourite character from *Romeo and Juliet* is Friar Laurence. I find Friar Laurence interesting for many reasons.

My first reason for finding him interesting is that he is easily the most talented and original character in the play. While most of the other characters appear to have little to do apart from enjoying their wealth, giving lavish parties, rioting in the streets and sword-fighting, we find Friar Laurence devoting his time to useful pursuits, such as giving helpful advice to wayward youths like Romeo and Juliet, and developing his talents as an expert botanist. When we first meet him he is filling a basket with herbs and plants that he is cultivating in order to extract useful cures and remedies for all kinds of ailments. I am very impressed by his learned comments on the properties of these plants.

Friar Laurence is also interesting to me because he is very unselfish. His main concern is for others, and he is prepared to put himself at risk to be of service to them. Every time he appears in the play, he is giving his time to those with problems, and coming up with novel solutions to help them. It is not his fault that these solutions do not always work out as he hopes.

He is also interesting for the manner in which he acknowledges the failure of his plans for Romeo and Juliet, and for his willingness to face whatever penalties the law may inflict on him, even death. He has good reasons for excusing his conduct, but he does not do this. I can only admire his attitude here. His humility, honesty and charity make him interesting to me because these are rare qualities in the play.

Finally, Friar Laurence interests me because I feel I can identify with him as somebody I could go to for advice if I had a personal problem that I could not deal with on my own. I feel that he is the kind of person who would listen with sympathy and understanding, and give me the benefit of his experience of life, as well as his wisdom and practical common sense.

(b) The relationship I would like to discuss is that between Friar Laurence and Romeo.

The relationship between these two characters starts from the fact that Friar Laurence is Romeo's confessor and spiritual guide. Because of this, Romeo is able to confide in Friar Laurence and open his heart and mind to him. Romeo tells him all his most intimate thoughts, feelings and problems. He can do this safely because he knows that the Friar will never betray his secrets to anybody else.

As well as being Romeo's confessor, it is clear that the Friar is also his close friend and acts as a sort of father figure to him. Their first meeting in the play shows this aspect of the relationship. Friar Laurence greets Romeo as 'young son', praises him by saying 'That's my good son', and advises him to 'be plain, good son'. The play does not show Romeo enjoying the same relationship with his own father, Montague. When Romeo is depressed over Rosaline, and Montague is asked by Benvolio why this is so, he makes a revealing reply: 'I neither know it nor can learn of him'. The play makes it clear that Friar Laurence knows, and has long known, all about Romeo's troubles.

Romeo has come to see Friar Laurence because he wants him to conduct his marriage to Juliet. The conversation between the two men shows how intimate and confidential their relationship is. They trust each other completely, as the events of the play show. Romeo is prepared to involve the Friar in performing a secret ceremony. Friar Laurence agrees to this because he believes it may eventually reconcile the Montagues and Capulets.

The relationship has another aspect. As well as being a friend, Romeo is also regarded by Friar Laurence as someone who needs moral and practical guidance. This is why the Friar calls him 'pupil mine'. Before he begins the marriage ceremony, Friar Laurence gives instruction to his 'pupil' not to indulge in 'violent delights', but to 'love moderately'.

This teacher–pupil aspect of the relationship becomes more and more obvious as the play goes on, and as Romeo finds himself in more serious situations. This is the case after he has been banished from Verona by the Prince. Friar Laurence is the one who brings Romeo the news that instead of imposing a death sentence on Romeo, which the law entitled him to do, the Prince has reduced it to one of banishment. Romeo flies into a rage, accusing the Friar of being heartless and inconsiderate when he points out that the Prince has shown him leniency. The Friar exerts all his strength of will to convince Romeo that he is fortunate not to have fared worse. The result is that Romeo sees sense, and on the Friar's advice goes to see Juliet.

Suitable for Ordinary Level

1 From a play you have read, describe a scene where something happens which makes one of the characters happy or sad.

    (a) What happens in the scene?

    (b) Which other characters were involved?

    (c) What made the character happy or sad?

The play I have read is *Romeo and Juliet*. The scene I have chosen is the one in which Capulet and Lady Capulet want to force Juliet to marry Count Paris. They do not know that Juliet has just married Romeo, who has been banished from Verona for killing Juliet's cousin Tybalt in a duel.

(a) The scene opens as Romeo is saying his last farewell to Juliet at daybreak. As he leaves, Juliet's mother, Lady Capulet, enters her room as if to wake her. Juliet is weeping. Her mother thinks she is sad because of her cousin's death. She cannot know that Juliet is weeping because of Romeo's banishment. She adds further to Juliet's misery by offering to have Romeo poisoned.

Thinking she is going to cheer-up Juliet, Lady Capulet offers her the 'joyful tidings' that she will soon be 'a joyful bride'. In fact, this is the worst news Juliet could hear. Her father has decided that she will marry Count Paris in two days' time. An angry Juliet, now deeply unhappy, swears that she will not marry Paris.

Juliet's father, Capulet, takes over. He cannot understand why Juliet does not want to marry such a wonderful man as Count Paris. He becomes ferociously angry. He verbally abuses her, calling her 'tallow-face' and 'baggage'. He threatens her that if she will not go willingly to the church to marry Paris, he will drag her there himself. Juliet's Nurse tries to defend her, but Capulet dismisses her as a 'mumbling fool'. Capulet then threatens to disown Juliet and to expel her from her home. Lady Capulet refuses to help her daughter.

When Juliet's parents leave the scene, the Nurse takes over and advises Juliet to forget her new husband, Romeo, and marry Paris. Juliet is horrified, and decides to have nothing more to do with the Nurse. With Romeo gone, she feels completely alone in the world.

(b) The other characters involved in this scene are Romeo, who leaves at the beginning; Juliet's parents, Capulet and Lady Capulet; and Juliet's Nurse.

(c) Everything in this scene gives Juliet a reason for being sad. At the start of the scene, she is profoundly sad when she is forced to part from Romeo. Her saddest thought is that she may never see Romeo again. Her sad mood continues as she realises how miserable she feels in facing the day without Romeo. She is sadder still when her mother gives her news that she is to be married, whether she likes it or not, to Count Paris.

This news adds a great deal to Juliet's misery. She is now trapped. She feels unable to tell her parents that she is already married. She does not know what they might do to her if she did. She is forced to disobey them and bring their anger down on her head when she refuses to marry Paris. What increases her sadness is the fact that her parents do not realise that if she were to obey their instructions, she would be committing bigamy.

As Capulet's bullying of Juliet continues, her sadness turns to desperation. She is abandoned by her mother, who refuses to comfort her, even after Juliet begs her not to cast her away. To increase her misery still further, her father declares that Juliet's birth was a curse upon her parents.

Then Juliet has to endure the saddest moment of all. This time the Nurse, on whom she has always depended, is the cause of her sadness. She advises Juliet to marry Paris, describing him as 'a lovely gentleman', and Romeo as a dishcloth in comparison to him.

Her parents and the Nurse have made her sadness so unbearable that the only comfort Juliet is left with is the knowledge that she still has the power to end her own life.

> **2** Name a play you've read that has suspense in it.
>   (a) Describe the suspense.
>   (b) Did the suspense add to your enjoyment? Explain your answer.
>   (c) How did the play end?
>   (d) Did you like the ending? Explain your answer.

The play I have read that has suspense in it is *Romeo and Juliet*.

(a) *Romeo and Juliet* is a strange play. We know from the Prologue that the two main characters will die by taking their own lives. The suspense comes from not knowing how this will come about. Some scenes feature more suspense than others. I will write about a few notable examples.

In the final scene of Act 1, Romeo enters the Capulets' house in disguise to attend the feast. We are left in suspense as to how he will fare. Will he meet his beloved Rosaline and win her over? The suspense increases when he is recognised by Tybalt. What will happen to him now? Then Tybalt asks for his sword. Is he about to wound Romeo? Tybalt complains to Capulet about Romeo's presence. Will Capulet throw Romeo out? Capulet defends Romeo and expels Tybalt, who vows revenge on Romeo in the future. Will he get his revenge? If so, when, and what form will it take?

When Tybalt makes his appearance at the beginning of Act 3, in fighting mood, the suspense increases. He seems about to pick a fight with Mercutio, Romeo's friend, but when Romeo arrives, Tybalt chooses him as his target. Will they fight? Romeo refuses to take up his challenge. Then Mercutio challenges Tybalt. How will this end? Romeo tries to stop the duel. Excitement mounts. Then Mercutio is wounded. We wait in suspense. Will he die? Will he recover?

As news arrives that Mercutio is dead, Romeo's anger boils over. When Tybalt returns, there is further suspense as Romeo and Tybalt are both determined to fight. Who will win? Romeo kills Tybalt.

We are again held in suspense when the angry Prince, the ruler of Verona, arrives. What will he do? He gets a detailed eye-witness account of the fights that resulted in two deaths. Will he sentence Romeo to death? He sentences Romeo to banishment.

This banishment creates further suspense. How will Romeo and Juliet cope? Romeo threatens suicide. There is further suspense as Friar Laurence and the Nurse combine to prevent him from carrying out his threat.

Then Juliet's parents decide to force her into marriage with Paris. How will she avoid this? Friar Laurence comes up with a solution: Juliet will take a drug that will make her appear dead. She will be buried in the family tomb, and when she wakes Romeo will be there to greet her. Will the plan work? We are once more in suspense when the plan goes wrong. Will Friar Laurence be able to act in time to prevent disaster?

(b) The suspense added greatly to my enjoyment of the play. It helped to maintain my interest in the events right through to the end. Without the suspense created by Shakespeare at different points in the play, it would have become dull and boring. Whether I am reading or watching a play I like to wonder what will happen next, and to be surprised and excited when something happens that I did not expect. This is what suspense is all about. I always remember two sentences from a play I saw: 'The suspense is terrible. I hope it will last.' This is the way I feel about *Romeo and Juliet*.

(c) The play ends tragically. Romeo gets false news that Juliet is dead. He decides to take poison because he cannot live without her. He reaches the tomb before the Friar does, takes the poison and dies beside Juliet. The

Friar arrives before Juliet wakes. She refuses to leave the tomb, and when the Friar leaves in fear, she stabs herself to death. Before he dies, Romeo has killed Paris, an innocent victim of the tragedy.

(d) I did not like the ending. I would find it hard to like an ending that involves the suicides of two such delightful people as Romeo and Juliet, and the terrible murder of Count Paris, who has never harmed anybody.

Those three deaths are undeserved, and offend my sense of right and wrong. I would have preferred an ending that involved the survival of these three characters, but I realise that this would have made the play a romance or comedy rather than a tragedy. One aspect of the ending I did like was the agreement between Montague and Capulet to end their feud, which promises a more peaceful future for Verona.

Higher Level questions to try:

1 Consider a character from a play you have studied. Choose a significant time of *either* good luck *or* bad luck which this character experiences.

   (a) Briefly describe this experience of good luck *or* bad luck.

   (b) Discuss how the character deals with it in the play.

2 Plays teach us lessons about life. Choose any play you have studied and explain how it has made you aware of any one of the following:

   Love **or** Death **or** Conflict **or** Harmony.

3 Name a play you have studied and state what you think is its main idea and/or message. Explain how this main idea and/or message is communicated in the play.

4 You have been asked to recommend a play for students studying for the Junior Certificate. Would you recommend the play you have studied for this examination? Give reasons based on close reference to your chosen text.

Ordinary Level questions to try:

1 Pick a scene you best remember from a play you have read, and write about:

   (a) What happened in the scene.

   (b) How any one character behaved.

   (c) How do you remember this scene?

2 Think about a play you have studied in which there are two very different characters.

   (a) Describe the differences between these characters.

   (b) How did their differences affect the outcome of the play?

   (c) Which of the two characters did you prefer? Explain why.

3 Think about a play you have studied. Pick a very dramatic moment and write about:

   (a) What exactly happened.

   (b) What characters were involved.

   (c) Why you found it dramatic.

4 Think about a play you have studied. Pick a scene where something happens to make one of the characters happy or sad:

   (a) What exactly happened?

   (b) What characters were involved?

   (c) What made the character happy or sad?

5 Think about a play you have studied. Use **ONE** of the following headings to write about the play:

   ■ Why I found the play enjoyable.

   ■ Why I did not enjoy the play.